The World of Architecture

The World of Architecture

KÖNEMANN

Copyright © 2000 Könemann Verlagsgesellschaft mbH
Bonner Strasse 126, D – 50968 Cologne

Project Management: Arco Editorial, S.A., Barcelona, Spain

Author: Francisco Asensio Cerver

Editor: Paco Asensio

Design and Cover Design: Mireia Casanovas Soley

Layout: Ricardo Álvarez, Jaume Martínez Coscojuela, Emma Termes Parera

Language Editing: Paco Asensio, Ivan Bercedo, Aurora Cuito

Cover (from top to bottom): Juri Havran, Eugeni Pons, Sasaki and Ass., Eugeni Pons

Original title: Atlas de arquitectura actual

Copyright © 2000 for this English edition:
Könemann Verlagsgesellschaft mbH
Bonner Strasse 126, D – 50968 Cologne

Translation from Spanish: G. Bickford, M. McMeekin, M. Reece and S. Wiles in association with First
Edition Translations

English Language Editing: Kay Hyman in association with First Edition Translations

Typesetting: The Write Idea in association with First Edition Translations

Project Management: Beatrice Hunt for First Edition Translations, Cambridge, UK

Project Coordination: Nadja Bremse

Cover Design: Mireia Casanovas Soley

Production: Ursula Schümer

Printing and Binding: Neue Stalling, Oldenburg

Printed in Germany
ISBN 3-8290-3564-0

10 9 8 7 6 5 4 3

WORLD CONTEMP...

HR to p. 56
(2nd p. of contents

Introductio

The current state of architecture, as well as that of many other human disciplines such as literature, industrial design, or fashion, is so complex that critics do not always manage to explain its intricacies using clear and meaningful criteria.

This review of the architectural world over the last decade reveals a huge variety of styles and trends, which has produced undeniable riches. This diversity defines all of these projects. They have been born out of the effort of individuals and groups, who, far from trying to make their work suit already existing premises, have fought to find functional and aesthetic solutions to real problems. Originality is the child of this search.

This vast selection, largely a compilation of the most significant buildings constructed over the last ten years, is not intended to do any more than demonstrate a certain quality common to a number of these architectural projects. We did not intend to make any kind of categorical judgement of personal views, but to introduce the public to this material by highlighting trends and analyzing their characteristics, with the sole aim of offering the reader, who might not necessarily be a specialist, a broad and up-to-date vision of the scope of architecture in the world today.

n

This volume has, therefore, a clear objective: to inform. It aims to orient the general reader, to bring them closer to the extensive, fertile, and hugely interesting subject of contemporary architecture.
Of course, it has not been an easy task to select the projects. The selection process was based on the proven quality and originality not only of the buildings proposed but also of the architects. In addition, we had to bear in mind that opinion is swaying towards a concrete time marker (the end of the decade and of the century), characterized by the concentration and defense of individualism. This is evidenced in the construction of buildings that are frequently personal and subjective expressions, by a heterogeneous group of master architects who establish a sincere, open, and clear dialog with architecture, the fruit of long and rich experience, as quickly as they construct strange, isolated shapes. Projects of great structural virtuosity follow, further removed and more casual than the much discussed relationship between architecture and the public. Between the two extremes, other technological or artistic contributions add to the broad range that contemporary world architecture offers us.
From among the group of buildings presented, there are some that

unconditionally extend theoretical modern schemes, such as, for example, some of the Nordic projects, with their obvious tradition and significance, which are a homage to a stylistic and functional architectural language.

In contrast, other works open the door to the future, to architecture for the year 2000, an architecture that tries to create a new reality divorced from its environment, and that gathers up all the troubled values of a uniform society controlled by international mass communication. Once again, architecture in North America seems to be becoming the paradigm to follow. This view, however, is not yet final

and will be accepted only with some hesitation and provisos.

Undoubtedly, these new departures will provide a breath of fresh air, allowing certain outmoded habits to be revised, and at the same time they will persuade people to view the current state of architecture in a new light. This is precisely the reason that, in preparing this book, a special effort has been made to include important projects built in the USA or designed by Americans.

The common thread running through all the projects here is their variety, reflecting today's multiplicity of tastes and trends: all architectural expressions seem to be accepted, as long as they produce a satisfactory and well-thought-out result, whether from the constructivist's optical point of view, or from the aesthetic or functional one. **It is a case of pragmatism carried to its logical conclusion.** This situation is certainly dependent on external factors such as the context in which the building is located, and on internal factors such as the weight of history and the professional and intellectual experience of each of the architects involved.

The element that binds all these aspects together in determining the outcome of any project is its subject. In other words, it is not the same to design and construct a church, a museum, a communications tower, a bridge, offices, a single family dwelling, or a theater. Each of the buildings included in this book has to meet strict functional requirements that the architect cannot avoid: they have to resolve them. The architect's contribution will be to endow the finished building with special worth, subject, of course, to the external and internal circumstances already mentioned above.

The buildings presented in this volume have been designed both by architects of established reputation, with a long professional record, and by younger practitioners who are now starting to define the state of architecture today and in the near future. It is interesting to be able to compare, through the 1000 pages of this book, the work of two different generations of architects – that of Antoine Predock, César Pelli, or Michael Graves, who are all now over 60 years old, and the work of those around 40 years old, such as Studio Granda, Christian Drevet, or Enrique Norten. It can be said, however, after analyzing all the works, that there is no break between the two. On the contrary, in some cases one can see fewer points in common between architects of the same era than between others with more than 30 years' age difference. In other words, the concerns of architects are a response not so much to their training as to their vision of reality. Ideas rush to all corners of the planet, affecting everyone equally. Architectural diversity is an undeniable reality, within which both traditionalist and frankly revolutionary attitudes coexist. A panoramic vision such as this book offers unleashes a cacophony of voices. Groups or movements do not feature strongly. Although certain materials or technical solutions are widely used, the approach to a project almost always springs from a personal and specific vision, not from the formal application of some accepted ideology or doctrine.

The publication of *The World of Architecture* aims to give the public access to material that until now has

been the province of specialists. We
hope we have achieved this.

Francisco Asensio Cerver

Urban planning and transport

Talking about transport and urban planning has become an essential activity in today's culture, and in most cases it is done from a position of ignorance of the principles that govern these disciplines so closely linked to the individual in society. The purpose of the first section of this study of contemporary international architecture is to show projects that have drawn up the rules of engagement for these two architectural disciplines, with a view to shaping the basic concepts. This will provide for the reader a more rigorous and reliable approach to this vast territory, comprising those transport and urban infrastructure facilities that define our current social behavior. Transport interchanges can be interpreted as redefining the hierarchical system between cities, from the moment they are erected as emblems of the development of a territory.

The economic expansion of the 1990s has brought with it an increase in the amount of international trade and the daily movement of people. All this, together with a blurring of frontiers, explains why the most widely used means of transport are the train and the plane, objects of study in this section of the book, together with the advantages and consequences of the use of urban transport. We also wanted to make a special mention of two types of construction that fall halfway between transport and urban planning: bridges and communications towers.

The term urban planning, for its part, applies not only to the study, planning, and construction of towns and cities, but also to their relationship with the surrounding region. In any case, their ultimate objective is to design the spatial environment where man carries on social activities. In this volume we will find a series of projects (squares, streets, urban parks, peripheral parks, land art, urban property, etc.) that tries to improve the urban environment by inspiring the person in the street, by reconnecting isolated neighborhoods, and by restoring and adapting heritage areas.

Airports

There are many varied factors involved in the design of airports, ranging from atmospheric conditions to accessibility of terrestrial transport, via the possible presence of other airports in the area, surrounding obstructions, or the presence of certain aeronautical requirements. All the projects in this section share the harmonious combination of the concepts of aesthetics and functionality, demonstrating that pragmatism in the selection of materials is not incompatible with beauty, distilled into suggestive forms, subtle structures, chromatic balance, and the surrounding landscape.

Denver Airport

Curtis W. Fentress

Location: Denver, Colorado, USA. **Date of project**: 1994. **Client**: Kaiser Bautechnick. **Associates**: Reinhold Meyer (structural engineering), Kaiser Bautechnik (works supervision), Roger Preston (mechanical and electrical engineering). **Photography:** Timothy Hursley, Nick Merrick (also pp 26/27).

A long building, with a large central hall, is divided into various levels, each associated with an independent function. On both sides, there are three blocks with a number of levels for parking. The spaces between these blocks become, on arriving at the central hall, the elements that connect the terminal's different levels. The hall is covered by an enormous canvas suspended from two lines of braced pillars. Direct access from outside is via two roads for wheeled vehicles on the upper level, that flank the hall just above the parking levels. Along both roads there is an access walkway covered with the same type of canvas that covers the central hall.

Fentress's ability to translate into architecture the vast prairies of Colorado with their horizons broken by the outline of the mountains bring the traveler into the city via a most poetic series of images.

Chek Lap Kok

Foster and Partners

Location: Hong Kong, China. **Date of completion**: 1998. **Design team**: Foster and Partners (architecture), Mott Connell Ltd (engineering), BAA plc (aerial plan). **Consultants**: Ove Arup and Partners (structural engineering), WT Partnership (costing), Fisher Marantz Renfro Stone (lighting), O'Brien Kreitzberg (construction program), Wilbur Smith Associates (traffic). **Surface area**: 516,000 m² (5.6 million ft²). **Photography**: John Nye, Airphotos International.

Hong Kong's new airport has the capacity of Heathrow and JFK combined in one. With 516,000 m² (5.6 million ft²) of surface area and a length of 1.27 km (0.8 mile), the Chek Lap Kok terminal is the largest covered space ever built. What is more, before constructing the terminal, it was necessary to create the site. In 1992, Chek Lap Kok was a mountain rising out of the sea. Construction of the airport has converted this island into a flat surface four times larger than it was, and 6 m (20 ft)

above sea level. The unifying element of this immense structure, which allows travelers to orient themselves in the immense halls of the terminal is the roof, which is made of a series of metal vaults. Norman Foster has developed here, on much larger scale, the same concept that he used so successfully at Stansted Airport: a light and luminous roof, an unrestricted open floor, and a basement level for housing services, equipment, and the baggage handling system.

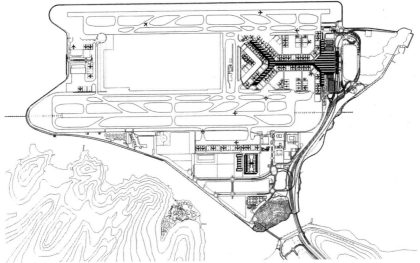

Kuala Lumpur Airport

Kisho Kurokawa Architect & Associates, Arkitek Jururancang.

Location: Kuala Lumpur, Malaysia. **Date of completion**: 1998. **Architects**: Kisho Kurokawa Architect, Arkitek Jururancag. **Surface area**: 400,000 m² (4.3 million ft²). **Scheme**: National and international terminals. **Photography**: Loo Keng Yip.

Faced with the challenge of building an airport to meet the country's economic growth, and ensure the organization of air traffic up to 2020, the Malaysian authorities saw the opportunity of turning this project into a symbol of an open door investment policy, of local industry's commitment to new technologies, and of putting money behind the national identity.

In spite of the preoccupation for developing a typically Malaysian style of architecture, which would make the building the visitor's first point of contact with the country's culture, responsibility for the project was given to the Japanese architect Kisho Kurokawa, though he did work in collaboration with the national firm Arkitek Jururancag.

The total surface area of the building is 400,000 m² (4.3 million ft²). The airport has been designed so that there is perfect symmetry between the two terminals (national and international), which are also symmetrical within themselves. The terminal building has an underground floor and five floors on a gradient. The most characteristic elements of the building are its roof and the structure of conical pillars on the top floor, the departure lounge.

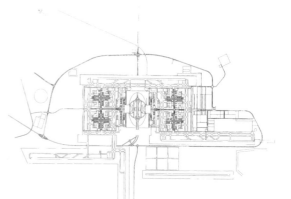

Kansai International Airport

Renzo Piano and Noriaki Okabe

Location: Osaka, Japan. **Date of completion**: 1994. **Architects**: Renzo Piano, Noriaki Okabe. **Client**: Kansai International Airport Co. Ltd. **Associates**: Peter Rice, Tony Stevens, Philip Dilley. Alistair Guthrie (Ove Arup & Partners); Kimiaki Minai (Nikken Sekkei Ltd.); Paul Andreu. Jean Marie Chevallier (Aéroports de Paris); Takeshi Kido, Misao Matsumoto (Japan Airport Consultants, Inc.). **Photography**: Sky Front, Yasuhiro Takawawa, Kanji Kiwatashi.

To build an island in the bay, with an area of more than 500 ha (1235 acres), a site had to be found that both provided enough free space and would avoid contamination. This meant that consolidation work had first to be done on the marine subsoil, which was very deep and unstable at this level. Sand was injected into the clay strata to increase strength, and then a consolidating infill was added. In less than five years the whole island was covered, using some 150 million m³ (5.3 billion ft³) of earth. Even though the degree of consolidation achieved was viable, there was still some yield, however, within acceptable limits. For this reason, the foundations had to be able to absorb any movement of the subsoil that might affect the stability of the building. The building was designed so that, despite its huge size – it stretches for more than 1.5 km (0.95 miles) – users can orient themselves at any time when they are crossing it: the keys to achieving this are absolute transparency, and adapting the corresponding scales to each zone in the structure.

United Airlines Terminal 1, O'Hare Airport

Murphy & Jahn

Location: Chicago, Illinois, USA. **Date of construction**: 1987. **Architect**: Murphy & Jahn.
Photography: Murphy & Jahn.

United Airlines Terminal 1 consists of three areas, two of which are joined by a very long corridor running the whole length of the complex. The two basic components, blocks B and C, form two linear structures each 460 m (1500 ft) long, separated by a free space of some 250 m (815 ft), which allows movement of several planes in both directions. Building C has a total of 30 boarding gates, while the other 18 gates are in Building B. The ticket area is in a large hall with 56 counters. This space has been topped with a barrel vault, which is highest at the entrance that gives onto the terminal, and slopes down towards the other end of the building.

The planning of the terminal is based on the concept of parallel volumes, a design that departs from the traditional Y shape that is prevalent at O'Hare. The walls, which are curved at the top, and the translucent roof, appear to be back lit with a wide range of colors. This gives the building a greater feeling of space.

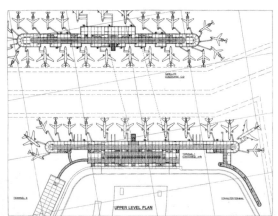

UPPER LEVEL PLAN

Terminal 2, San Diego Airport

Gensler

Location: San Diego, California, USA. **Date of construction**: 1998. **Architects**: Gensler Architecture Design & Planning Worldwide (Santa Monica office). **Scheme**: Nine boarding gates, ticket sales hall, baggage collection area, shopping areas, restaurants, and services. **Surface area**: 11,000 m² (120,000 ft²). **Photography**: Marco Lorenzetti, G. Cormier.

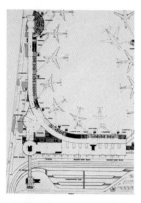

Gensler received the commission to expand Terminal 2 for the final of Superbowl XXXII.

The terminal is L-shaped, and in the angle Gensler has placed interconnecting rotundas, containing the waiting areas, cafeterias, and shops. The two arms of the L house the arrival and departure halls. The façade consists of an inclined glass plane, with a structure of heavy concrete columns supporting a metal roof that is rather evocative of the wings of an aircraft. The extensive use of glass allows one to enjoy the view out over San Diego Bay. Inside, Gensler has chosen a range of colors inspired by the local landscape: gold (sand), green (trees), and blue (sky and sea), giving a pleasing natural effect.

Stuttgart Airport

Meinhard von Gerkan

Location: Stuttgart, Germany. **Date of construction**: 1992. **Architect**: Meinhard von Gerkan. **Photography**: Richard Bryant/Arcaid.

In Stuttgart Airport, the pillars are trunks that divide into extended branches and the roof is a thick foliage that filters the light and allows only some rays to pass through. In this way some of the most emblematic symbols of technology are converted into melancholic beings and landscapes longing for the natural world.

The roof which von Gerkan designed allows both natural light to come in through skylights, and artificial light from lamps installed in boxes.

The inclined roof and the stepped levels of the hall give an impression of latent movement, in an image that has been compared with the mythical Birnam wood in *Macbeth*. In order for the roof to be better appreciated, von Gerkan placed the air-conditioning ducting over the ticket sales counters and the blocks containing elevators.

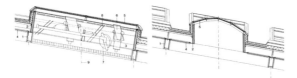

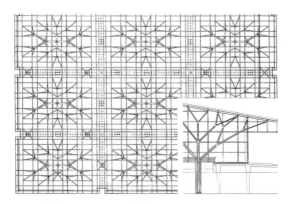

Charles de Gaulle Airport, interchange module

Paul Andreu, J. M. Duthilleul

Location: Roissy, Paris, France. **Date of construction**: 1994. **Architects**: Paul Andreu, Jean–Marie Duthilleul. **Scheme**: Interchange module for connections between terminals. **Photography**: Paul Maurer.

The airport of Roissy-Charles de Gaulle looks like some living organism, such as a sponge under a microscope. Inside, there is constant fluid movement. There is no single concept of space in Roissy, but many different strata: scales, networks, circuits, and contrasting dimensions, into which a number of gaps break. The TGV (High Speed Train) station is part of the airport's module 2, an interchange module that will become the center of the airport when it is finished. This module allows renewal of the spatial scheme. Since its beginning (in 1974) the airport has grown as a juxtaposition of elements: Terminal 1, Terminal 2, train station, parking areas. With the advent of the High Speed Train new installations had to be built, which are now used for the internal transport system, under an immense glass roof. Roissy is a complex, yet at the same time easy to use, place which maybe reflects the sentiment of a century.

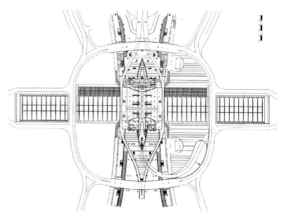

Stansted Airport

Sir Norman Foster & Associates

Location: London, UK. **Date of completion**: 1990. **Architect**: Sir Norman Foster & Associates. **Scheme**: New terminal for Stansted Airport: departure and arrival terminals, platforms for connection with train and underground network, banks, shops, kitchens, medical facilities, offices, and services. **Photography**: Richard Davies.

In the early 1980s it had become vital to build a new terminal in the southeast of England to satisfy the urgent requirements of air traffic in the London area. The building in question is square, measuring 200 x 200 m (660 x 660 ft). The opposing sides on the southeast and northwest, which are transparent, are set back in relation to the roof. The remaining two sides are reflective in contrast to the transparency of the others. The roof complements the floor architecturally and constitutes an important structural part of the complex. It is supported over the hall by six groups of pillars, 36 m (120 ft) apart. A tree-shaped structure lends a solid configuration and the strength to bear all the technical systems: heating, ventilation, lighting, and air-conditioning. All the services included on the ground floor (banks, shops, kitchens, medical facilities, etc.), are contained in easily removable modules. With an initial capacity of eight million passengers annually, Stansted has potential for growth up to 15 million users a year.

Schiphol Airport

Benthem Crouwel NACO

Location: Amsterdam, The Netherlands. **Date of construction**: 1993–1995 **Architect**: Benthem Crouwel NACO. **Scheme**: Airport facilities, shopping center, and train station. **Photography**: Jannes Linders, Claes de Vrieselaan.

The first phase of the new Schiphol airport dates from 1967. The new facilities replaced an old airport nearby, known today as Schiphol-Oost. The project was inspired by the terminal at O'Hare (Chicago) and featured the novelty of a departures hall raised above the runways, with all-glass façades, so that passengers awaiting flights could see the planes

taking off and landing. This idea has subsequently been widely used. The architects have discovered that one of the most moving and poetic activities at an airport, surely, is to sit and watch the planes coming in and flying out.

The Schiphol terminal is an example of the relationship between the new and the modern in architecture. Two years after finishing the work on Terminal 3, the new shopping mall, Schiphol Plaza, also designed by Benthem Crouwel NACO, was opened. Built in the central

triangle formed by the different terminals, this space is the main access route to all of them, as well as to the train station. A series of metal pillars, triangular in section, supports an inclined roof garden with skylights set in it. The interior of the mall is designed like a real town square: an open and free space for people.

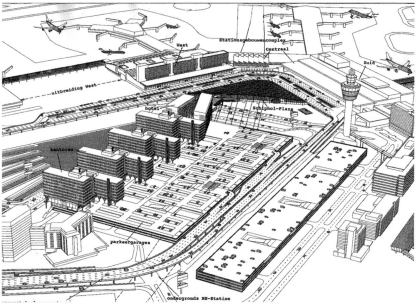

Train stations

With the dawn of the 21st century, the purpose of the railroad is changing. With the population moving from the cities to the suburbs, the train has become the means of connecting the residential periphery to the commercial center. Designers of train stations, however, often restrict themselves to planning the building in terms only of the flow of travelers and the immediate functional demands. They do not take into account the urban dynamic that can turn the station into one of the differentiating elements of a city, into the building that forms a special image, a mark of identity. The tendency is still to enclose new stations. But we have included examples that are most representative at an international level, which will help over the next few years to clarify the new image of the station.

TGV station at Lyon-Satôlas Airport

Santiago Calatrava

Location: Lyon, France. **Date completed**: 1996. **Promoter**: Lyon Chamber of Commerce and Industry and SNCF. **Architect**: Santiago Calatrava i Valls. **Associates**: Alexis Burret, Sebastien Mémet (chief architects), David Long, L. Burr (assistants). **Photography**: Ralph Richter/Architekturphoto.

In the TGV (High Speed Train) station of Lyon-Satôlas Airport, Santiago Calatrava uses his two favorite compositional mechanisms: symmetry and duality. Symmetry is provided by the desire to simplify the plan. His architecture is based on the construction; for this the essential aspect of his projects is the

sectional view. For Calatrava, the plan is order and the section beauty. Duality or dialogue give tension to the project, but also give it unity. The station covers two perpendicular movements with two different structures that demonstrate that crossing point. A vaulted roof, made of an oblique mesh of white concrete beams and

rhomboidal glass skylights, covers the six railroad tracks for a length of half a kilometer (one third of a mile). This roof is crossed above by a large triangular-shaped hall connecting the main entrance in one corner with the main complex and the taxi and bus terminals, and at the other end with a conveyor belt that takes passengers 180 m (600 ft) to and from the airport's passenger terminal building.

Two gigantic steel arches each rest on the corner of the triangle by the entrance and, respectively, on the two corners on the opposite side, defining the north and south façades. A structure of steel and glass sections is built on these, which rotates to improve ventilation in the hall.

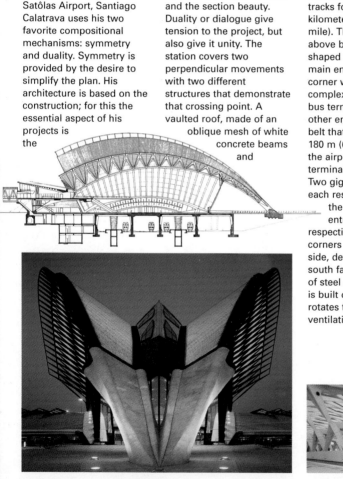

Stockholm Bus Station

Bengt Ahlqvist, Ralph Erskine, Anders Tengbom

Location: Stockholm, Sweden. **Date of completion**: January 1989. **Client**: Municipality of Stockholm and Stockholm Railroad Company (S J). **Architects**: Bengt Ahlqvist, Ralph Erskine, Andera Tangborn. **Scheme**: Central bus station, indoor public plaza, cafeteria-restaurant, hotel, restaurant, office complex, and connection with the central railroad station. **Photography**: Kjell Appelgren.

The building is 270 m (890 ft) long and is divided into four blocks, the spaces between which correspond to existing streets. Each block consists of one tall building facing the city and a lower one that faces the outer part of the esplanade. The stair and elevator wells join these spaces to form four patios or atria with curved, transparent glass roofs. Internal connection between the patios is via a gallery located on the same level as the office complex. The first of the atria has a reception area and a panoramic view over Stockholm. The second atrium, which is the biggest, is the one that opens out onto the terminal. The third is the center of the office complex and the entrance hall of the World Trade Center. It is designed as an indoor public plaza, with a café-restaurant. The fourth atrium is the north entrance hall, with garden terraces and escalators, leading to another restaurant and the hotel included in the complex. The roof is made of sheet metal panels.

The architectural concept is based on the great classic railroad stations, and is intended to represent the apogee of the age of glass buildings; a modern version of the great passenger hall, sharing light and space with the local business premises.

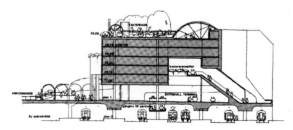

Atocha Station

José Rafael Moneo

Location: Madrid, Spain. **Date of construction**: 1990. **Architect**: José Rafael Moneo. **Scheme**: Local train station, high speed train station, bus station, subway station, parking, and remodeling the old station as an entrance hall. **Photography**: Luis Casals.

Atocha Station is in the center of Madrid, a short distance from the Reina Sofía and Prado museums. The huge glass and steel roof of the old 19th-century station had to be conserved and restored and, at the same time, the new building had to house a high speed train station and stations for local trains, buses, and the subway, in addition to a large area for parking. Moneo approached this complex program by breaking down the different elements, and playing around with different levels for each of the stations. His intention was that, in spite of the size of the building, the station should not alter the scale of the city nor of the old 19th-century structure to be converted into an entrance hall-cum-conservatory. There are very few new elements to be seen from the outside: an access rotunda and a clock tower. The other areas of the station are hidden thanks to clever sectional work.

Nagasaki Port Terminal

Shin Takamatsu

Location: Nagasaki, Japan. **Date of construction**: 1995. **Architect**: Shin Takamatsu. **Consultants**: Mitsubishi Estate A & E (building and installations). **Surface area**: 3950 m² (425,000 ft²). **Scheme**: Waiting rooms, ticket sales area, hall, offices, and services. **Photography**: Nacasa & Partners·

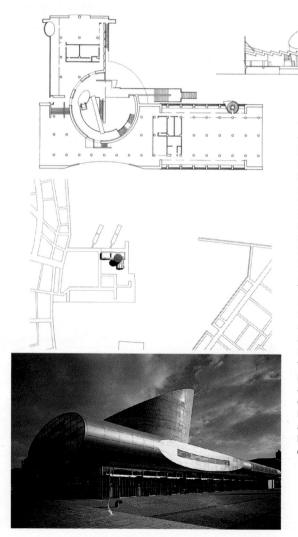

The port of Nagasaki, in the south of Japan, has historically always been very important since it was traditionally the only port open to foreign countries. A series of projects is being undertaken in Nagasaki following the Nagasaki 2001 Urban Renewal plan, supervised by locally based architect Hideto Horiike.

The ferry terminal is located in the Mofune area, in the center of the port, surrounded by mountains and sea, so that the project had to consider the distant view from both places. This privileged location makes it a symbol within new urban development. Takamatsu has planned the project as a crossroads traveled over by people from different cultural backgrounds.

Charles de Gaulle Airport, interchange module

Paul Andreu, Jean Marie Duthilleul

Location: Paris, France. **Date of construction**: 1994. **Architects**: Paul Andreu, Jean-Marie Duthilleul.
Photography: Paul Maurer

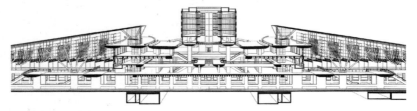

This building is a crossroads: railroads, internal communication, channels between installations. The different elements are located at different levels: the viaducts on top, and underneath, successively, are the services relating to the terminal area, the internal transport system, the hall of the railroad station, and, finally, the platforms under the first floor, forming a trench with the viaducts for taxis. Only the hotel rises between the tracks as a solid opaque mass. The glass roof and the absence of a tunnel over the train tracks means that the interchange routes are easily recognizable. Development of the visual relationships is based on the handling of the light, which is one of the main materials in this project, together with steel and concrete elements.

Liverpool Street train station

A & DG

Location: London, UK. **Date project begun**: 1979. **Date of completion**: 1991. **Client**: British Rail. **Architect**: A & DG. **Scheme**: Remodeling of an old train station: facilities, new connections with the subway, platforms, hall, ticket offices, offices, and services.

It was planned to demolish Liverpool Street station and replace it with a modern construction, but in 1979 it was agreed to remodel it, and final approval was obtained in 1983. The chief objectives laid down by British Rail (the former British state railroad company), who gave the project to A & DG, were to modernize and improve the station's facilities, and its connections with the subway and the approach roads to the station. The platforms had to be the same length (the existing ones were all different) and there was to be a new hall, respecting the historical and aesthetic demands of the existing structure. With this rebuild, Liverpool Street station has become a model for the new spirit of public-private cooperation and skillful fusion of the best of the past with the best of the future, preparing it for the 21st century.

Slependen Station

Arne Henriksen

Location: Baerum, Oslo, Norway. **Date of construction**: 1993. **Architect**: Arne Henriksen. **Scheme**: Access, train station, parking, ticket area, offices, and services. **Photography**: Jiri Havran (also pp 50/51).

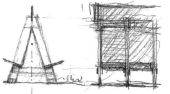

There was the chance to create an architectural milestone at Slependen Station in Baerum, outside Oslo. The landscape was highly dramatic thanks to the steep slope and the number of different levels. To connect all the existing routes with the station platforms, it was necessary to construct ramps and stairways. So Slependen Station has a large number of buildings and singular elements: two ramps, one straight and the other curved, a rotunda, a stairway, a ramp-stairway, and two bridges. The concrete represents the heavy, while the wooden structures constitute the light and active components of the design. The rotunda, with its spiral ramp constructed from elements of dark concrete, is a very special structure. Both the outer curve of the wall, and the slope of the ramp, as well as the architectural image itself, are coded in the element that constructs the rotunda.

Solana Beach Station

Rob Wellington Quigley

Location: Solana Beach, California, USA. **Date of construction**: 1995. **Architect**: Rob Wellington Quigley
Scheme: Train station, parking, installation of soundproofing. **Photography**: Richard Barnes.

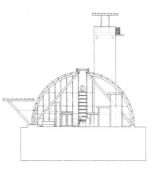

participated along with the architects in the design of the city center.

From the start, small workshops were organized which sought to reach a consensus between community and professionals on decisions about the project: the traffic, the parking, the mechanisms for soundproofing, the size of the buildings, and the relationship between commercial and residential buildings.

The station building is the first phase of an urban project of some 35,000 m² (454,000 ft²), destined to become the new city center for Solana Beach in the next few years. In addition to the station, the complex includes a large parking lot, a park, businesses, restaurants, cinemas, low-cost homes for the aged, and lofts for artists. The complex is in the form of a rectangle measuring approximately 70 m (255 ft) wide by 500 m (1780 ft) in length, bordering Route 101, which connects with the center of San Diego, and with the train tracks. The project was conceived in a completely different way from normal, more openly and democratically, since the inhabitants of Solana Beach themselves

Urban transport

This chapter is dedicated entirely to subway and bus stations for city use. These are projects in which architects have found a new arena for their creativity: places that can join streets and underground galleries, neoclassical façades and tunnels, in a form that encompasses the different levels of the city. Although bus stands are normally mass produced, those shown here are designed from the point of view of their relationship to the urban context. Each of these projects has been designed as a particular object linked to a particular location, as if it were a sculpture. They clearly show a capacity to enrich the city with minimal architectural detail – such possibilities are all too often ignored.

Subway station in Bilbao

Norman Foster

Location: Bilbao, Spain. **Date of construction**: 1996. **Architect**: Norman Foster. **Scheme**: Access canopy, exit module, lighting, signing, roof, offices, and services. **Photography**: Luis Sans.

Bilbao is a city that has traditionally been affected by the environmental consequences of its heavy industrial plants.
Foster has achieved a situation in which, inside the subway, travelers sit within the earth, conscious of the singularity of the place they are in.
The tunnels are the principal theme of the project. Measuring 16 m (53 ft) wide by 8 m (26 ft) high, they were dug using the Nat system (the new Austrian method of tunnel construction). To avoid weather problems, Foster wanted to create a space at the entrances to the subway that, although enclosed, was light and transparent. This gave rise to his idea of designing glass canopies with a stainless steel structure, so that, while they offer protection to passengers, by night they become enormous lamps that light up the city – inescapable landmarks.

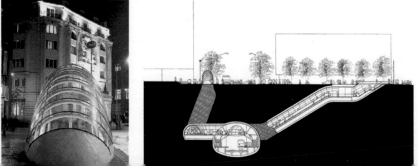

Subway station in Valencia

Santiago Calatrava

Location: Valencia, Spain. **Date of construction**: 1995. **Architect**: Santiago Calatrava. **Scheme**: Subway station, ticket offices, services, litter bins, entrance canopy. **Photography**: Paolo Rosselli (also pp 70/71).

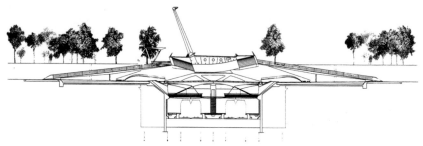

Alameda subway station is located below what was once the bed of the river Turia. Though underground, the station maintains a link with the exterior through a ribbed, translucent roof which is in turn the floor of the square above the station.

The station is divided into three levels: the entrance, the ticket offices, and the platform. The access level consists of an escalator in a steel tube at each end of the station, leading to the ticket offices, from where can be seen both the double height space of the platform as well as the shape of the roof.

The structure is of white reinforced concrete. The translucent glass skylights are supported in metal frames. In addition to allowing light and air to enter, by night the lines of skylights define the limits of the square in the busy center above ground.

Subway station in Lyon

Jourda & Perraudin

Location: Lyon, France. **Date of construction**: 1993. **Architect**: Jourda & Perraudin. **Scheme**: Subway station, offices, and equipment. **Photography**: George Fessy.

The subway station of Vénissieux-Parilly is situated in a little urbanized suburb at the intersection of a number of important roads. The mixture of different geometric shapes forms a structure of concrete arches and vaults based on diagrams of

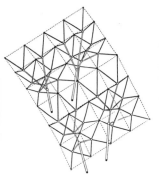

energy transmission from the ground floor to the level of the platforms. All the elements (columns, capitals, vaults, and arches) were designed according to the manufacturing techniques used: metal form-work, on-site concreting, and prefabricated vaults. This project involved underground architecture using large-scale excavation. It took advantage of the plasticity of the concrete and the expressive lines of force of the arches and the inclined side columns. Natural light penetrates thanks to two apertures in the main entrance hall.

Vuosaari subway station

Esa Piironen

Location: Helsinki, Finland. **Date of construction**: 1998. **Architect**: Esa Piironen. **Scheme**: Platforms, ticket offices, and services. **Area**: 4394 m² (47,000 ft²), **Photography**: Veikko Niemelä.

Vuosaari station in Helsinki evokes transparency. Esa Piironen has been concerned mainly with the roof and the glass façades, as well as with integrating the structure into the surrounding landscape. In section, two structures are superimposed one on the other: the first is of concrete, and supports the platforms, and the second is of steel and glass, forming the roofs. As with much of the architecture of the north of Europe, transparency is identified with democracy, closeness with the citizen, and compromise with the user: a literal harmony. Clearly, this huge structure of glass and steel acts as a conservatory which, though extremely beneficial in Finland, would be unthinkable in other, more southerly latitudes.

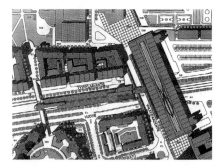

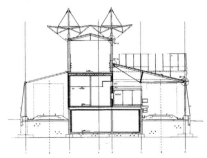

Nils Ericson Bus Station

Niels Torp

Location: Gothenburg, Sweden. **Date of completion**: 1996. **Client**: GLAB – Stefan Ekmann. **Architect**: Niels Torp AS Arkitekter MNAL. **Associates**: ABACO Arkitektkontor AB; VBB Markplanlaggare (landscaping); RF Byggkonsult (construction). **Area**: 4500 m² (48,000 ft²). **Scheme**: Terminal for the Gothenburg central bus station. **Photography**: Hans Wretling.

This project is the result of a competition held in the 1980s. It initially consisted not only of the construction of this terminal but also a new train station that had to contain a shopping mall and cafeterias, as well as a small business center. In addition, Nils Ericson square was redesigned as an urban park and became a splendid green open space, a contrast with the raucous traffic.

Passing through the rectangular entrance to the terminal one can connect with a tram stop, SJ line trains, metropolitan buses, and a taxi rank.

The scale and intimacy of this reception area relate to other parts of the complex, which retain the same importance and functionality as at the start of construction.

The main building includes an arcade which looks out onto the park outside, and gives protection from the wind and cold. It is right here that the terminal meets the city.

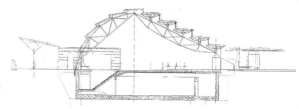

Tram station in Strasbourg

Gaston Valente

Location: Strasbourg, France. **Date of construction**: 1994. **Architect**: Gaston Valente. **Scheme**: Tram station, parking, access, commercial gallery, and services. **Photography**: Accent Visuel, Stéphane Speck, Rob Fleck, L. Lecat.

The station in the Place de la Gare is the main hub of the new tram line promoted by Strasbourg's local government in order to replace traditional forms of transport with other less contaminating ones. The tram line runs at a depth of 17 m (56 ft). Gaston Valente has divided the station into four levels. The upper two are organized around an empty central plaza, where two lines of trees have been planted. This has been covered over with a structure of steel and glass. Like a classic atrium or as in one of the famous shopping arcades of the 19th century, numerous shops have been built along the perimeter on both levels. On the platforms and escalators, the American artist Barbara Kruger has installed huge concrete beams on which, in enormous capital letters, she asks travelers:

Where are you going?
Who do you think you are?
Where is your head?
Who laughs last?

Tram station in Strasbourg   83

Stuttgart Station

Günter Behnisch & Partners

Location: Stuttgart, Germany. **Date project begun**: 1985. **Date of completion**: 1991. **Architect**: Günter Behnisch & Partners. **Associates**: Manfred Sabatke (supervisor), Ulrich Mangold, Matthias Tusker (project architects). **Scheme**: Train station, protective canopy, passenger platforms, ticket offices, pedestrian tunnel, litter bins, and remodeling of the pavement outside. **Photography**: Christian Kandzia.

It was not possible to make any major structural changes, so the architects had to adopt other less radical approaches, based on transforming existing components: in particular a defensive bunker, whose huge bulk stands out in the middle of the complex, making it the focal point of the new station/square's design. This design has cleverly integrated a number of components of great lightness of form and aesthetic value into a canopy. Two passenger platforms have been placed beside the tracks on which the local express runs, protected by pergolas of steel and acrylic. Finally, a convenient pedestrian tunnel was installed under the street that joins the city center with the autobahn.

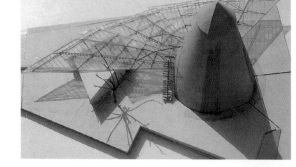

Tram station in Hanover

Alessandro Mendini

Location: Kurt-Schumacher Strasse, Hanover, Germany. **Date of construction**: 1994. **Designer**: Alessandro Mendini. **Scheme**: Canopy, signboards, and elements of urban decoration. **Photography**: Thomas Deutschmann.

In the course of the 20th century, squares and avenues have been subtly taken over by sculptures, which have become points of reference, giving their environments added meaning. Sculptures have been superimposed on buildings and embedded in the texture of façades. They present flowing images, add associations with their angles, they act as symbols.

The idea of converting bus, subway, and tram stops into singular pieces, each one conceived as an isolated and independent work of art, linked to a specific site, somehow revives the lost tradition of combining the two disciplines: sculpture and architecture. Mendini is someone who, since the 1950s when he was responsible for Casabella o Domus, has worked avidly

to promote an art that is close to society, close to the working methods of advertising and mass communications media. Mendini's popular art is based on symbolic and historical references that appeal to the collective imagination. Paradoxically, his tram station in Kurt-Schumacher Strasse turned out to be his most polemic work to date.

Greenwich North subway station

Alsop & Störmer

Location: Greenwich, London. **Date project begun**: 1991. **Date of construction**: 1998. **Architect**: Alsop & Störmer. **Associates**: JLE E + M (services engineering). **Scheme**: Train station, ticket office, escalators to platforms, ventilation system, offices, and services. **Photography**: Roderick Coyne

The initial design consisted of an open station that would allow passengers to enter from the ticket sales area, located on the upper floor and facing west, through a walkway suspended from the concrete roof by cables to both sides of the station. The location of this entrance allows views to the waiting platform that connects with the entrance area by means of two passenger escalators going up and down.

The public areas (60 x 13 m, 200 x 43 ft) are open, which allows natural ventilation and good lighting. The ventilation ducts are also suspended from the roof.

The generous size and simple elegance of the structure has been emphasized by the use of ultramarine blue on walls, floor, and roofs. The air ducts and escalators are of stainless steel.

Greenwich North subway station 89

Bridges and communications towers

For a better understanding of each of the works in this chapter of *The World of Architecture*, we must mention the complexity that accompanies the planning and construction of bridges and communications towers. They need to be a balanced combination of aesthetics and pragmatism and, at the same time, of architecture and engineering. For this reason, each of the projects included has been analyzed in terms of how it satisfies functional requirements (structures, antennas, technological elements, beams, arches, and so on) and how it meets harmonic criteria, on which the concept of beauty depends. Thus, when examining all these structures, it becomes clear that architecture and engineering cannot be separated and, consequently, architects must apply their knowledge to both disciplines simultaneously.

Normandy Bridge

Charles Lavigne

Location: Honfleur-Le Havre, France. **Date of completion**: 1995. **Client**: Chamber of Commerce and Industry of Le Havre. **Architect**: Charles Lavigne. **Associates**: F. Doyele (director of works), Quadric, Sogelerg, Eeg (viaduct), Seee (concrete structure), Sofresid (metal structure), Onera, Cstb, Eiffel, Sogelerg (wind effect), Cete (foundations), Yann Kersalé (lighting). **Photography**: S. Soane/architekturphoto.

Just where the fresh water of the Seine meets the salt water of the English Channel, between the cities of Le Havre and Honfleur, the construction of the Normandy Bridge represents an important development that eliminates the 58 km (37 mile) round trip that used to be necessary to cross the river by the Tancarville Bridge further inland. Together with route A29, the project will establish a north–south axis that will open up the Normandy region and contribute to the development of the city of Le Havre as a logistical center. This will help in the diversification of its industrial base, reinforce its position as an important port, and encourage new activities in the estuary. The architects' most important consideration was continuity throughout the length of the bridge. The slope was not to exceed 6%. The cross section of the platform is identical for both the pre-stressed concrete sections and for the central metal section. Aerodynamic performance is improved by a blue painted aluminum cornice along the edge of the bridge which also serves to unify the two sections. The structure can withstand wind speeds in excess of 300 km/h (190 mph). Each of the A-shaped towers rises from the ground on two legs, between which the traffic passes, which then become a single anchoring mast rising to a height of 210 m (690 ft). Constructed out of pre-stressed concrete with steel reinforced tops, the towers are extremely rigid and ensure transmission of forces to the foundations. The piles, which are also of concrete, reach down deep into the banks of the Seine, while the viaducts are supported on a layer of limestone for added stability.

Höfdabakkabrú Bridge

Studio Granda

Location: Reykjavik, Iceland. **Date of completion**: September 1995. **Client**: Public roads administration. **Cost**: $1.73 million. **Architect**: Studio Granda. **Associates**: Línuhönnun (structural engineering), Landslagsarkitekar (landscaping). **Photography**: Sigurgeir Sigurjónsson (also pp 92/93).

The Höfdabakkabrú Bridge is a road interchange between a secondary road and the highway to the city of Reykjavik.

The form of the bridge is predetermined in practical terms by the precise route that vehicles must follow and by the structural logic that the engineers have laid down. In other words, in this case the architecture was not part of the origins of the project, but had to be adapted to previously made decisions and grafted on later as an additional aspect of the work. According to the architects themselves, their principal objective for this project was to smooth the impact of such a large structure on the immediate surrounding area.

The containing walls flanking the bridge follow the shape of the ground and the slopes have been planted with trees and bushes to assist this integration process.

In a contrasting strategy, brilliant black artificial stone was chosen for the finish of the walls, in order to form a background that would reflect the colored flashes of the cars speeding by. In the center of the bridge's intrados, the metal pillars have been painted in bright colors. In the darkness of the tunnel they flash like vertical brush strokes of yellow, orange, and red.

Eastern Scheldt Project

West 8

Location: Eastern Scheldt Delta, The Netherlands. **Date of construction**: 1991–1992. **Client**: Directoraat generaal Rijkswaterstaatdirectie Zeeland. **Architect**: West 8. **Associates**: Adriaan Geuze, Paul van Beek, Dirry de Bruin (model). **Scheme**: Construction of a barrier bridge as part of the Delta Project: closing the estuaries and inlets in the southwest of the Netherlands; integral landscaping project. **Photography**: Hans Werleman, Mectic Pictures Rotterdam, Bart Hofmeester.

This is the largest hydraulic engineering work of its kind in the world. In 1953, following serious floods over much of Zeeland, it was decided to return half of the land to the sea, erecting dikes along the old coastline. The construction of the final part of the project destroyed a unique

ecosystem and there was wide-scale opposition to this destruction from both ecologists and the producers of mussels and oysters. At the end of 1974, the government heeded these protests and decided that the mouth of the Eastern Scheldt would remain partially open, but provided with a system that could completely close it off in case of emergency. The integral landscaping project by West 8, following up the construction work on the barrier and its two ends, could be no less sophisticated and it was decided to form a series of enclaves in the landscape. Especially typical of this

work were the "shell beds": after flattening all the zones to the level of the surroundings, West 8 covered them with shells, produced from the neighboring shellfish beds. White and black shells were placed alternately, to form contrasting black and white designs of squares and lines. Located 13 m (43 ft) above sea level, the highway that follows the gentle curve of the delta protection barrier now offers a spectacular panorama over the watery landscape of Zeeland.

Ohnaruto Bridge

Honshu-Shikoku Bridge Authority

Location: Honshu-Shikoku, Japan. **Date of completion**: 1990. **Architect**: Honshu-Shikoku Bridge Authority.
Scheme: Bridge connecting islands, landscaping to blend the structure in, and respect for marine fauna.

The Honshu-Shikoku Bridge Authority was formed in 1970, to be responsible for designing the rail and road networks connecting the islands of Honshu and Shikoku. This corporation considered it important to integrate the project into a magnificent landscape. For this reason it was decided to build a suspension bridge (1,629 m, 5300 ft) after considering the geological conditions of the sea bed. The most important considerations for the design of a suspension bridge were typhoons and earthquakes. In this regard, preliminary studies were done to estimate vibrations from the wind and to construct superstructures capable of withstanding earthquakes of up to force 8 on the Richter scale. Once research into safety had been carried out, the design of the bridge was divided into two parts: the infrastructure (anchoring techniques to fix the system of cables) and the superstructure (the vertical elements for suspending the supports). The cables are the essential part of a bridge: in total the bridge has 19,558 wires with a diameter of 5.37 mm (0.2 in), which, if joined together, would go around the world twice.

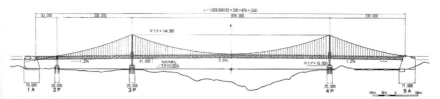

Vasco da Gama Bridge

Location: Lisbon, Portugal. **Date of construction**: 1995–1998. **Photography**: Paco Asensio.

Organization of the last World Fair of the 20th century was the driving force behind the transformation of Lisbon, through major structures such as the Vasco da Gama bridge over the Tagus. The candidature for holding the Expo in the Portuguese capital went hand in hand with the opportunity to explore location options that were both on the periphery of Lisbon and on the water. Two alternatives were proposed: one to the east and one to the west of the modern hub of the city.

The eastern option, on both sides of the Tagus, had serious infrastructure, housing, and environment problems, precisely in the place selected for the fair, bolstering the argument for regeneration. It was proposed to renovate this area and it became vital to improve all the access routes to and from the city. The most significant operation in this respect was the construction of the Vasco da Gama Bridge, which joins Lisbon to its outskirts on the peninsula over the water.

This project has provided new access into Lisbon, which before could only be reached by a bridge located a long way from the center, necessitating a much longer journey. Structurally the bridge consists of pillars from which are hung metal cables that support the elements closest to land. The central section consists of a platform on pillars with no additional support.

La Barqueta Bridge

Juan J. Arenas y Marcos J. Pantaleón

Location: Seville, Spain. **Date of completion**: 1992. **Architects**: Juan J. Arenas and Marcos J. Pantaleón. **Scheme**: Bridge connecting the island of La Cartuja to the historic center of Seville. **Photography**: Fernando Alda/ Expo '92 photo archive.

La Barqueta bridge was erected to link the historic city of Seville with the island of La Cartuja, where the vast complex of Expo '92 was developed. The triangular porticoes at the ends of the bridge platform, as well as solving the problem of stability, became a formidable entrance to the Expo site.

One of the most outstanding aspects of its design is the fact that its central arch stretches freely over the platform and that it also has, as a starting reference, a number of triangular points, heavily emphasizing its strong three-dimensional and aerodynamic nature. As to materials, steel has been used, in contrast to the general trend of using concrete or some other similar material.

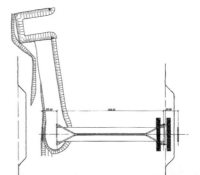

Montjuïc Tower

Santiago Calatrava

Location: Barcelona, Spain. **Date of completion**: 1992. **Client**: National Telephone Company of Spain. **Architect**: Santiago Calatrava. **Scheme**: Communications tower and surrounding gardens. **Photography**: David Cardelús

The Montjuïc telecommunications tower was erected as one of the symbols of the spirit of the Barcelona Olympics. The idea proposed by Santiago Calatrava materialized as a white figure 119 m (390 ft)

in height. Its inspiration was anthropomorphic, its attitude one of offering. The column is inclined at an angle of 17° to the vertical, which is the angle of the summer solstice in the city, so that the tower became a monumental sundial. A semicircular corona completes the tower's natural imagery. The Montjuïc tower had to perform various functions: firstly, it had to be a node in the fixed radio communications service, as part of the infrastructure in support of small capacity short-range radio links; secondly, it had to provide

connections for automatic mobile phone services; and, finally, it had to be a substitute for the old Montjuïc Radio Station. Once the hectic Olympic games were over, it was no longer of use, and the tower has now become just a decorative element of the city landscape.

Collserola Tower

Sir Norman Foster & Ass.

Location: Barcelona, Spain. **Date of completion**: 1992. **Client**: Municipality of Barcelona. **Architect**: Sir Norman Foster & Associates. **Scheme**: Telecommunications tower, restaurant-observation platform, and parking lot. **Photography**: John Edward Linden.

The project is a mixture of a traditional television tower with a concrete column and metal masts supporting the radio antennae themselves, all passing through a high tech filter characteristic of the architect.

The tower combines three basic elements: a concrete column, 4.5 m (15 ft) in diameter and 209 m (686 ft) high; a central body with 13 platforms, the height of a 23-story building, which houses the electronic equipment; and the cables that support the structure.

This communications tower, designed by Norman Foster, involved a complex engineering operation. Situated on one of the hills in the Collserola range, the structure occupies 10 ha (25 acres) of land situated 448 m (1470 ft) above sea level. The tower itself occupies only 3.5 ha (8.5 acres), while the rest of the site is a huge parking lot.

Squares

The concept of the square as a feature
planned in a single stroke is recent in the
history of town planning. Moreover, an
expansion of this idea has occurred in both
the functional and spatial senses. A square
is no longer just a wide part of the street
surrounded by buildings. The word now
implies more ambiguous concepts that
make the square a location. In addition,
many squares now have no specific use,
and are intended to do no more than
provide a pleasant meeting place and give
some character to areas that are run down
or otherwise uncared for. This chapter is
dedicated to the recent design and
construction of squares internationally.
Here we find not only cases of
rehabilitation, but also projects that create
a topography or have particular uses. And
there are other projects that generate their
own independent arguments in respect of
their surroundings and in this way
revitalize space. All these have one thing in
common, however: the wish to create
worthwhile spaces where people can meet
and just be.

Federal Tribunal Plaza

Martha Schwartz, Inc.

Location: Minneapolis. Minnesota, USA. **Date of construction**: 1996. **Architect**: Martha Schwartz. Inc. **Area**: 4,645 m² (50,000 ft²). **Photography**: George Heinrich.

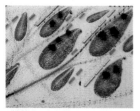

In the center of the city of Minneapolis, opposite the old city hall, this plaza has been developed in front of the new US Federal Tribunal, recently finished by the leading New York firm of Kohn Pederson Fox. The idea was to give the plaza a character that would speak for the city as a whole. It would be one large civic space that would also allow individual activities to be carried on. Elements of the actual landscape of Minnesota have been used, and these have acquired a new value when placed in the plaza. When taken out of their context, elements become sculptural, and these are capable of symbolizing both the natural features of Minnesota, and the way man has manipulated them for his own purposes.

The most characteristic element of the space is a number of oblong tumuli, covered in vegetation, running east–west.

The long tree trunks used for benches are evocative of one of the state's most important economic activities: it has a long timber industry tradition. These two main elements are placed on a neutral plane that takes up nearly all of the plaza: a pavement of bands running towards the Federal Tribunal building itself.

The plaza is especially sensitive to the Minnesota climate's abrupt changes of season. In winter, the snow leaves only the edges and the central path visible. In spring and summer the tumuli are full of color. Some are permanently green, while others are covered with white narcissi or blue squills, setting off the blue banding of the pavement surface.

Schouwburgplein

West 8

Location: Schouwburgplein, Rotterdam, The Netherlands. **Date of design**: 1990. **Date of completion**: 1992–1995. **Architects**: West 8. **Scheme**: Public space. **Photography**: Jeroen Musch.

Schouwburgplein occupies a prestigious position in the center of the Dutch city of Rotterdam. Surrounded by stores and offices, and close to the central train station, it is one of the cultural centers of the city. In addition to the municipal theater and a complex of concert halls, it now includes the recently built Pathé multiscreen cinema. What West 8's team of

architects found before undertaking the project was a place of little character, much affected by the existence of a very run-down underground parking lot below the square. The purpose of the scheme was to encourage wider use of the square. The renovated space retains the quality of emptiness that already existed. The way the sun passes over the square throughout the day determined how it should be divided up into different sections, with different materials used for the pavement in each one. As an additional attraction, four enormous hydraulic post-cranes more than 35 m (115 ft) in height take up different positions throughout the day. People can put a coin in the control panel and direct them as they wish, thus constantly changing the appearance of the square.

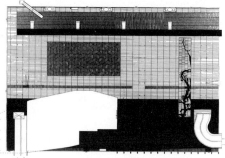

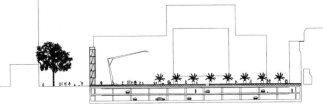

Citizens' Square

Kenzo Tange Associates

Location: Tokyo, Japan. **Date of construction**: 1991. **Architects**: Kenzo Tange Associates. **Photography**: Osamu Murai, Shinkenchiku Shashiubu.

The Tokyo Municipality's headquarters and square are located in a district of Tokyo called Shinjuku, on three adjoining blocks belonging to the Municipality that join Shinjuku park to the west, surrounded on the remaining sides by office blocks along edges of the multilevel highway.

One of the project's most important features is that this huge civic space was planned for the middle of a landscape of high-rise buildings, in a city that has hardly any parks, and where the pedestrian feels lost among huge office blocks, stores, parking lots, and urban highways. There are no other examples of squares in Tokyo and so it is inevitable that reference should be made to the historic squares of Europe, where great civic buildings traditionally have public spaces in front of them, and where an important part of city life is played out.

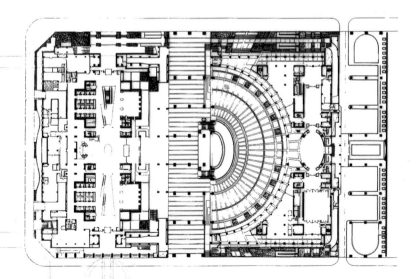

Solid Square

Nikken Sekkei

Location: Kanagawa, Japan. **Date of construction**: 1995. **Architects**: Nikken Sekkei. **Photography**: Kokyu Miwa Architectural.

Solid Square forms part of a complex of offices, apartments, and services next to Kawasaki station in the Japanese city of Kanagawa, 20 minutes from Tokyo station. It serves both as an entrance atrium for the 100 m (330 ft) high office blocks and, in the transition zone between the interior and exterior of the building, as a place for relaxation. Inside the atrium is a large pool, 27 m (90 ft) across, which dominates the space and holds the visitor's attention. Every hour, the silence of this circular sheet of water is interrupted by a gentle bubbling as the water in the pool is replaced. The sound breaks the dominant silence. The water, which is only 7 cm (3 in) deep, can be drained and the whole area converted into a large arena that can be used for other events. Apart from the water, light is the other element that plays an important role in this atrium. Up the vertical walls from ground to first floor level, a large unbroken glass surface gives an unobstructed view of the gardens outside.

Pershing Square

Legorreta Arquitectos

Location: Los Angeles, USA. **Date of construction**: 1994. **Architects**: R. Legorreta, N. Castro, V. Legorreta, G. Alonso. **Photography**: Lourdes Legorreta.

Pershing Square, more than 120 years old, is a historic plaza in the city of Los Angeles, California. The square is a rectangle with proportions of approximately 1:2, surrounded by streets with very dense traffic. On all four sides, there were previously entry and exits ramps leading to the underground parking lot underneath. The plan was simple: locate the entrances on the four corners, away from the square, allowing easy access; concentrate vegetation around the edges in an attempt to protect the square from noise; and, at the same time, hide the cars entering and leaving the parking lot, thus freeing the central area for the enjoyment of the people in the neighborhood.

The result of these decisions is a square slightly lower than the surrounding streets and with planting all around, which separates it from the buildings. Onto this area the architects have projected a plan for a plaza as if they were founding a new city, as a metaphor for and homage to the foundation of the Spanish cities in America, and, in particular, to the origin of Los Angeles. The first step in this development of the square was to trace out two imaginary lines in the form of a cross: the longer arm runs north–south and the smaller one east–west. On this primary plan are placed the elements of the plaza in the same way that public buildings are placed on the grid of Spanish towns in the traditional way.

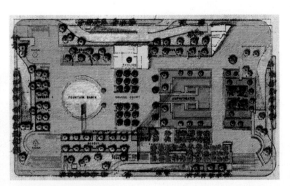

Plaça de la Constitució

J. A. Martínez Lapeña, E. Torres Tur, J. Esteban, A. Font, J. Montero

Location: Girona, Spain. **Date of construction**: 1993. **Architects**: J. A. Martínez Lapeña, E. Torres Tur, J. Esteban, A. Font, J. Montero. **Photography**: Lourdes Jansana.

In 1983 the Municipality of Girona decided to dedicate a plaza to commemorate the Spanish Constitution of 1978. For this they chose a triangular plot of land located in the outskirts of the city. Limited on one side by the Gran Vía de Jaime I and the new building of the Banco de España, on the other side it borders a college and an access ramp for an underground parking lot. The architects have built the plaza on the basis of a metaphor: "The plaza is a flowerpot in the city." The planners wanted to be faithful to this image and their first job was to think of the shape that a flowerpot might take; how it had to be able to hold fragments of nature in the middle of the city, in the same way that a flowerpot does in a house.

But walls are made not of clay but of concrete. They are not soft, smooth shapes that adapt to the hand, but have sharp angles that can harm it. These walls express the result of all the tension generated between the fragment of nature, fenced in and constrained, and the city that encircles it. These long polyhedral shapes are like tectonic folds rising from the earth that, unable to support the forces they are subjected to, break into crystalline forms that immediately solidify on contact with the air.

Place des Terraux

Christian Drevet

Location: Lyons, France. **Date of construction**: 1994. **Architect**: Christian Drevet. **Photography**: Eric Saillet.

This square is located in the middle of historic Lyons, and is the largest public space in the city. The buildings around it have grown up gradually since its creation in the 17th and 18th centuries. The project has tried to minimize the amount of work carried out on the square, with each decision prudently thought out, and full recognition given to the values of the location

The first job was to slide the sculptured Bartholdi fountain gently from the middle of the square to the north façade and turn it through 90° so that it faces the Palais St-Pierre.

This minimal movement achieved surprising results: it gave order and clarity to the undifferentiated space of the square and suddenly gave emphasis to the façade of the Palais St-Pierre. The next step in Cristian Drevet's reasoning was simple: change the look of the square, so that all the different elements are linked, to give some level of civic cohesion and make this public space justify its existence.

He has used only two materials to do this: water and light. Sixty-nine fountains have been set into the paving, with their jets forming a spurting forest. The murmur of the sprinklers, like the whisper of leaves, competes with the urban traffic. This is a place for strolling, chatting and relaxing.

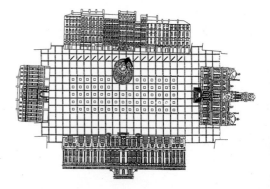

Tanner Fountain

Peter Walker

Location: Cambridge, Massachusetts, USA. **Date of construction**: 1985. **Architect**: Peter Walker. **Associates**: SWA Group. **Scheme**: Design and construction of an urban square. **Photography**: P. Walker, A. Ward.

The space chosen for the Tanner fountain was a loosely defined area where a number of paths crossed. It was an empty space between the Georgian brick buildings of Harvard, the modern science center planned by J.L. Sert, and the commemorative Victorian Gothic assembly hall. However, since it was one of the few open spaces on campus, the area was heavily used.

The challenge for Peter Walker was to make people aware of the place and its identity without restricting the usual movement through the locality.

There are 159 round stones measuring 1.2 x 0.6 x 0.6 m (4 x 2 x 2 ft) set haphazardly like cobbles in a circle 18 m (60 ft) in diameter between the asphalt and the lawn of a parterre. They are placed with no geometric relationship with each other or even with the asphalt path.

A fine mist some 6 m (20 ft) in diameter and 1.5 m (5 ft) high rises from the center of the stone circle, formed by five concentric rings of water sprinklers buried in the asphalt. In winter, when the temperature drops below zero, the water mist is replaced by steam from the heating system of the adjacent science center. The snow that falls on the ground melts at a different speed from that falling on the stones, but the resulting configuration is impossible to predict since wind and shade from the trees also have an effect. The water in its different forms becomes fire at night, when the mist or steam reflects and refracts the light projected upwards from the ground.

Plaza de Olite

Francisco José Mangado Beloqui

Location: Olite, Navarre, Spain. **Date of construction**: October 1996 – January 1998. **Client**: Municipality of Olite. **Architect**: Francisco José Mangado Beloqui. **Associates**: Fernando Redón, Arturo Pérez (supervisor). **Scheme**: Design and construction of urban plaza with access to underground galleries, street furniture, landscaping, and lighting. **Photography**: Francesc Tur.

The site is in the medieval village of Olite. The architect had to take into account the existence of old galleries constructed in the 11th and 12th centuries, of great historical importance, that were probably the entrance to the cellars of a palace. There were three problems to be solved by the architects. Firstly, they were obliged to make uniform a geometrically asymmetrical shape that had arisen from random urban growth; it was also decided that the underground galleries should be able to communicate with the outside, even though they had remained hidden for centuries. Lastly, there was the issue of the juxtaposition of old and new materials. Three sections can be seen on

the ground: the steps into the plaza, the boulevard, and the plaza space itself. The geometric configuration of the boulevard is completed by street furniture, benches, lights, and fountains, laid out in a line, achieving a horizontal effect, in contrast with the verticality of the foot of the walls. As to materials, it was decided to use quarried stones with a grayish tone, a contrast

with the original that confers autonomy on the new creation. With the geometrical theme continued by means of pyramids, circles, and cones, the whole layout of the complex is unified.

Plaza Berri

Peter Jacobs, Philippe Poullaouec-Gonidec

Location: Montreal, Quebec, Canada. **Date of completion**: 1992. **Client**: Municipality of Montreal. **Architects**: Peter Jacobs, Philippe Poullaouec-Gonidec. **Associates**: Beauchemin, Beaton, Lapointe Inc.; Consultants Geniplus Inc.; Montreal City Council. **Scheme**: Urban square for public use in the center of Montreal. **Photography**: Philippe Poullaouec-Gonidec.

The Place Berri is located right in the middle of the Latin quarter. This inclined plane, covered with lawn and framed by lines of silver maple trees and thorn trees, which forms a green open space like the eastern slope of Mont Royal, symbolizes the terraced foot of the mountain that the city has erased. The water that runs at an angle to the space symbolizes that other watercourse which gushes out of old terraces and disappears into the city to flow later into the invisible river. Melvin Charney's sculptures, metaphorically crossed by bridges and streets that remind one of the structure of the city, take action physically as cascades which cross the square. The main area, paved with hundreds of pink granite slabs, placed some 90 cm (3 ft) below the level of the sidewalks, leads to an immense ice rink open five months of the year. A retaining wall of polished black granite, 40 cm (1.3 ft) wide, separates the square itself and the inclined plane; 46 cm (1.5 ft) high and running the whole width of Place Berri, it is also used as a bench for eating. An area with reddish gravel, under the shade of three rows of silver maples, runs along the whole north façade. The square has become a meeting place invoking ample and diverse use of the whole space.

Promenades and streets

This chapter is dedicated to analyzing streets and promenades. It includes observation and interpretation of the most interesting landscaping proposals in the contemporary urban context: all those streets, avenues, promenades, or any urban roadway that makes up the city landscape. All the projects presented meet the criteria and principles that qualify them for this book: that can be summed up as the way in which they possess certain physical, cultural, historical, or humanistic characteristics. All these examples have been included because of their special attention to the resources provided by nature (light, water, vegetation) as well as for their understanding of the changing rhythms of life.

Public spaces in Nantes city center

Bruno Fortier & Italo Rota

Location: Nantes, France. **Contest**: 1991. **Date of construction (1st phase)**: 1992–1994. **Client**: Municipality of Nantes. **Architects**: Bruno Fortier, Italo Rota. **Associates**: Jean-Thierry Bloch (engineer), Roger Narboni (lighting), Jean-Claude Hardy (landscaping). **Photography**: Phillippe Ruault.

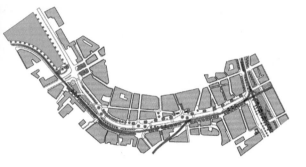

This project by Bruno Fortier and Italo Rota is the result of a contest announced by the Municipality of Nantes in 1991 for the renovation of an important area of public space in the center of Nantes. This was occupied by large stretches of parking lot and the remains of earlier commercial and even military activities, utilizing the two rivers, the Loire and the Indre, that form the basis of this urban wasteland.

The fact that this extensive area had previously been wide open, "a large emptiness," meant that this great expanse of space, much larger than one's normal idea of urban space, should be preserved, but at the same time properly cleaned up and organized according to the uses to which it was to be put. There had to be some way of directing the various kinds of traffic that would pass through it. Using street furniture and all kinds of urban accessory constructively the project managed to create an atmosphere totally opposite to the former disorder and desolation. The area was adapted to the functional needs of the contemporary city machine: traffic flow and transport requirements.

Overtown Pedestrian Mall

Wallace, Roberts & Todd: Gerald Marston

Location: Miami, USA. **Date of construction**: 1994. **Architects**: Wallace, Roberts & Todd: Gerald Marston. **Photography**: Gary Knight & Associates (also pp 112/113).

Overtown is the name used for the African-American district of Miami, where this pedestrian zone project is now located.

The Overtown pedestrian zone is part of a policy of revitalization, both economical and cultural, to stimulate both private investment and community pride in this historic district. The project and its execution were carried out in the record time of four months, all the more commendable considering that the process involved public bodies, residents' associations, and such groups as landscape architects, civil engineers, and even a local artist, Gary Moore. The latter, together with Gerald Marston, the landscape architect of the firm Wallace, Roberts & Todd, were the leading lights behind the genesis and coordination of the project's basic concept, in which special importance was given to historical and cultural references, the sense of African-American vibrancy, and the use of metaphoric meaning.

The project consists of two elements: one involving the closure of a section of the public highway to traffic; and the other, perpendicular to the first, running under the Dade County Railroad.

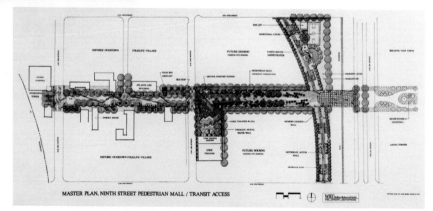

MASTER PLAN, NINTH STREET PEDESTRIAN MALL / TRANSIT ACCESS

Sea Front Promenade in La Barceloneta

J. Henrich, O. Tarrasó, J. Artigues, M. Roig, A. M. Castañeda

Location: Barcelona, Spain. **Date of construction**: 1996. **Architects**: J.Henrich, O. Tarrasó, J. Artigues, M. Roig, A.M. Castañeda. **Photography**: David Cardelús, Josep Gri, Jordi Henrich, Juli Espinás, David Manchón (also pp 136/137).

The Plaza del Mar and the new Paseo Marítimo occupy an area that until 1994 was full of public restrooms, snack bars, and sports clubs. These took up the entire front of La Barceloneta, the old fishing quarter, and cut off any relationship with the sea. Thanks to the Coastal Law it was possible to clear all

areas of the coast that came under public domain. Once the structures had been removed from the beach, the streets of La Barceloneta looked out to sea with no intervening obstacles; preserving these perspectives was the most important aim when it came to deciding the level of the new promenade. In order to integrate the two fully, it would be the same as that of the fishing quarter. With no need to worry about differences of level, the pedestrian can reach the large area of promenade from any street around.

The whole promenade is paved with gray-green

quartz, which has textures and reflections very reminiscent of the sea; the stones are placed in lines of different widths which extend to the limits of the La Barceloneta area. The irregular edge of the promenade on the built-up side, with little plazas looking out to sea, offers many more possibilities than a promenade with a uniform cross section. These variations in dimension by themselves define the diverse character of the spaces, which is underlined by the location of the street furniture.

Champs Élysées remodeling

Bernard Huet

Location: Paris, France. **Date of construction**: 1994. **Client**: Municipality of Paris. **Architect**: Bernard Huet. **Associates**: Olivier Bressac, Jean-Baptiste Suet (project designers); Omnium (engineering); Jean-Michel Wilmotte, Marc Dutoit (street furniture); GTM-DS (parking lot construction). **Photography**: Alessandro Gui, Alexandra Boulat.

Without doubt, the Arc de Triomphe is a memorable focal point from any perspective. But in regard to the architecture flanking the Champs Élysées it is above all the alignment and dimensional unity, rather than the somewhat modest quality of its façades when considered separately, which contribute to the coherence of this urban composition. As Bernard Huet says, the chief factors in this context are, for instance, the surface of the paving, the alignment of the trees, and the design of the street furniture.

The sidewalks, which are all at the same level, and therefore needed a proper drainage system designed, have been organized into two groups differentiated by the treatment of the paving. The pedestrian promenade, which is completely empty except for the exits from the subway and parking lots, has been designed with large light-gray granite slabs, punctuated by small blue-gray tiles. In the second group of sidewalks, between the new line of trees and the street furniture, the rhythm is marked by small light-colored tiles, cut by a series of darker double bands going across, in line with the trees. This system serves as a basis for the urban furniture. This concept and the unity of aspect, color, and material

sought by the project designers should reinforce the perception of space and the coherence of an urban plan to which contributions throughout the centuries have been the fruit of the same unique straight thinking in this regard.

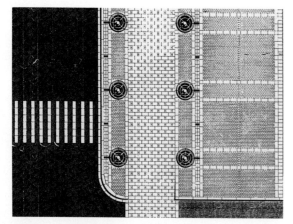

The Citadel

Martha Schwartz

Location: City of Commerce, California, USA. **Date of construction**: 1990–1991. **Architect**: Martha Schwartz. **Photography**: G. Leadmon.

Landscaping design is a doctrine, a way of perceiving the human being and our relationship with nature and the universe. Martha Schwartz starts with the idea that man, especially in North America, has used and abused Mother Earth; by becoming materialistic and losing contact with nature, we have lost a large part of our perception of ourselves. The apparent dislocation operating in the human environment does not, however, cancel out

our inspiration. Rather, it constitutes our starting point for working.
In the Citadel, the origin of the inspiration is in the form of the old factory of UniRoyal Tire and Rubber. On a piece of ground paved like a checkerboard in tones of gray, green, and ochre, lines of date palms planted in whitened tire like containers converge towards a plaza that takes us to another time and a different place.

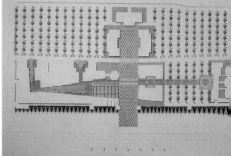

East Couplet Street urban improvement

Randall D. Beck, Carol F. Shuler, Kevin Berry

Location: Scottsdale, Arizona, USA. **Date of construction**: 1995. **Client**: Cities of Scottsdale and Phoenix. **Architects**: Randall D. Beck, Carol F. Shuler, Kevin Berry. **Associates**: Sandy Gonzales Conner (design and construction contracts administrator). **Photography**: Richard Maack, Carol Shuler.

The renovation undertaken in the East Couplet Street area comprised the development of a garden which winds along the paths, providing spaces of different sizes. The objective was to convert

this garden zone into a bird sanctuary. The planting was selected with the aim of providing cover and food for a wide variety of bird species. Trees and bushes were planted to act as windbreaks, deaden the noise of the traffic, and provide shade to people using the area. In the center of the Hummingbird Garden, five steel sculptures were installed, a little over 4.5 m (15 ft) high, which evoke the form of flower corollas. The configuration of the walks reproduces on the ground the shape of these flower sculptures. Low winding walls have been built along the walks and mini-plazas for people to sit, while the pavement has been painted red and ochre, the colors of the flowers alluded to by the sculptures. The effect achieved contributes to the transformation of an area previously not particularly pleasant for walking and leisure into a place of relaxation, with a highly original concept of modern aesthetics.

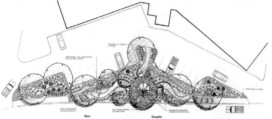

Cleveland Gateway

Sasaki Associates Inc.

Location: Cleveland, Ohio, USA. **Date of construction**: 1994. **Architect**: Sasaki Associates Inc. **Scheme**: Sports complex, baseball stadium, basketball stadium, and parking lot. **Photography**: Sasaki Associates.

The client was a foundation which contracted Sasaki Associates Inc. to design and construct an urban sports complex in the center of Cleveland. The project, which was located on an 11 ha (27 acre) plot of land below Public Square, included: an open-air baseball stadium for the Cleveland Indians, with a capacity of 45,000 spectators; a multi-use stadium for 20,000 spectators used by the Cleveland Cavaliers basketball team; a residential zone and a parking lot for 2100 vehicles next to it. One important objective of the original project was the incorporation of this entertainment and sports area into the financial center of the city, at the same time obtaining a space that would allow the economic development of the zone to continue.

Sasaki Associates was responsible for the final design of the plan, the formal documentation, and the administration of the construction phase in all the locations, including plazas, streets, signage, and designs for traffic flow and control.

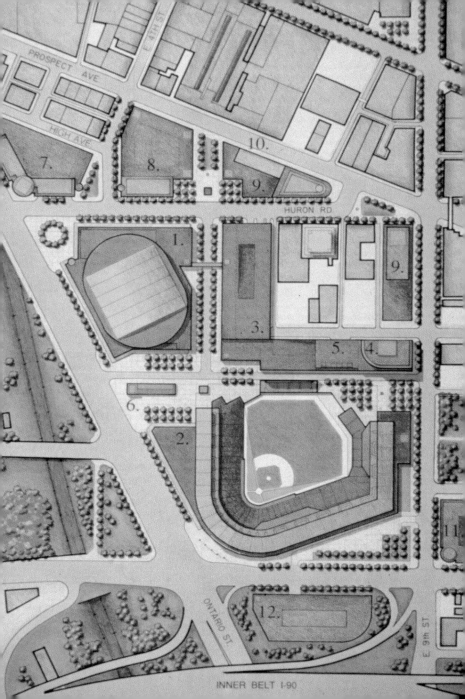

Schiedgraben and Hirschgraben in Schwäbisch Hall

Wilfried Brückner

Location: Schwäbisch Hall, Baden-Württemberg, Germany. **Date of construction**: 1990–1992. **Client**: Municipality of Schwäbisch Hall. **Architect**: Wilfried Brückner. **Associates**: Rolf Kronmüller (architect); Stiefel Engineering Office (surveying); Volker Ellsässer (landscaping); Edgar Gutbub and Michael Turzer (artistic collaboration). **Photography**: Wilfried Dechau.

The city's architecture is characterized by its ancient historical center: half-timbered houses and a city wall with bridges and turrets. Following ecological principles, materials from the project and from other demolition sites was collected, sorted, and used on the surfaces, materials which could both be reused and provide the basis for a diverse flora to flourish. A flight of steps rising from

the inner wall of the city joins two old defensive structures; steel structures that the sculptor Turzer designed together with the architect have been erected on these ruins. The weight and naturalness of the stone is dissolved in the transparency and technical perfection of the steel, so that the observer feels at the same time and in the same way both horizontal tranquillity and vertical

growth. The continuity of the trench and the high walls of natural stone are interrupted by modern constructions: stairs, doorways, and roofs made of steel appear in spots that mark the ruined towers. The bases of these are made from the ashlars in the original walls, while the transitional layers to the foot of the steel construction are made of treated stones. A work made of steel bars forms a figure with an aeronautical air, partly covered by perforated sheets and a colored, varnished board. The bodies form rhythms in conjunction with the wall. The aesthetic effect complements the functionality of this architectural work which, conscious of its meaning, uses the historical substance and develops it from the original idea.

Christiania Quartalet urban remodeling

Niels Torp

Location: Oslo, Norway. **Date of completion**: 1994. **Client**: Aspelin Ramm AS. **Architect**: Niels Torp Arkitekter MNAL. **Associates**: Pal Ring Giske, Per S. Schjeldsoe, Trine Rosenberg, Lina Hyll; Selmer AS (contractor). **Area**: 20,000 m² (215,000 ft²). **Scheme**: Remodeling and construction of space for offices in a new development in the historic center of Oslo. **Photography**: Jiri Hayran, Hans Wrettling.

The urban area known as Christiania Quartalet forms part of a neighborhood in the ancient heart of Oslo dating from 1624. The colors, materials, and details used in the project reflect the historical importance of this part of the capital city.

Before starting the remodeling, the architects found themselves with a series of buildings with very little in common as far as size and height were concerned. It was aesthetically desirable to concentrate more on the façades facing the street than on the street itself. For this reason, the various walls on the block had to be dealt with differently depending on the surrounding environment. Obviously, one of the most important aspects of the project was the construction of a large new building opposite the Norges Bank (Royal Bank of Norway). In this case, the budget meant that prefabricated concrete elements had to be used in place of blocks of natural stone (as had been planned in the original project). Once again, in order not to be out of tune with the surroundings, the walls were painted the same color as the neighboring bank. Once more, the old was inspiring the new.

Indiana White River State Park Promenade

Angela Danadjieva & Koenig Associates

Location: Indianapolis, USA. **Date of completion**: 1988. **Client**: White River State Park Development Commission. **Architect**: Angela Danadjieva & Koenig Associates. **Scheme**: Recovery plan for the riverside. **Photography**: T. Hursley, J.F. Housel, A.Danadjieva

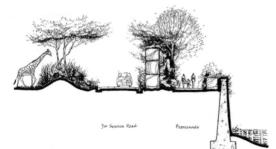

3 m Service Road   Promenade

Floodwall

The promenade projected by Angela Danadjieva on the bank of the White River is part of a vast urban plan aimed at recovering the riverside as it passes through the center of Indianapolis. The specifications from the White River State Park Development Commission concentrated on accessibility for the public, by mixing leisure with the historical and cultural identity of the place and encouraging wider integration through the recurrent and symbolic use of Indiana limestone. The promenade is nearly 5 m (16 ft) wide and follows the gentle curve of the White River, flanked by 1272 irregular blocks of Indiana limestone, placed in such a way that they form an environment that is a combination of rustic naturalism and sculptural abstraction. The smoothly undulating outline allows different sequences to be created along the route, and the resulting variety of perspectives, textures, and sensations is one of the principal achievements of the project.

Different species of tree help to suggest the formal division of the promenade, articulated in four landscape variations: the amphitheater, the rose gallery, the bas-relief and one dedicated to the geological history of the limestone. These four sectors link the recreational purpose of the promenade with an educational impulse to the project.

Rose Window Gallery

Voie Suisse

Georges Descombes

Location: Lake Uri, Switzerland. **Date of completion**: May 1991. **Client**: Municipality of Geneva. **Architect**: Georges Descombes. **Associates**: C. Chatelain, B. Spichiger (botanists), A. Coboz (urban development), H. Cauville (writer and critic), A. Leveille, R. Schaffert (architects and town planners), F-Y. Morin (art critic), M. Pianzola (art historian), B. Tottet (geographer), J.P. Cetre (civil engineer). **Scheme**: Routing and renovation of a footpath around a lake in Switzerland. **Photography**: Georges Descombes, Françoise Goria, Herve Laurent.

The Voie Suisse is a 35 km (56 mile) footpath around Lake Uri. The 26 cantons of the Swiss Confederation were involved in routing and building it. Each of them assumed responsibility for a section, without losing sight of the communal sense of the project. The extent of the stretches awarded to each canton was decided in terms of the number of inhabitants. Different types of action were suggested. The idea was to preserve the substance of the path while ensuring its accessibility to users; thus a great number of different levels were explored, with steps of wood and grass built into slopes so that people could feel and observe the landscape from high up. In other instances, there was a desire for reevaluation: introduced in this respect was the work of the musician Max Neuhaus, who installed a sound system with loudspeakers in a clearing in the woods which allowed one to listen to the life hidden within. In 1991, after the celebrations to mark 700 years of the Swiss Confederation, many of the more ephemeral elements of this project disappeared; the site became overgrown, but a discreet trace remains, ready to be rediscovered on some future occasion.

Gavá Walk

Imma Jansana

Location: Gavá, Barcelona, Spain. **Date of completion**: 1992. **Client**: Municipality of Gavá and Biology Faculty of the University of Barcelona. **Architect**: Imma Jansana. **Associates**: S. Juan, J. Navarro (special planning), Bet Figueras (landscaping), F. Giro (botanical supervision), C. de la Villa. J. Lascurain, N. Abad, M. Jorba (works supervision). **Scheme**: Restoration of a 20 km (12 mile) stretch of coastline in Gavá. **Photography**: David Cardelús.

For many years, Barcelona has maintained a slender and marginal relationship with its natural coastline. One of the recent efforts undertaken to protect what remains of this delicate ecosystem was the new coastal walk at Gavá, an operation forming part of an ambitious plan which includes the restoration of 20 km (12 miles) of coastline. The contribution from the town has been centered on simply tidying up a number of footpaths that run along the beach and across a landscape of dunes held in place by vegetation. In an environment where we can also find younger dunes, built up by the wind, two winding paved paths were designed that, flirting with the shore line, run parallel to the sea. The ecological impact from the construction of the path was minimized by rescuing all those plants affected by the route of the new paved areas and transferring them to a nursery.

San Francisco tram stop

Sasaki Ass. Inc.

Location: San Francisco, USA. **Date of completion**: 1998. **Architects**: Sasaki Associates Inc. **Scheme**: Canopy for a tram stop, signage, and pavement. **Photography**: Sasaki Associates.

The electric tram line of the San Francisco Municipal Company represents an important link in this city's public transport system. At the same time, it constitutes an element in the redevelopment of the southern Embarcadero seafront promenade. The initial designs for this canopy, consisting of a series of curves on the roof, was strongly criticized by locals and some shopkeepers in the area, who thought that the construction would block their precious view of the bay. Sasaki Associates. Inc were contracted by the Municipality in 1994 as urban design consultants to lead the team responsible for designing the canopy and coordinate the different public and private groups involved in the project. Sasaki identified three principal objectives in the design, starting with the urban context of the project and the needs of the seafront promenade. The canopies had to contribute to the civic and commercial revitalization of the neighborhood and at the same time preserve the bay views, so they were finally made of transparent plate glass. Finally, a modular system had to be used to reduce the cost of construction. The curved shape of the roof is the work of the artist Anna Murch and alludes to the dynamism of the waves of the bay and the distant hills beyond.

Urban parks

The projects grouped together in this
chapter are here because of a terminology
that is as broad as it is ambiguous: the
term urban park has a complex meaning
derived from the disproportionate growth
of cities as well as the typological
confusion generated by this urbanization.
This selection of contemporary projects is
intended only to outline the semantic
breadth of what should be understood as
an urban park.

Le Jardin Atlantique

François Brun, Michel Pena

Location: Paris, France. **Date of construction**: 1994. **Architects**: François Brun, Michel Pena. **Photography**: J.C. Ballot, P. Marechaux, M. Pena.

Le Jardin Atlantique is located literally on top of the train stations of Montparnasse and Pasteur, adding a surface area of 3.5 ha (8.5 acres) to Paris, won back from the railroad. Totally removed from the traffic flows and surrounded by recently constructed buildings, there is nothing to link it to traditional Parisian city gardens.

The project had to solve particularly complex problems, both technical and environmental, such as the depth of the soil and the load limits, a 700 space parking lot located over the railroad but under the garden, the presence of a hundred openings for lighting the spaces underneath, the ventilation shafts, and the shadows cast by the surrounding tall buildings.

The distribution of the park on the ground was organized around a large central square surrounded by a strolling area that separates it from the other zones. The garden is built on strips of land around this central lawn area, on the edges of which, on one side, are areas planted with trees, featuring a linked series of smaller themed spaces and, on the other, sports installations.

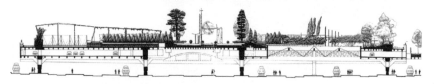

Vertical landscape: four projects in Manhattan

West 8

Location: New York, USA. **Date of construction**: 1996. **Architect**: West 8. **Scheme**: Design of four alternatives for urban revival in Manhattan. **Photography**: Jeroen Musch.

We had heard talk of this vertical city. We had seen pictures of its skyscrapers and looked forward, in its sublime expression of high rise construction, to finding striking pieces of vertical landscape, parks as ambitious as the Chrysler Building, the Empire State Building, the Rockefeller Center and others.
The first one we discovered was Central Park, the perfect empty space. A landscape sharply defined by 150 blocks, which enlivens the Manhattan skyline and satisfies the city's desire to expose itself to the sun. The remaining green spaces of Manhattan are in the form of Hanging Gardens of Babylon. The roof garden of the RCA building, the bamboo garden of the IBM building,

the interior cascades of Trump Tower, planting in the air and in the plazas: these can be considered genuine attempts to bring green inside and onto buildings and make it a part of the great spectacle that is Manhattan. However, this Babylonian ambition is revealed as superficial and deceptive

when it is examined more carefully. In order to awaken the potential of Manhattan, we explored the possibilities of using netting and the Manhattan principles of ambition and limitless verticality in landscaping projects.

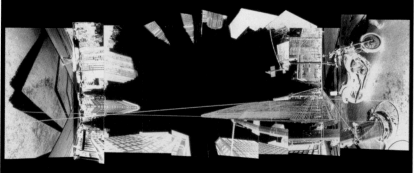

Santo Domingo de Bonaval Park

Alvaro Siza Vieira & Isabel Aguirre

Location: Rúa da Caramoniña, Santiago de Compostela, Spain. **Date of project**: 1990. **Client**: Consortium of the City of Santiago de Compostela. **Associates**: Alessandro D'Amico, Xorxe Nuno, Carlos Muro. **Photography**: Tino Martinez (also pp 166/167).

The convent of Santo Domingo de Bonaval enjoys a fine situation on a hill to the north of the city of Santiago. De Bonaval Park, with a surface area of 3.5 ha (8.5 acres) occupies the same land as the convent, which dates from the 12th century, and is divided into three clearly differentiated areas. One is a terraced kitchen garden, the second an old oak grove, and the third an old cemetery. Working to transform such special surroundings into a public park meant respecting pre-existing features: remains of walls, ruins, old paths, tombs, and, above all, stone and water. Cleaning out the streams and fountains, the water was left to run where it wanted, this time to give life to the park itself.

In the lower part of the kitchen garden zone a small geometrically shaped garden used by the convent was restored. There were traces of old platforms at different levels, joined together by ramps. A sculpture by Eduardo Chillida, "The Door of Music," was placed on one of these platforms, against the walls of the enclosure, in a terraced area on the steep slope. The upper area, which is less populated, will house the Eugenio Granell Museum Foundation. Going through a door under an enormous lintel carved with the letter omega, one reaches the old cemetery, in the shape of an octagon.

The chosen materials and the way they were used bear witness to the extreme care with which the work has been done. These were the same materials that existed before – granite, grass, moss, water – even to the extent that the combinations of them are kept almost in the same plane as before.

Doosan Centenary Park

Sasaki Associates

Location: Seoul, Korea. **Date of construction**: 1993. **Architects**: Sasaki Associates. **Scheme**: Design and construction of a small urban park. **Photography**: Sasaki Associates.

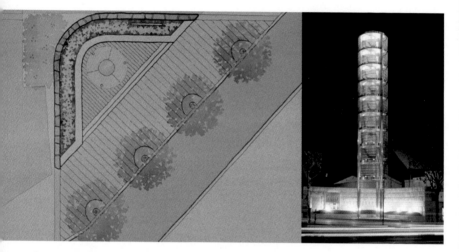

Sasaki Associates undertook the conceptual design of a small park in the historical center of Seoul. The park, situated on the site of the original Doosan store, was constructed on the occasion of the 100th anniversary of the Doosan Corporation, the oldest company in Korea. The idea behind the project was to use this historical place to create a memorable and lasting monument and to celebrate the past, present, and future successes of Doosan. The program for the project included a representation of the original store front, a time capsule, and a representation of the numbers 100 and 27, to indicate the number of years and the number of Doosan subsidiaries, respectively. The company wanted the park to be made from the best materials available and to be easily maintained.

The park, which measures some 94 m² (1000 ft²), consists of a continuous parabolic wall of granite, a bed of flowers just in front of the wall, and a cylindrical tower 25 m (82 ft) high located in the center.

The wall provides a vertical space for the names of the 27 subsidiary companies, symbolizing unity (in a single wall) and at the same time the originality of each company. Parallel to the wall and the flower bed, there is a continuous bench on which to sit.

Story Garden

Doug Macy

Location: Waterfront Park, Portland, Oregon, USA. **Date of construction**: 1993. **Clients**: City of Portland. **Architects**: Doug Macy, Larry Kirkland. **Associates**: David Oldfield (child psychologist).

Doug Macy and Larry Kirkland have created with their Story Garden a unique landscape for the Waterfront Park of Portland. Fables, myths, and reality are intertwined in a fantastic maze which is, in itself, an authentic metaphor for the journey of life. This is a surprising environment that entertains visitors by encouraging them to follow the route, posing them questions and offering them answers.

The Story Garden is a two-dimensional maze measuring 18 m (60 ft) across, built on the luxuriant lawn of the Waterfront Park. Inside, the granite paths take a series of turns that never converge at a central point, but offer a huge variety of alternative routes. Dominating the area where the maze is situated is a small mound on which there is a throne of red granite, which looks down impassively on the tortuous paths of the monument. At the other end, there is a stone platform on which a door is built out of small geometrical stones, reminiscent of one of the construction kits in children's games. The perpendicular axis formed by these two figures is finished off by granite statues representing a tortoise and a hare, in a clear allusion to the fable. Thus, the four cardinal points of the maze are defined by the throne, the doorway, the tortoise, and the hare, and the whole perimeter is framed by a series of cubes similar to those used for the door.

Macy and Kirkland interviewed child psychologists, parents, the police and people responsible for the maintenance of parks and gardens. The Story Garden is not simply a decorative element, a visual fancy; it could almost be thought of as a mental exercise, a simple hieroglyph full of symbolic elements and representations: a place that entices one in for leisure and reflection in equal measure.

Battery Park

Hanna & Olin, Paul Friedberg, Child Associates

Location: New York, USA. **Date of construction**: 1984–1995. **Architects**: Hanna & Olin, Paul Friedberg, Child Associates. **Client**: Municipality of New York and the Urban Development Corporation of the State of New York. **Associates**: Cooper Eckstut and Associates. **Photography**: Esto.

This park is an ambitious residential and commercial project on a 37 ha (92 acre) piece of land, located in Lower Manhattan alongside the World Trade Center and the Hudson river. The operation can be divided into two basic phases, and comprised the planning of an open public space that includes a mile long walk along the river and several miles of avenues and streets, as well as a considerable number of plazas and parks. The original space, which had no natural cohesion or urban identity, made the designers undertake a series of preliminary studies in order to find a way to connect this new public space with the urban and cultural idiosyncrasy of the city. In this way, it was proposed to integrate, for example, works of art in an everyday urban context.

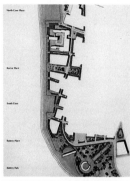

André Citroën Park

Jean Paul Viguier, Jean Francois Jodry, Alain Provost, Patrick Berger, Gilles Clément

Location: Paris. France. **Date of completion**: 1992. **Client**: Municipality of Paris, Department of Parks and Gardens. **Architects**: Jean Paul Viguier, Jean François Jodry, Alain Provost, Patrick Berger, Gilles Clément. **Scheme**: Restoration of a plot of land for the construction of a multifunctional park in the center of Paris. **Photography**: Alain Provost.

The Citroën Park is above all a conceptual garden of many parts: rejecting the idea of a multicultural forum or recreational use, it was built as a place for the contemplation of nature. Its current configuration dates back to the international competition to create gardens on the land spoiled by the Citroën car company. André Citroën Park, together with La Villette, is the most important green space created in Paris since the Second Empire. The central area, of 11 ha (27 acres), includes a wide esplanade on a gentle slope, closed off by two enormous hot-houses, a large rectangular parterre, and a series of levels that descend to the edge of the park. Flanking the end of the park furthest from the river, like two large ears, are the Black Garden and the White Garden. The first, thickly wooded, has an empty space in the middle; the second, very stony and light, with white flowering plum trees and plants with light-colored leaves, has no space in the middle.
To the northeast of the park, where the Black Garden ends, there is an area with many gardens, particularly the *jardins sériels*, poetic and intimate and laid out in a line. On the other side of the diagonal there is a more stony area, dotted about with towers and granite nymphs, and with a large canal feature.

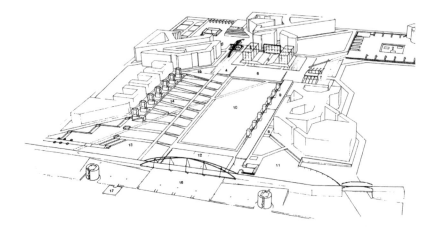

La Villette

Bernard Tschumi

Location: Paris, France. **Date of completion**: 1991. **Architect**: Bernard Tschumi. **Photography**: J.Y. Gregoire.

La Cité des Sciences, la Géode, le Grand Hall, le Parc de la Villette and la Cité de la Musique occupy the same area on the outskirts of Paris. This was one of the great urban debates of the 1980s and a much discussed subject in publications at the time. The construction of the monumental and scenic Cité de la Musique brought its architect, Christian de Portzamparc, the Pritzker Prize. The La Villette project was one of the star competitions of the 1980s yet, nevertheless, the celebrated scheme of the Swiss-French Bernard Tschumi seems today a landscape in decline. This area is in competition with La Défense to be the least happy urban planning experience in Paris.

Place Stalingrad

Bernard Huet

Location: Paris, France. **Date of construction**: 1990. **Client**: Municipality of Paris. **Architect**: Bernard Huet. **Scheme**: Plaza for public use: landscaping, access bridge to the upper terrace, and street furniture. **Photography**: Francesc Tur.

The Place Stalingrad project was at first strictly related to the La Villette program, and was part of the Parisian plan for restoring the canals. Bernard Huet's strategy for this remodeling project can be summed up in five points, in order of priority: improving the image of the square as a public area, the only function of which is to be available for use by all; emphasize the spirit of the place, its essence and historical significance; carry out the great urban project formulated by Ledoux (and, especially, the later one by Girard) without resorting to strategies of continuity that make it appear totally finished; avoiding vulgar and direct pragmatic solutions, given that the role assigned to architecture is one of sublimating and emphasizing these aspects; and, finally, consciously refusing to give the same answer to every question, so that each part of the project can be dealt with in accordance with the stylistic language most appropriate to its nature.

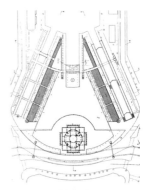

La Vall d'Hebrón Park

Eduard Bru

Location: Barcelona, Spain. **Date of completion**: 1992. **Architect**: Eduard Bru. **Clients**: Municipality of Barcelona. **Scheme**: Urban park for public use, sporting installations, changing rooms, office, and services. **Photography**: David Cardelús, Eduard Bru.

The 1992 Olympic Games in Barcelona gave the city a unique opportunity for urban renewal within the metropolitan area. The Olympic Ring provided the space that the sporting event so rightly deserved and bequeathed to the city a series of recreational areas. One of these is now the La Vall d'Hebrón Park: a complex of sports installations, equipment, and buildings that needed to be fitted in with neighboring development. This uncontrolled peripheral growth, which had been taking place for decades up to the limit of the Collserola hills, had to be rationalized.

Today this is a beautiful park for the public, in which all the sporting facilities left as a legacy of 1992 are used extensively.

Piccolo Giardino at Gibellina

Francesco Venezia

Location: Gibellina, Trapani, Italy. **Date of construction**: 1985–1988. **Client**: Municipality of Gibellina. **Architect**: Francesco Venezia. **Associates**: Giuseppe Taibi (works assistant). **Scheme**: Remodeling a public plaza in a historical center. **Photography**: Mimmo Jodice.

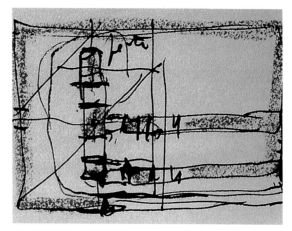

The city of Gibellina, destroyed in an earthquake in 1968, was the object of a series of plans which tried to reorganize its urban image. The Italian architect contributed to this reconstruction by means of a small public garden in which he has managed to reconcile concepts that are not usual in an urban setting. The small area is situated in a zone characterized by a slight slope up the hill dominating the location. Here has been located the central plaza, with the market, the library, houses, and the garden that closes off the island. The project was conceived as a difficult combination of a building and a park, as a public space, and, at the same time, a private one. This means architectural continuity of front elevations, creation of an accessible inner space that is in contact with the natural urban environment and that, finally, invites introspection and reflection, a dialog between the past and the present, carefully avoiding a clash of styles.

Peripheral parks

The only unifying parameter which the projects included here share is that of their location: the works chosen are situated halfway between urban area and nature, in an ambiguous no man's land. It is precisely this definition of location that distinguishes them from urban parks or squares. However, these projects also display a number of differences with respect to other aspects of landscaping, since peripheral parks do not insist on forced integration of green spaces into the city. The adjustment of the periphery aims to dignify marginal areas, create ecosystems that are fully valid both ecologically and aesthetically, and build a more intimate connection between the individual and nature.

El Besós Park

Culhuacán Historical Park

Xochimilco Park

Candelstick Point Cultural Park

Byxbee Park

Papago Park

Princess Sofía Park

Le Domaine du Rayol

Le Jardin des Retours

Poblenou Park

El Besós Park

Viaplana & Piñón Arquitectes

Location: Barcelona, Spain. **Date of completion**: 1987. **Client**: Municipality of Barcelona. **Architect**: Viaplana & Piñón Architects. **Scheme**: Urban park for public use, sculptural trail. **Photography**: David Cardelús.

With the intention of returning lost space to the city, it was proposed to restructure this area according to a series of urban planning and landscaping criteria that have presided over the whole project: on the one hand, linking the park to the framework of the urban fabric, not only in a physical and material sense, but also in its most abstract and spiritual aspects, whether typological, tectonic, or landscaping; and, on the other hand, creating an area for collective enjoyment, emphasizing it as a place for dialog with the environment and one that is available to the people of the city.

In the planning stage, as well as considering physical factors, it was suggested there was a need to recover the identifying values of the place, both from the cultural point of view (typological tradition) and from the natural (selection of different species of vegetation in accordance with the climate and the landscape). At the same time, special emphasis was placed on the definition of spaces suitable for collective enjoyment, with a distribution of functional areas to be used for walking and for talking.

Culhuacán Historical Park

Grupo de Diseño Urbano

Location: Iztapalapa. Mexico. **Date of construction**: 1992. **Clients**: Culhuacán Community Center (National Institute of Anthropology and History). **Architect**: Grupo de Diseño Urbano. **Associates**: Elsa Hernandez (archeology), Juan Vanegas (history). **Scheme**: Design and construction of a historical theme park. **Photography**: Gabriel Figueroa

Recovering the history of a people is, sometimes, the prime objective of the landscape architect. The Culhuacán park uses historical and archeological remains as elements for organizing the space, where they are integrated into contemporary local culturural activities.

The basic objective consisted of recovering the historical character of the place and at the same time promoting the traditions of the local inhabitants. To achieve this, three thematic fields were established: the rescue of memory (the Aztec ruins), reevaluation of existing buildings (the former convent), and the creation of new areas. These three levels also had to re-create the type of environment of ancient Tenochtitlán's age of splendor. The overall compositional scheme adopted had to be orthogonal, in accordance with the urban outline and also with the orientation of the convent. As an element to generate interest in the site, a pool was proposed – a historical reference to the Aztec waterway – framed by the ruins of the ancient walls. An open air theater, with seating for 250, was built in the southeastern part of the park.

The special geometry of the different spaces and the use of local materials contribute to the way the park blends in with its surroundings. As an extension of buildings and historical remains that already existed, the Culhuacán park is a peaceful and tranquil spot which is also permanent, far from the vicissitudes of the present day.

Xochimilco Park

Grupo de Diseño Urbano

Location: Xochimilco, Mexico. **Date of construction**: 1992–1993. **Client**: Municipality of Xochimilco and Department of the Federal District. **Architects**: Grupo de Diseño Urbano. **Associate**: Jorge Calvillo. **Scheme**: Urban park for public use, sporting areas, greenhouses, information center, exhibition hall, shops, cafeteria, services, and offices. **Photography**: Jorge Sandoval.

The 280 ha (690 acres) of the park were used to create a natural bird sanctuary, a botanical garden with an area for gardening demonstrations, a recreational area with boating, a new lagoon, as well as a market selling plants and flowers, sports areas, greenhouses, and a visitors' information center. The information center is located in the access plaza, the heart of the park, a multifunctional building

which houses a small museum, an information post, a hall for temporary exhibitions, shops, cafeteria, services, and offices, in addition to a viewing point on the roof. The reddish concrete used is an allusion to tezontle, the local stone of the region, traditionally used for building. All the buildings are integrated into the landscape and are surrounded by paths, pergolas, vines, and brushwood fences, thus helping to preserve the natural character of the park's location.

Candlestick Point Cultural Park

Hargreaves Associates

Location: San Francisco, California, USA. **Date of construction**: 1985–1993. **Architecture**: Hargreaves Associates. **Associates**: Mack Architects, Doug Dollis. **Scheme**: Design and construction of an urban public park. **Photography**: Hargreaves Associates

The project arose in 1985 out of a joint initiative of the California Arts Council, the department of parks and the office of the architect for the state of California. Their objective was to integrate architecture, landscaping, and art in one location. The site is on the edge of the city of San Francisco, on some land reclaimed from the sea, in an industrial area buffeted by high winds. The plot, of 7.3 ha (18 acres), excluding an enormous area of open parking lot, is in the middle of a featureless urban landscape next to a sports stadium. There is a gentle grass-covered slope that extends directly down to the water. Depending on the direction of the wind, the conditions can be like a wind tunnel, and this intensifies the experience of visiting the cultural park.

Byxbee Park

Hargreaves Associates

Location: Palo Alto, California, USA. **Date of completion**: 1991. **Client**: City of Palo Alto. **Architect**: Hargreaves Associates. **Associates**: P. Richards, M. Oppenheimer (sculptures), Robert L. Davies (architect), Emcon (engineering). **Scheme**: Converting a garbage tip into a suburban park. **Photography**: Hargreaves Associates.

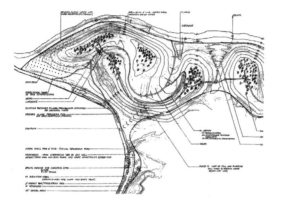

Byxbee Park is an interesting experiment in landscape recycling, inasmuch as it consists of the transformation of a 60.7 ha (150 acre) garbage tip into a coastal park on San Francisco Bay.

Hargreaves's plan was to clean up the landscape and place sculptures to highlight the qualities of the location, such as the light and the breeze. The first step was to seal the garbage with a 60 cm (2 ft) layer of earth and 30 cm (1 ft) of clay. The upper layer of clay is shaped to produce mounds some 18 cm (7 in) high at the base of the slope to avoid erosion. To prevent this cover from cracking, and in view of the risk of toxic substances escaping due to the growth of large roots, it was decided not to plant trees. Instead, most of the park is covered by dense short grass, native to the area. The paths of crushed shells, some 1.8 m (6 ft)

wide, wind along the contours of the park, and produce a special crunch when walked on. An earth wall, with a gap in it, marks the transition between the north part of the park, open and exposed, and the more sheltered areas, next to the marsh. Along the edge of the marsh, a series of tables and benches are sheltered from the wind and from here visitors can enjoy the view and watch the large population of migratory birds in this area of the park.

Papago Park

Steve Martino

Location: Phoenix. USA. **Date of completion**: 1992. **Architect**: Steve Martino. **Associate**: Jody Pinto. **Scheme**: Design and construction of a peripheral park and its irrigation system. **Photography**: R. Maack, S. Martino.

The progressive urbanization of the area and an uncontrolled demographic explosion of small mammals, together with a total lack of maintenance and protection in this natural park, were the reasons for the ecological disaster here. Having arrived at this situation it was necessary to take some sort of action that would serve as a catalyst for any future operations and give an indication that the park was going to change direction. The scheme included the elevation of a sculpture at the entrance to the park, a landmark in the immensity of the desert. The

highways, marking the limits of the park where they cross in one corner, only add harshness to the already arduous task of defining and giving content to the zone. Martino and Pinto's work makes a simple yet forceful contribution to the landscape: set against the speed of the highway, this is a static sculpture of sufficient dimensions to be seen and, set against the arid climate, it uses stone and native plant species as materials for expression. The structure consists of an aqueduct nearly 200 m (650 ft) long, with seven branches, small walls that spread sinuously across the adjacent terrain, irrigating the dry land.

Princess Sofía Park

José Antonio Martinez Lapeña-Elías Torres Tur

Location: La Línea de la Concepción, Cadiz, Spain. **Date of construction**: 1990–1993. **Client**: General Directorate of Town Planning, Andalusia Board, Public Land Company. **Associates**: Iñaki Alday, Nuria Bordas, Arturo Frediani, Marisa García, Clara Jiménez, Eduard Miralles, Joaquín Pérez, Inés Rodriguez, Quim Rosell. **Technical Architects**: José Maria Hervas. Carlos Sánchez. **Construction**: Fomento de Construcciones y Contratas. **Photography**: Fernando Alda (also pp 192/193).

In addition to one of the two zones projected for open air shows, these photographs show the general lighting system for the park: a number of masts, which are also used for irrigation, carry the lights that are suspended above the park.

The basic idea of the remodeling project is based on respecting and reevaluating the existing trees by means of a new area of park. There are four winding strips of land that follow the existing palm trees, planted between the lawn and edged by metal plates. In addition, new palm trees are planted to fill in the empty interstices to form continuous lines. These strips run the length of the park from north to south and, being separated, they define other similar strips that are paved with white gravel, in which the other, existing trees appear in haphazard order. Superimposed on these are two straight paths, also running north to south and paved with asphalt, that make the large area of the park more accessible to traffic. Another street, also asphalted and wider than the first, which is designed to be the axis for activities inside the park, crosses it from east to west. Eucalyptus trees are planted alongside this, taking advantage of the proximity of the water table, which makes the promenade a suitable area for the annual La Línea fair. To give better accessibility to the far reaches of the park there are a number of 3 m (10 ft) paths, parallel to the main promenade and crossing the strips of lawn. To the south of the promenade of eucalyptus there are two concrete buildings that are used for small open-air spectacles. There are also two large canopies, also made of concrete, to protect the temporary installation of kiosks or bars.

Le Domaine du Rayol

Atelier Acanthe & Gilles Clément

Location: Le Rayol Canade, France. **Date of project**: 1988–1997. **Landscape Architects**: Gilles Clément and Philipe Delian. **Associates**: François Macquert-Moulin (conservationist), Jean-Laurent Felizia, Jean-Michel Battin (gardeners), Albert Tourrette (imports). **Client**: Conservatoire du Littoral. **Area**: 25 ha (62 acres). **Scheme**: Botanical garden. **Photography**: Alexandre Bailhache.

Underwater garden and marine habitat.

Mexican desert landscape.

The splendor of exotic plants.

Le Domaine du Rayol occupies a particularly beautiful area of the Côte des Maures, on the French Mediterranean coast. Clément proposed to the Conservatoire the creation of an "austral garden," by which he meant, in his own words, "a complex for life's compatibility," where the real inhabitants are the flora planted in it, and which could also become a place for experimenting with the behavior of the different species when all are living together and in relationship with the climate. So, Clément divided the land into a small number of sectors, each one corresponding to a different area of the planet: Australia, New Zealand, Tasmania, South Africa, Chile, Mexico, California, and China. Many of the species planted over the six years of work were found in Europe, although a few were brought from their places of origin; others were planted by seed. The project was proposed as the creation of a garden for the improvement of plants: removing them from their natural habitats and replanting them in Le Domaine, the universal method of removing an organic element from its context and trying to maintain its vitality outside it, one of the best procedures. Clément calls La Domaine "a garden to understand," a place where the vitality and full growth of vegetation are the chief protagonists. He does not seek to create landscapes, but rather this is an operation of "ordered and planned reforestation," in the sense that the species recovered have clear autonomy with respect to man's colonizing experience in their area.

Le Jardin des Retours

Bernard Lassus

Location: Rochefort-sur-Mer, France. **Date of completion**: 1995. **Client**: Municipality of Rochefort-sur-Mer. **Landscape Architect**: Bernard Lassus. **Associates**: D. Anglesio, P. Aubry (landscaping), P. Donadieu (agricultural engineer). **Scheme**: Landscaping and historical restoration. **Photography**: Bernard Lassus, B. Poitevin

Starting with this landscaping operation, the architect tried to create a garden as a starting point for the cultural revitalization of this French city. Thus, Lassus proposed the idea of making a link between the city and the sea, giving a different scale to the connection between the town and the river Charente, without forgetting the important relationship with the historical past. With the planting of species of plant commonly considered to be from the interior, it has been possible to evoke the places of origin of those species and the historical period when they were introduced. Consequently Lassus calls them "plants for landscapes." A pedestrian link (357 m, 390 yds) was created between

the town and the Corderie building. There is a parallel access in the form of a ramp (140 m long by 21 m wide, 460 by 70 ft), which follows the ancient wall of Rochefort, parallel to the old industrial buildings. Nearby is the Maze of Battles, a landscape, a mediation between the river, the dikes, and the plants. This undulating garden can only be enjoyed from the inside and step by step. Finally, this garden also offers a simple walk by the river bank, in contact with the natural vegetation which borders it, principally comprising local woodland plants and trees.

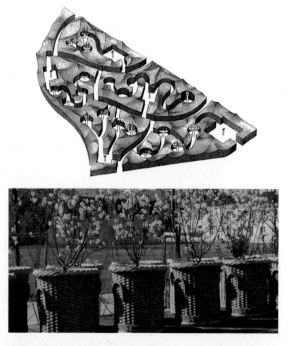

Poblenou Park

M. Ruisanchez and X. Vendrell

Location: Barcelona, Spain. **Date of completion**: 1992. **Client**: Municipality of Barcelona. **Architects**: M. Ruisanchez and X. Vendrell. **Associates**: S. Pieras, E. Prats (architects), M. Colominas, J. Consoia (agricultural engineering). **Scheme**: Recovery of an old industrial zone for the construction of an urban park. **Photography**: David Cardelús.

The old part of Poblenou forms part of the industrial expansion of the city of Barcelona that began at the end of the 19th century. The land consisted of waste material and was occupied by a number of industrial installations and a railroad station. Poblenou Park's configuration follows dunes running from the beach inland, through a break created between two walks. A Mediterranean woodland has been planted consisting of masses of bushes and groups of flowering trees.

The structure of the pedestrian walks in the park are in the form of a grid: longitudinally, a series of winding paths following the topography; across these, paths have been designed that are extensions towards the beach from the old streets of the neighborhood. These paths all have different surfaces, from colored concrete to impacted earth, depending on where they are and the directions they run. Each section of the grid has a different type of lighting: low beacons beaming onto the pavement or standard lamps that project their light onto a small curved screen beyond.

The park has a system of water cannons that can provide irrigation in a way very much like the natural process of rain, while at the same time reducing the harmful effects on the vegetation of salinity brought by the wind from the Mediterranean.

Urban monuments and land art

It is difficult to judge the relationship between art and nature from the appearance of land art at the end of the 1960s. Now, nature is art. Now, not only mountains, valleys, and atmospheric phenomena but even open urban spaces have become support, material, and subject of new forms of artistic intervention. Land art arose linked to the minimalist idea that tried to break with the decorative function of sculpture and was nourished by the wish to dematerialize works of art. The ephemeral nature of works of land art (this is the principal difference between the two types of works included in this chapter) opened the doors to the idea of art as an experience. The examples that follow form a diverse panorama which shows locations dedicated to art in the search for new connections between nature, art, and urban life.

Mount Tindaya

Wrapped Reichstag

Tower of the Winds

Ice Walls

Boundary Split, Annual Rings, Formula Compound

Iceland Project

Fieldgate, Oak Tree, Elm Leaves, Red Pool

Bird's Nest, Empty Nest, Groups of Flowers

Toronto Project, Prefabrications, Frauenbad

Triangular Pavilion

La Grande Arche

Capsa de Mistos

Mount Tindaya

Eduardo Chillida Juantegui

Location: Fuerteventura, Spain. **Date of project**: 1996. **Architect**: Eduardo Chillida Juantegui. **Associates**: José A. Fernandez-Ordoñez, Lorenzo Fernandez-Ordoñez, Luis Ignacio Bartolomé Biot. **Photography**: Lorenzo Fernandez-Ordoñez (also pp 216/217), Daniel Diaz Font.

Making space in the bowels of Mount Tindaya means for Chillida creating a place between heaven and earth, from where to contemplate the horizon and deliver oneself up to light and the architecture that it creates.

The work on Mount Tindaya is on a world record scale for light in underground spaces, though these achievements are nearly always surpassed.

The space is located within the mountain in such a way that it is not affected by any of the currently known diaclases and dikes. Given the huge size of the hall excavated, an area of the mountain had to be found that would be unaffected by any sort of geological fracturing.

The opening for the sun was located on the south side of the mountain and that for the moon on the north, since a colder light was required. The opening that looks out to the horizon, to the infinity of the sea, has been hidden in a fold in the west side of the mountain, making use of a quarry and an existing road, which will serve as access. In order to preserve a clear vision of the horizon from the hall, the entrance tunnel has been located at a level a few meters lower than the hall.

In this way, visitors entering and leaving the monument will not appear in the line of sight to the horizon, out to sea from the space inside Mount Tindaya, but rather there will always be a neat horizon on view.

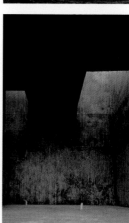

Wrapped Reichstag

Christo & Jeanne-Claude

Location: Berlin, Germany. **Date of realization**: 1995. **Architects**: Christo & Jeanne-Claude. **Associates**: Michael S. Cullen, Roland Specker Wolfgang Volz, Sylvia Volz. **Scheme**: Wrapping of the German Parliament building. **Photography**: Wolfgang S. Wewerka.

For 14 days, from 24 June to 7 July 1995, the German Parliament in Berlin, the Reichstag, was wrapped in a metallic fabric, tied down on all sides as if it were a parcel. Christo and Jeanne-Claude had been pursuing this idea since 1971. Twenty-four years of work and perseverance, involving the public and many institutions in the project, permitted them to realize their ambition with this emblematic new work. A contract was signed between the city of Berlin, government authorities in Bonn, and the artists whereby the artists had to provide:
– insurance for all the personnel and property involved with the city of Berlin and the federal government;
– complete and satisfactory removal of all the wrapping material;
– full cooperation with the Berlin community;
– personnel contracted from among the local inhabitants;
– communication with and access to the daily activities of the Reichstag during the process of the work.
The work was entirely financed by the artists, as on other occasions, when projects have been paid for by the sale of drawings, preliminary studies, collages, etc., thus dispensing with the need for sponsors, and guaranteeing the independence of the work. The artists used 10 ha (25 acres) of aluminized polypropylene material and more than of 16 km (10 miles) of cord of the same material, in order that, for a number of days, they could hide the Reichstag, the true symbol of German democracy, from public view.

Tower of the Winds

Toyo Ito & Associates

Location: Yokohama, Kanagawa, Japan. **Date of construction**: 1986. **Client**: Committee for the 30th Anniversary of Yokohama West Station. **Architect**: Toyo Ito & Associates. **Associates**: Gengo Matsui + O.R.S. (structure); TL Yamagiwa Inc. (lighting); Masami Usuki (programmer). **Photography**: Sinkenchiku-sha, Tomio Ohashi.

The Tower of the Winds is located on an urban center of accelerated energy typical of Japan's major cities, which are immersed in the vortex of the twin paradox about architecture that we are proposing.

The primitive ventilation and water tower that existed in the bus terminal square of Yokohama station has been re-covered, following its restoration, by an elliptical cylinder of perforated aluminum some 21 m (70 ft) high. When night falls, its surface loses all form. All that can be seen is a network that traps the essence of each moment, filters all the available environmental information, and interweaves it to produce the fabric that is the reality of the place.

The direction and speed of the wind as well as the intensity of the traffic noise are transformed into electrical impulses to become an ephemeral architecture of light. The tower is a mirror of its circumstances, and thus is not material. The tower is never the same, which makes it ephemeral, changing in essence.

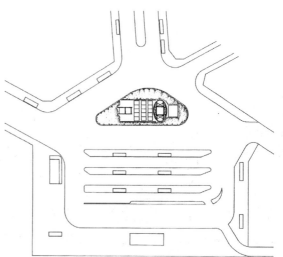

Ice Walls

Michael Van Valkenburgh Associates

Location: University of Harvard, Cambridge, Mass., USA. **Date of construction**: 1987. **Architect**: Michael Van Valkenburgh Associates. **Scheme**: Ephemeral installation in the form of a wall of ice. **Photography**: Hansen, C. Mayer, Michael Van Valkenburgh.

Michael Van Valkenburgh graduated as a landscape architect from the University of Illinois in 1977. He is professor and president of the department of landscaping of the Graduate School of Design of the University of Harvard (Massachusetts). In 1987, he undertook an experiment at Harvard which culminated in the installation, the following year, of a series of ice walls on the Radcliffe Yard of the campus. The design consisted of vertical panels, each 15.2 m long by 2.1 m high (50 ft by 7 ft). Made from a galvanized stainless steel mesh with a water channel along the top edge, the surface was sprayed to encourage the formation of small blocks of ice that finally finished up as a whole wall of ice. The extreme precariousness of the ice and the conditions of maintenance required certain techniques to be respected. So, with a view to the need to make repairs, the supply of water was located where it could be easily reached.

The channels were made of rubber, to make them less affected by the expansion of the water freezing inside and because, at lower temperatures, they were more flexible than plastic or metal. A heating cable, supplied by electricity or heat from the sun, controlled the freezing under extreme conditions. Both the increase in weight due to ice and the action of the wind introduced a factor of instability which was controlled by balancing the verticality using hydraulic jacks.

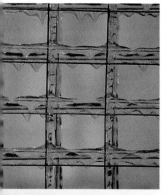

Boundary Split, Annual Rings, Formula Compound

Dennis Oppenheim

Location: St. John River. USA; US/Canada border; Potsdam, New York, USA. **Dates of realization**: 1968, 1968, 1982. **Artist**: Dennis Oppenheim. **Scheme**: Three ephemeral works of land art. **Photography**: Dennis Oppenheim.

Minimalism, land art, body art, conceptual art, installations, pieces, objects...Oppenheim has concentrated on the land art experience and so-called earthworks, especially during the periods between 1967 and 1969, and from 1973 onwards. In these, the works leave the galleries and museums and are transported to the great outdoors. The mountain, the sea, the countryside, even at times the city itself, will provide a new context for artistic creation. Land art, that in its time was considered as "the Anglo-Saxon variant of peasant art," originates from suggestions similar to those of minimalism and endows the procedure and the material to be transformed by a value greater than the end result of the work. In accordance with this spirit, Oppenheim maintains that the important thing is not so much "what one does, but what drives one to do it," predicting moreover that "the movement of sensory pressures from the object to the place will be the greatest contribution of minimalist art." His interest in change urges him to experiment with deviations of course, transplants of material, transformations of energy, and the

breakdown of substances found in the natural world.

Iceland Project

Magdalena Jetelová

Location: Iceland. **Date of project**: 1992. **Architect**: Magdalena Jetelová. **Photography**: Werner Hannappel

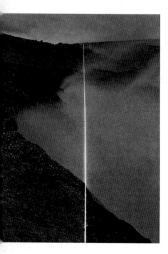

A line traced by a laser separates the American and Eurasian continents. The Atlantic oceanic ridge is visible for more than 350 km (560 miles) in Icelandic territorial waters.

After a detailed study of the geography of Iceland, a concept was developed for a visualization of the intercontinental frontier that separates Eurasia from America. This island is the only place where it is possible to see, on the surface for more than 350 km (560 miles) the Atlantic mountain chain, which divides the two continental plates and runs more than 15,000 km (24,000 miles) under the ocean.

In the summer of 1992, Magdalena Jetelová went to Iceland with a small team of technicians to identify and represent the geological line between America and Europe.

Across the mountain range, from one end of the island to the other, this dividing line was redrawn using a laser beam. The photographs have become a document of the frontier, traced by laser across the rocky landscape, up and down the masses of lava or dissolving and disappearing into the steam from the geysers. But the artist's objectives did not stop there. She considers this work as part of a global process and not an end in itself: the division, the fracture into two, like the hope of renewal. The surprising act of cutting Iceland in two gives it a renewed beauty. The luminous line dividing the earth becomes part of the island; without it, the island could not exist in this way, and its power to fascinate resides in this total interdependence.

Fieldgate, Oak Tree, Elm Leaves, Red Pool

Andy Goldsworthy

Location: Poundridge, Dumfriesshire, Scotland. **Dates of realization**: 1993, 1994, 1994, 1995. **Artist**: Andy Goldsworthy. **Photography**: Andy Goldsworthy.

The work of Andy Goldsworthy (from Cheshire, UK, born 1956) is nourished by his immediate natural environment. The impact produced by direct contact with such elements as real as cold and rain, the weight of rocks, the vastness of sand, and the brightness and softness of other materials is nowadays restricted to the very limited worlds of children and artists, but, as Goldsworthy himself admits, "I need the effect of touch, the resistance of the place, the materials and the time...." Working directly with natural materials from the environment itself and without the artificial prosthesis of tools, he associates the triangular coordination of eye, hand, and mind with the world of the infantile state, with a child's admiration for minute things, their first attempts to handle small twigs and leaves. Goldsworthy weaves simple patterns and lines with colored leaves and thorns, superimposing them on the complex orders of slowly evolving nature. Lines drawn with leaves along the heavy branch of an oak are immediately recognized as human. The leaves of an elm extended the length of a rock remind one of the labors of a hardworking caterpillar on a summer's afternoon. But, he maintains, "I am not representing the primitive."

Bird's Nest, Empty Nest, Groups of Flowers

Nils-Udo

Location: Bavaria; Raimes Forest; Reunion Isles. **Dates of realization**: 1990, 1993, 1994. Artist: Nils-Udo.
Scheme: Various installations with reference to forms from nature. **Photography**: Nils-Udo.

"Nature interests me only so much!"
This defines the attitude of photographer and sculptor Nils-Udo, born in 1937 in the Bavarian town of Lauf. Since 1972 he has had exhibitions and installations in various places throughout the world and among the titles of his works is constant reference to forms from nature such as the sun, water, woods, valleys, bamboo, maize, or flowers. In some of his work notes, Nils-Udo expresses a series of ideas: "Draw with flowers. Paint with clouds. Write with water. Record the May wind, the fall of a leaf. Work for a storm. Anticipate a glacier. Bend the wind. Orient water and light...." There is, therefore, an evident desire to capture and record the currents of energy in the movements of nature, subject them to stress, and transform them into the power of expression.

Toronto Project, Prefabrications, Frauenbad

Tadashi Kawamata

Location: Toronto, Canada; Tokyo, Japan; Zurich, Switzerland. **Dates of realization**: 1989, 1992, 1993.
Artist: Tadashi Kawamata. **Scheme**: Three constructions of ephemeral art. **Photography**: Tadashi Kawamata

Kawamata uses recycled wood as his raw material, and his work (social attitudes and shapes that transform the urban environment) speak to us of time, space, and the confrontation of rhythms. Four months of work were needed for the Toronto Project (1989), an open space between two neoclassical buildings located opposite a large shopping center. Following his usual method, Kawamata establishes a dialogue of contrast between static buildings and his own dynamic and ephemeral constructions of recycled wood.

Prefabrications (Tokyo, 1992) is a good example of his work. This is an installation in the gardens of the Setagaya Museum of Art. Another of Kawamata's recent projects is *Frauenbad* (Zurich, 1993), in which the artist's work starts with the presence of some old bathing huts located on the river Limmat and the Helmhaus. In this case, his associates have been participants (alcoholics and drug addicts) in a rehabilitation program. His participation

consisted of building two new bathing huts, the symbolic purpose of which was to make an ironic statement on Protestant morality, which puts up walls so that the users cannot be seen: so, one of the bathing huts has been put into the river, far from the bank, so that it cannot be freely used; the other has been installed inside the museum, with the intention of showing the complex relationship between the inside and the outside. All of Kawamata's creations explore an ambiguous land of nothing, that seems to swing between urban land art and ephemeral architecture in form.

Triangular Pavilion

Dan Graham

Location: Museum of the Prefecture of Yamaguchi, Japan. **Date of realization**: 1990. **Architect**: Dan Graham. **Scheme**: Ephemeral work: triangular pavilion on a grid of wood and glass. **Photography**: Dan Graham.

Along with many American artists who emerged in the 1970s, Dan Graham challenges any attempt to classify the dominant styles of that period. Neither pop art, nor minimalism, nor conceptual art offer a sufficiently flexible profile act as a label. The openings and multiplications that Graham has practiced on the prototype of the minimalist cube have been considered as a caricature of modernity and a criticism of the growing privatization of public spaces. Constant use of glass and two-way mirrors defines the interest that Graham places on the sociopsychological perception of individuals. In 1990 he was invited to undertake one of his projects in the Museum of the Prefecture of Yamaguchi (Japan), and he introduced a typical

wooden grille, so widely used as partitions in Japanese homes. This triangular pavilion with wooden panels had a two-way mirror that functioned as an optical frontier in opposition to the physical barrier represented by the latticework. Visual relationships can be affected when the viewer opens or closes the sliding doors of the mirror. In the

same way, their location parallel to a glass wall belonging to the museum provoked kaleidoscopic repetition and visual pleasure as an antidote to the alienating and monolithic effect of two-way mirrors in offices.

La Grande Arche

J.O. von Spreckelsen & Paul Andreu

Location: La Défense, Paris, France. **Date of construction**: 1989. **Architects**: Johan Otto von Spreckelsen (winner of the competition), Paul Andreu (Aéroports de Paris). **Consultants**: Coyne & Bellier (structural engineers), Peter Rice (design), Trouvin (air-conditioning), Serete (electrics), Commins (acoustics), CSTB Nantes (aerodynamic studies), Clair Roof (lighting), André Putman, and Jean-Michel Wilmotte (interior layout). **Scheme**: Viewing point, meeting and conference room, exhibition areas, offices, and services. **Photography**: Stockphotos, G. Fessy.

The major urban development of La Défense wanted to involve historical Paris, so the complex of skyscrapers and office buildings was organized around the same axis that joined the Louvre with the Arc de Triomphe. In this way, the Champs Élysées were extended to the periphery. Within this strategy, the Grande Arche was built as a visual landmark that would allow La Défense to be identified from the center. The design competition was won by Johan Otto von Spreckelsen, and the fundamental decisions concerning the project are his, but the premature death of Spreckelsen and the involvement of Aéroports de Paris in the construction of the building brought in Paul Andreu to be responsible for the final project. Although the function of the Grande Arche is basically monumental, the building houses offices, conference and meeting rooms, and exhibition areas, downstairs, upstairs and in the sides, making full use of the structure.

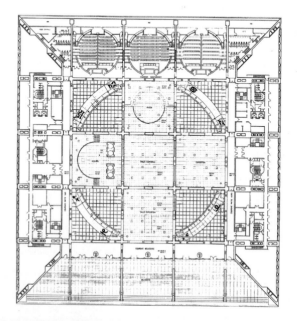

Capsa de Mistos

Claes Oldenburg and Coosje van Bruggen

Location: Barcelona, Spain. **Date of realization**: 1992. **Architect**: Claes Oldenburg and Coosje van Bruggen.
Scheme: Sculpture in an urban plaza in commemoration of the Olympic Games. **Photography**: David
Cardelús.

Claes Oldenburg and Coosje van Bruggen are two figures paradigmatic of the art of the second half of the 20th century who, starting with pop art, have brought a new vision of what they themselves call "private art in public spaces." One of the clearest examples is that of Capsa de Mistos. Since 1987, the idea of the matchbox presented itself in the artists' minds, as a result of a series of reflections on Spanish and Catalan culture. The formal composition of the box, with its profiles elevated, inclined, fallen, disseminated, and the palette of pure colors (red, blue, yellow, and black) make various symbolic references: the traumatic memory of the Spanish Civil War; the metaphor of Quixote; the colors of the Catalan and Spanish flags; or refer to the sculpture of Picasso for the Chicago Civic Center and the unfinished Sagrada Familia cathedral of Antonio Gaudí. But the clearest symbology is the commemoration of the Olympic Games of '92: the matches are like athletes and sportsmen, metaphors of triumph, power, strength, sacrifice, and, above all, the emblem of fire and the Olympic torch. The work has become one of the landmarks of post-Olympic Barcelona, a symbolic and commemorative element that, without resorting to traditional ideas of monuments, transforms the scale of landscape of the city, conferring on them a strange new dimension.

Cultural facilities

The 20th century has seen the
development of architecture where new
technologies have played a determining
role, an architecture that, apart from cost,
has no limits, succeeding in materializing
the wildest desires of clients and
designers, an architecture of ego.
Architects who have enjoyed greatest
recognition have become celebrities, idols,
metaphors for the purest kind of creation.
So, administrations have contracted such
personalities to plan the cities of the
future: in addition to providing a guarantee
of quality, they lend prestige to the project.
In this regard, the last few decades have
seen many types of cultural facility
flourish, the majority of which have
become the symbol of the place they
house, tourist attractions that are now
generators of profit. The flow of visitors to
museums, cultural centers, and art
galleries has increased enormously thanks
to the reworking of their image.

Previously, museums were repositories
where works of art were held, and
decontextualized. Nowadays, such
buildings offer spaces with their own
character, that appear like an extension of
the works they exhibit. There is a double
treat on offer here: contemplation of
sculptures, pictures, and displays, plus the
appreciation of quality architecture.
Buildings both functional and unusual
have been created that respond positively
to client and user requirements and offer
spaces that combine multiple sensations
for the delight of the viewer. The four
chapters included in this section hope to
give an overall view of this species of
building, presenting contemporary projects
that have managed to become
architectural standards: emblematic
buildings, not only because of the unique
works they contain, but also because of the
quality of their construction, their singular
aesthetics, and their perfect functionality.

Museums

Art galleries

Cultural centers and foundations

Schools and universities

Libraries

Religious buildings

Museums

If there is one idea that symbolizes modern thinking, it is that of the museum. The technological revolution brought about by computers and communications media has in the last few years meant a new transformation of our way of life and, likewise that of museums. Nowadays people are opening museums of every sort: of places, of wine, of coffee, or of art and, at the same time, traditional museums are being expanded out of all proportion, which makes it impossible to see all in a single day. On the other hand, they are being equipped with leisure in mind. They house shops and restaurants, they organize seminars and postgraduate courses, they are the monuments that identify and differentiate one city from another, they become tourist attractions, they act as market places for art, they promote some artists to the detriment of others, they anticipate fashions by organizing temporary exhibitions...and, in addition to all this, museums can now be visited not only physically, but also on the Internet or via the numerous documentary programs shown on television. The museum has without doubt become a temple to the turn of the century.

Neanderthal Museum

Zamp Kelp, Julius Krauss, Arno Brandlhuber

Location: Mettmann, Germany. **Date of construction**: 1994–1996. **Client**: Stiftung Neanderthal Museum (Neanderthal Museum Foundation) **Architect**: Kelp, Krauss, Brandlhuber. **Associates**: Thomas Gutt (coordinator), Astrid Becker, Marko Glashagen, Carlos González, Alex Kouzmine, Götz Leimkühler. **Surface area**: 2,800 m² (30,100 ft²).

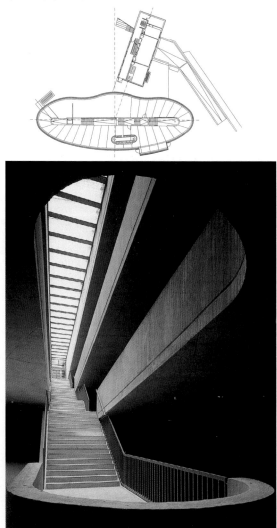

Near Düsseldorf, there is a museum that houses the remains of Neanderthal man, discovered in 1859. The museum premises consist of two independent buildings connected by an underground passage, one dedicated to administrative and management functions, and the other for the exhibit itself. The museum runs up a ramp and is lit centrally by a skylight system.

Domus. Home of Man

Arata Isozaki and Cesar Portela

Location: Corunna, Spain. **Realized**: April 1995. **Architects**: Arata Isozaki and Cesar Portela. **Associates**: T. Tange, M. Hori, N. Ogawa, I. Peraza, A. Casares, F. Garrido, J.L. Gahona, P. Sánchez, F. José, A. Suárez. **Photography**: Hisao Suzuki.

The building is designed to be a landmark that can marshal a response to the nearby Hercules lighthouse, act as a punctuation mark on the coastline, and hold the gaze of the observer. It was to be constructed in a simple but forceful shape when seen from afar. Added to these considerations are the climatic characteristics of the Galician coast: a solid building was necessary to withstand this harsh climate. Meeting these two premises, climate and scale, a curved wall was built, with very few openings since a large part of the interior is planned to be an exhibition hall. To the rear, there is an open granite wall, reminiscent of a Japanese screen, the height and dimensions of which are in accordance with the urban scale and the needs of pedestrians using their cultural facilities. The interior is one continuous exhibition space, which is adapted to the topography by a series of ramps that successively join the three levels of the museum, in accordance with a linear itinerary that runs parallel to the walls. This ends in the event halls, where films can be shown and conferences held, at the same time that exhibitions are on. On the upper floor there are offices and study areas. On the floor immediately underneath the exhibition hall, an extended restaurant is planned, with a glass terrace offering a stunning view of the bay.

Natural History Museum of Rotterdam

Erik van Egeraat

Location: Rotterdam, The Netherlands. **Date of design**: 1991. **Date of completion**: 1995. **Architect**: Erik van Egeraat. **Associates**: Francine Houben, Birgit Jürgenhake, Jeroen Shipper. **Photography**: Christian Richters.

The Natural History Museum is in the "Museums Park" in the city of Rotterdam. The old Villa Dijkzigt, built in 1851 by F.L. Metzelaar, which houses the Museum, had become too small. So, when the old villa was to be restored, it was decided to build an annex that would solve the problem of space for the Museum's exhibits.

The new building has a large temporary exhibition hall on the first floor, while the offices and library are on the second floor. This leaves the two main floors of the villa dedicated exclusively to exhibits.

From Villa Dijkzigt one can reach the entrance to the annex by means of a covered walkway. The annex has its own double-height hall space, where the skeleton of a whale hangs to great effect. The annex is a simple building, perfectly rectangular in plan. The façade has been conceived, according to van Egeraat, as the sum of three different skins. The first of these is of concrete and encloses the exhibition halls. The second is of glass and acts as a membrane around the body of concrete. The third skin is of brick. It acts as an element of protection from an excess of sun on the glass façades.

Chikatsu-Asuka Historical Museum

Tadao Ando

Location: Minami-kawachi, Osaka, Japan. **Date of design**: 1993. **Date of construction**: 1994. **Architect**: Tadao Ando. **Photography**: Shigeo Ogawa.

This museum has an undeniable likeness to the great works of protohistorical cultures: pyramids, ziggurats. Chikatsu-Asuka, to the south of the prefecture of Osaka, was the social center of the country during the first period of Japan's history. In this area Japan's main complexes of tumuli (*kofun*) were to be found: more than 200 tombs and cenotaphs, including four Imperial tombs. The purpose of the Chikatsu-Asuka Historical Museum is to study and provide education about the culture of the *kofun*. In order to integrate the museum into the tumuli, it was conceived as a stepped hill, from which the visitor has a panoramic view of the necropolis. The roof can be used for theatrical shows, music festivals, or other types of performance. Inside the building, the exhibition areas are dark and the objects are exhibited as they would be found in the tombs. Visitors have the sensation of entering into a tomb and being submerged in history.

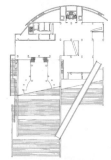

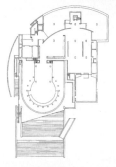

Wakayama Prefecture Museum of Modern Art

Kisho Kurokawa

Location: Wakayama, Japan. **Date of design**: 1991. **Date of construction**: 1994. **Architect**: Kisho Kurokawa. **Associates**: Tasuaki Tanaka, Akira Yokohama, Hiroshi Kanematsu, Kazunori Uchida, Masahiro Kamei, Seiki Iwasaki, Nobuo Abe, Yukio Yoshida, Ichoro Tanaka, Naotake Ueki, Iwao Miura. **Photography**: Tomio Ohashi (also pp 246/247).

The museum is located very near to the castle of Wakayama, in the gardens that surround it, now divided into two areas. The project comprises two buildings: the largest holds international modern art exhibitions, both temporary and permanent; the smaller, exhibitions of regional or local interest. The architecture of this museum is in sympathy with traditional Japanese forms. There are curved eaves in reference to the roofs of the castle, but they are made of modern materials, since they are more daring structurally. Between the two buildings, which are joined at the basement level, there is a gap, a space. This space, according to Japanese tradition, is the expression of the very essence of basic existence.

Both the art museum and the prefecture museum have been designed in simple geometric shapes. This simplicity and continuity of space in the plan becomes more complex and unequal towards the edge, the façade. This is not a continuous, smooth line, but discontinuous, with gaps which give the surface an articulate and expressive form.

Shoji Ueda Museum of Photography

Shin Takamatsu

Location: Kishimoto-cho, Tottori, Japan. **Architect**: Shin Takamatsu & Associates. **Date of design**: 1993. **Date of completion**: 1995. **Associates**: Yamamoto-Tachibana Architects & Engineers (structural engineers), Architectural Environmental Laboratory (mechanical engineers). **Photography**: Nacasa & Partners.

Traditional Japanese architecture has a marked horizontal direction, and its spaces are not only not geometric, they are irregular. It might be said that this is architecture without form, in which work and nature are integrated, producing a kind of floating space. Located in a bucolic environment with views of the Daisen volcano, this museum exhibits the work of the photographer Shoji Ueda, born in the Tottori area. In the Shoji Ueda museum there is a sequence of four concrete rooms alternating with three empty spaces in which a surface of water has been placed. This reflective floor captures the image of the volcano and its environment in the manner of a photograph. In this way the landscape is captured, introduced into the architectural composition, and is presented to the visitor as a further exhibit in the museum's collection. Each room has an exhibition space lit by vertical and horizontal slits, through which a framed landscape is filtered. Time and the museum separate art from its context and allow us to appreciate it as a formal game. The photography holds its own with reality.

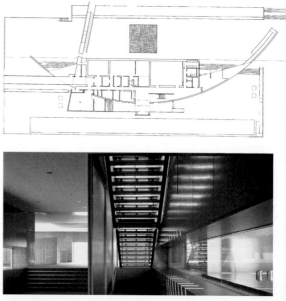

Okazaki Museum of Art and History

Akira Kuryu

Location: Okazaki, Aichi, Japan. **Date of design**: 1992. **Date of completion**: 1996. **Architect**: Akira Kuryu. **Associates**: Toshihiko Kimura + Kimura (structural engineers), Hanawa (structural engineers), Sogo (mechanics), Placemedia (landscaping), Fujie Kuzuko Atelier (furniture). **Photography**: Nacasa & Partners.

The Okazaki Museum of Art and History is in the central park of the city. Surrounded by greenery, it is located on the slope that goes down to Lake Kuryu. Two axes extend as if they were two tapestries of nature, one of water, the other of wind.

The visitor, after slipping down the water tapestry, encounters the transparent volume of the entrance hall. On the first level are the restaurant, the library, and the entrance hall, designed as an enormous skylight. On the intermediate level, a large central exhibition hall surrounded by a gallery forms the central body of the museum. The lower level, some meters above the level of the lake, is nearly all taken up by storage areas.

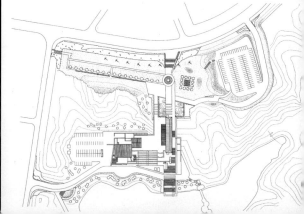

Serralves Museum

Alvaro Siza

Location: Serralves Park, Oporto, Portugal. **Date of completion**: June 1999. **Architect**: Alvaro Siza. **Scheme**: Exhibition galleries, administrative offices, bookshop, gift shop, auditorium, restaurant, terrace and exterior landscaping. **Photography**: Luis Ferreira Alves.

The Serralves Museum of Contemporary Art is the first major museum in Portugal dedicated exclusively to current art. Designed by Alvaro Siza, the permanent collection as well as the exhibitions planned at the new museum will be dedicated to international and Portuguese artistic expression that has taken place from the 1960s until the present day.

This cultural program is run in a mansion dating from 1930 (the Casa de Serralves), surrounded by an 18 ha (44 acre) park including gardens, woods, and agricultural land, situated right in the center of Oporto city.

The complex is celebrated for its outstanding Art Deco architecture and in 1996 it was declared a national monument. The museum is located approximately 500 m (550 yds) from the Casa de Serralves, in the middle of the park.

The plan designed by Siza concentrates on the flexible spaces required by much of art since the 1960s. The size of the building (12,700 m², 137,000 ft²), with an exhibition area of 4500 m² (48,400 ft²), is proof of this. The exterior of the building is of granite and stucco. The ground floor contains galleries, the bookshop, and the gift shop. The remaining galleries, which all communicate with this central space, are designed with different criteria of scale, proportion, and light. The museum also has an auditorium for 300 spectators, a restaurant, and a terrace with panoramic views of the park. The landscaping project has 3 ha (7 acres) of land and will conserve the most important plant species. The aesthetics of the museum reflect its contemporary style, putting the new in contact with the classical forms.

Omegna Forum

Atelier Alessi / Atelier Mendini

Location: Parco Rodari 1, Omegna (Verbania), Italy. **Date of construction**: 1996–1998. **Architects**: Atelier Alessi. **Associates**: Andrea Balzani, Giovanni Bertolini, Raoul Cilento, Bruno Gregori, Jacopo Ninni, plus leading producers: Alessi, Bialetti, Lagostina, and Piazza. **Scheme**: Museum of household objects, auditorium, premises for congresses and meetings, stores, workshops, shop, bar-restaurant, and gymnasium. **Photography**: Atelier Mendini.

The Omegna Forum (Verbania) is a building that was born from the ruins of an old iron works characterized by its long linear structure. It is an industrial building with three floors, which was recently extended and restored, according to a plan drawn up by the Atelier Mendini.
Two parallel buildings are joined together by a wide and very interesting vault,

in the center of which the auditorium is suspended. Inside and all around the old building, which is of great interest to industrial archeologists, there are now new functions: in addition to the auditorium for some 150 people, the household museum, premises for meetings, stores, workshops, a shop, a bar-restaurant, and the gymnasium area.
The surrounding green area has been designated as a public space with the installation of a children's adventure park.

The Forum hosts a permanent collection of household objects, a real Museum of the House, with historical and contemporary objects, molds, utensils, prototypes, documents, books, etc. The museum has managed to achieve all this with the participation of leading companies in the area, such as Alessi, Bieletti, Lagostina, and Piazza.

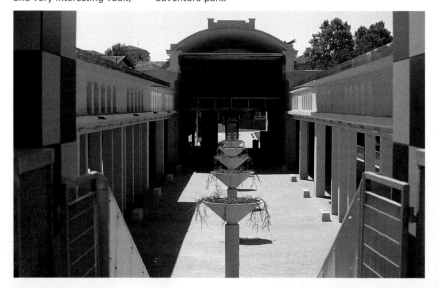

Art galleries

The interest in systematically collecting
works of art from all periods, including
those more distant in time and space, is a
recent phenomenon and one that is
inseparable from modernity. No previous
civilization has looked back to the past in
such an analytical and structured way. The
gallery and museum of art were born at
the same time as the consolidation of
scientific thought and the publication of
the first treatises on history. The examples
that have been included in this section are
an attempt to show the evolution of the
different ways of understanding
architecture in relation to these cultural
spaces which have proliferated.

Palais des Beaux-Arts de Lille

Jean Marc Ibos and Myrto Vitart

Location: Lille, France. **Dates**: March 1990 (competition); 1990–1992 (executive plans); 1992–1997 (construction). **Client**: Municipality of Lille. **Associates**: Pierre Cantacuzène (coordinator), Sophie Nguyen (façades and museography), Khephren Engineering (structure), Y.R.M. Antony Hunt & Ass. (façades), Alto Engineering (fittings). **Scheme**: Renovation and extension of the Palais des Beaux-Arts de Lille. **Surface area**: 28,000 m² (300,000 ft²) in total, of which the extension project is 11,000 m² (117,000ft²).

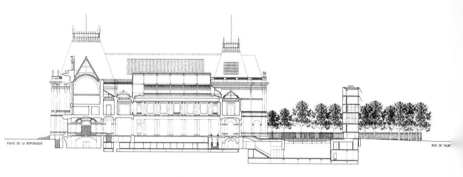

PLACE DE LA REPUBLIQUE

RUE DE VALM

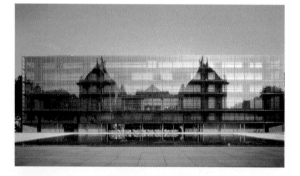

Ibos and Vitart have constructed a building/screen on whose glass façade the existing museum is reflected, thus duplicating its image and reviving the original project of 1895 that proposed a building double the size of the current one. The new temporary exhibition hall is buried in an artificial pool of glass, which is surrounded by one of water. On the southern façade, a system of probes measures the sunshine, temperature, and wind strength, and automatically activates external sun shades. The glass roof has a slope of 1%. Between the beams, an automatic system of blinds allows the amount of sunshine to be controlled and adjusts the level of natural lighting to the requirements of the work being exhibited.

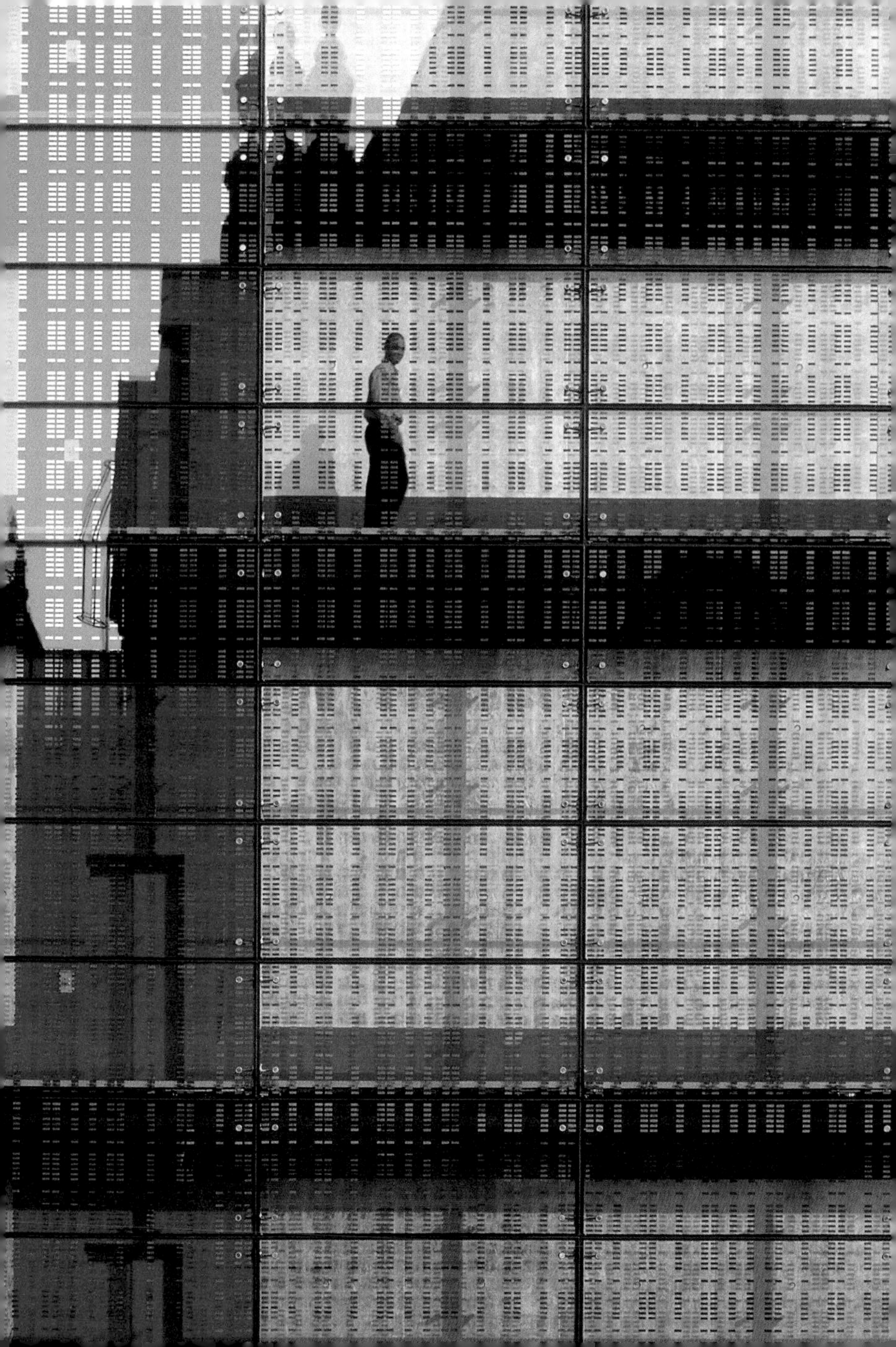

Guggenheim Museum

Frank O. Gehry

Location: Bilbao, Spain. **Date of design**: 1990. **Date of completion**: 1997. **Architect**: Frank O. Gehry. **Associates**: Randy Jefferson, Vano Haritunians, Douglas Hanson, Edwin Chan. **Scheme**: Museum of contemporary art: exhibition halls, conservation rooms, auditorium, restaurant, shops, stores, and outdoor plaza for public use. **Photography**: Eugeni Pons.

The museum is on a bank of the river, beside a very much used suspension bridge that Gehry coopted as a further element of the museum project.

Due to the peculiar shape of the building, a great number of comparisons can be made but, according to the architect himself, his references were: the film *Metropolis* by Fritz Lang, the sculptures of Brancusi, the image of a quarry, and, above all, the contained force transmitted by the city of Bilbao. What most affected the final shape of the building was the actual modus operandi of Gehry, who started with sketches and free models, which were translated almost literally to the computer screen, then analyzed mathematically and any technical or structural matters resolved.

The museum consists of a large central atrium, with a height of 50 m (165 ft), crowned by a metal flower, and three wings facing east, south, and west. To the north, the museum borders on the river, and the virtual fourth wing is cut off, leaving in its place an enormous glass door.

The permanent collection is located in the southern wing, in a succession of square halls. The collection of living artists is in the west wing, in seven galleries of unusual shape and varying sizes. Finally, the temporary exhibitions are on show in an extended great hall (130 x 30 m, 426 x 98 ft) which stretches out to the east.

Stockholm Museum of Modern Art

Rafel Moneo

Location: Stockholm, Sweden. **Date of completion**: 1998. **Client**: Swedish National Board of Public Works. **Architect**: Rafel Moneo. **Associates**: Michael Bischoff, Robert Robinowitz, Lucho Marcial. **Scheme**: New museum of modern art: exhibition halls, cafeteria, offices, store, and services. **Photography**: Wenzel.

More than a designer, Rafel Moneo is an architectural scholar. Either because of his academic profile or his interest in history, each of his projects has a theme that reflects on the city, the topography, and classical typology. It is often said of his works that there are never two the same and this is precisely what Moneo stands for: trying not to fall for the sensation one gets when looking at instances of contemporary architecture which have been destroyed and reconstructed with the sole intention of creating paradigms, while real problems are ignored. The Stockholm Museum of Modern Art is an example of Moneo's wish to integrate his work into its context, which he does in this case by adapting some of the architectural characteristics of the existing buildings that surround the museum. The project started with a typological study of the exhibition galleries inside. It was decided to design four exhibition halls on a square plan, featuring pyramid roofs with a skylight in the middle to filter the sunlight. Another interesting aspect of the museum is the large glass roof over the area used for the cafeteria terrace.

Chicago Museum of Contemporary Art

Kleihues + Kleihues

Location: Chicago Illinois, USA. **Date of construction**: 1994–1996. **Architects**: Kleihues + Kleihues. **Associates**: Ove Arup (engineering), Claude R. Engle (lighting), Daniel Weinbach & Partners (landscaping). **Surface area**: 10,000 m² (108,000 ft²). **Scheme**: Museum, services, parking lot, and exterior landscaping. **Photography**: Hélène Binet, Steven Holl, Hedrich Blessing.

The architects' attention concentrates, basically, on the modernist dialog with tradition and the relationship between their two aesthetic codes. With regard to design there was a wish to reflect the pragmatism that characterizes the city of Chicago and its architecture. At the same time, they tried to ensure that the building showed something of its "poetic rationalism." The characteristics that define the museum are simplicity, space, calm, silence, and the play between transparency and content.

One can reach the building from Michigan Avenue and see the lake from its central axis. Otherwise one can go in from the other side (the Sculpture Garden), in which case one will see the Water Tower and Michigan Avenue. In any case, when entering the exhibition halls visitors find themselves facing only art. They can enjoy the exhibits without having to be distracted by people moving up and down access ramps or stairs or by the cries of people lost and trying to find part of their group from a balcony.

Arken Museum of Modern Art

Søren Robert Lund

Location: Ishøj, Denmark. **Date of design**: 1993. **Date of construction**: 1996. **Architect**: Søren Robert Lund.
Associates: Helgi Thoroddson, Jorgen Erichsen, Mette Andersen, Finn Bogsted. **Photography**: Friedrich
Busam/architekturphoto (also pp 268/269).

Robert Lund's project
shows the influence of the
"new empiricism" of Alvar
Aalto: this architectural
current is a reaction
against the excessive
schematism of 1930s
architecture. On the other
hand, the Arken Museum is
also influenced by the
"new formal abstraction."
This trend generates an
architecture that,
paradoxically, is both

abstract and figurative at
the same time.
The proportions of the
museum's entrance are
squeezed down until they
take on an almost domestic
size. From this point there
are two alternative routes,
both on the same level: the
art route leads the visitor
through a sequence of
exhibition galleries
designed as differentiated
spaces; from the foyer, a

second route runs through
areas where activities
complementary to the
exhibitions are held.
Robert Lund is sensitive to
the harshness of the
environment and chooses
concrete to give texture to
the building. The rough
surface contrasts with the
façades and the metal
skylights, giving a greater
richness to the whole
complex structure.

Hamburger Bahnhof, Museum of Contemporary Art – Berlin

Kleihues + Kleihues

Location: Berlin, Germany. **Date of design**: 1990–1995. **Date of construction**: 1992–1996. **Architects**: Kleihues + Kleihues. **Associates**: Schon + hippelein (façade), Linder Ag. (construction), Scholz & Herzog (electrics), Max Sange (elevators), A. Kuhn Gmbh (locksmiths). **Surface area**: 10,000 m² (107.640 ft²). **Scheme**: Restoration of the old train station as a museum; exterior landscaping. **Photography**: Kleihues + Kleihues.

There are three important aspects in the design of this project: firstly, the correct analysis (not nostalgic but rational) of the existing structure of the old Hamburg train station and remembering its importance to the architectural history of the city; secondly, the intention to create simple, transparent spaces; thirdly, the technology of museums: high ceilings in the new galleries that combine natural with artificial light; integration of electrical systems into the older parts of the building using false ceilings; use of materials such as aluminum, granite, wood (particularly oak), and sandstone; walls painted in matte white so as not to affect color perception.

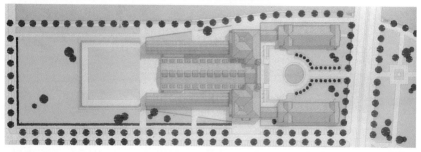

San Francisco Museum of Modern Art

Mario Botta

Location: San Francisco, California, USA. **Date of construction**: 1991–1995. **Architect**: Mario Botta. **Associates**: Hellmuth, Obata & Kassabaum, Bechtel International Company. **Surface area**: 20,900 m² (225.000 ft²). **Photography**: Robert Canfield.

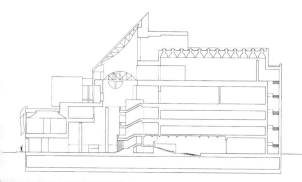

The main theme of all Mario Botta's work is the revival of monumentality. His projects try to invoke this quality in modern architecture: although it is often absent, it has been associated with this art for many centuries.
In the San Francisco Museum, Botta uses many of the architectural resources of this type of construction: simple, ascetic spaces, huge shapes lined with brick or stone, which provide no information about the look of the interior.
The lighting is provided through gaps or holes in the wall, since one cannot actually call them windows in any recognizable form.

The central atrium connects all the rooms, which makes it easy to find one's bearings and select the rooms to be visited. Botta has achieved one of his original ideas: to illuminate the majority of the rooms with natural light, which he has implemented by using a stepped section design. On the first floor one finds all the independent activities: bookshop, cafeteria, auditorium, temporary exhibition halls, and main entrance hall. On the second floor are the proper exhibition halls. Botta uses the scaling of the building, from the main façade to the rear façade, to locate rooms only in areas that have no floor above, and he leaves the rest of the floor for offices or conservation rooms.

P.S.1 Museum

Frederick Fisher

Location: Long Island, New York, USA. **Date of construction**: 1997. **Architects**: Frederick Fisher, David Ross, Joseph Coriaty. **Floor area**: 7800 m² (84,000 ft²). **Photography**: Michael Moran.

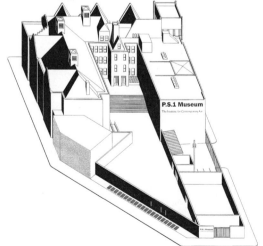

Fisher's method of tackling an art museum project is more akin to that of an artist or gallery owner who is occupying a space to keep and show his work, than that of an architect who has received one of the most juicy commissions of his career (a museum) and is trying to demonstrate his ability to create spaces and invent new images.

This is a former school, located in an industrial area near the Queens district of New York. The main value of the building lies in the wide variety of spaces available.

Therefore, the strategy of the project consisted of integrating the facilities into the existing structure of the building.

The second floor has kept the mythical galleries, to preserve the tradition of the P.S.1 as an alternative exhibition area. In the same way, the "art in residence" facility (several artists living and working in the museum) has importantly been retained.

MACBA

Richard Meier

Location: Barcelona, Spain. **Date of construction**: October 1990–March 1995. **Client**: Consorci del Museu d'Art Contemporani de Barcelona **Architect**: Richard Meier. **Associates**: Thomas Phifer (design team), Renny Logan, Alphonso Perez (architectural design), Fernando Ramos, Isabel Bachs (associate architects), Obiols Brufau, Moya Arquitectos (structural engineers), F. Labastida (installations), Fischer, Marantz, Renfo & Stone (lighting technology), Secotec SL, Intecasa (quality control), Ibering, Estudis I Projectes SA, Gerard Esteban (consultancy), COMSA (construction) **Scheme**: Museum of Contemporary Art: exhibition halls, open air courtyard, offices, and services. **Photography**: Eugeni Pons.

The Barcelona Museum of Contemporary Art falls within the characteristic plastic idiom of Meier, based on clear rationalism in which straight and curved lines are combined to produce a harmonic dialog between the interior spaces and the exterior light through wide galleries and windows. Meier designed an elongated building measuring 120 x 35 m (394 x 115 ft), inside which he placed a circular room which crosses it vertically. He thus created a contrast which gives the whole a very particular appearance and acts as an axis around which the exhibition areas revolve. The virtually sculptural aesthetics of the building are conjugated with the provision of the latest technical innovations in terms of exhibition, convenience, and maintenance. Its bright, luminous appearance makes it one of the most attractive museums of the decade, paying off the debt that Barcelona owed to its famous, international contemporary art.

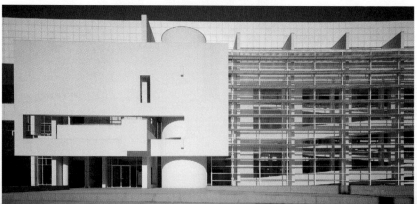

Kunsthal

Rem Koolhaas

Location: Rotterdam, Netherlands. **Date of construction**: 1987–1992. **Architect**: Rem Koolhaas.
Associates: Fuminori Hoshino, Tony Adams, Isaac Batenburg, Leo van Immerzeel, Herman Jacobs, Edu Arroyo, Jim Njoo, Marc Peeters, Ron Steiner, Jeroen Thomas and Patricia Blaisse (interiors and garden)
Photography: Lock Images.

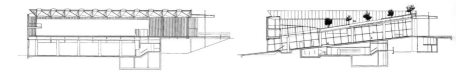

There is an essential objective that motivates the work of Koolhaas, from his writings to his designs and buildings, and which determines every decision on every level, from the domestic to the urban, from diagram to detail. The objective is to discover the real collaboration that can be established between architecture and freedom. The museum's relationship with the great city is fascinating, although not free from criticism. Within the Kunsthal is a "deliberate exploitation of penetration." The building becomes a disorganized and superconductor body, capable of restructuring itself, allowing itself to be crossed by different flows in different directions, such as pedestrian flow and traffic flow. The space is generated by travel and many speeds are established by juxtaposing or diversifying their interconnections. In this design, the structural strategy employed is also a way of breaking up the space. It uses functionally specialist structures within a single space. The inclined columns defy the laws of gravity to align with the topography generated in the design, in a radical declaration of freedom and independence from the natural order.

Bonn Art Gallery

Gustav Peichl

Location: Bonn, Germany. **Date of completion**: 1992. **Client**: Bundesministerium für Raumordnung, Bauwesen und Städtebau. **Architect**: Gustav Peichl. **Associates**: M. Kolhbauer, J. Guth, R.F. Weber. **Scheme**: Exhibition halls, art galleries, gardens, cafeteria, terrace, offices, shops, conference rooms, and library. **Photography**: Soenne/architekturphoto.

The Bonn Exhibition Hall and Art Gallery is a simple building on a square base with 96 m (315 ft) sides. It is raised 11 m (36 ft) above ground level, with a garden for exhibitions and three sharply pointed conical towers, which decorate the open countryside and are the logo of the institution, as well as being three attractive skylights for the building's interior.

The main entrance is on the northwest side, facing a row of 11 carved pillars representing the 11 regions which contributed to the project. From here a wide, grand staircase leads to the roof. The first floor is 9 x 9 m (30 x 30 ft), divided into a perimeter strip and four inner areas: the foyer/entrance, the forum/auditorium, the great hall, and the atrium. The exhibition area provides a system of small, medium, and large halls which can be used individually, in parallel, or combined in various ways. The exhibition area in this project is a synthesis of modern multifunctional containers and traditional museums with aisles and rotundas.

Menil Collection Museum

Renzo Piano

Location: Houston, Texas, USA. **Date of construction**: 1981–1986. **Architect**: Renzo Piano. **Associates**: S. Ishida, M. Carroll, M. Downs, C. Patel, B. Plattner, C. Susstrunk. **Photography**: Hickey & Robertson.

In 1981, Dominique de Menil commissioned from Renzo Piano a new building to house his collection of surreal and primitive art, one of the largest in the world. The museum was to be located in a residential area of Houston containing small, single family, wooden houses built in the 19th century. Piano's design is an example of a museum on a human scale, a building which dispenses with any monumental intention and integrates perfectly with virtually domestic surroundings. The scale of the building and the selection of finishes fits with the local tradition and background without, however, giving up the purified technological resolution of its building materials.

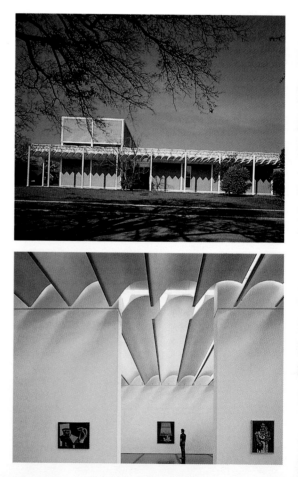

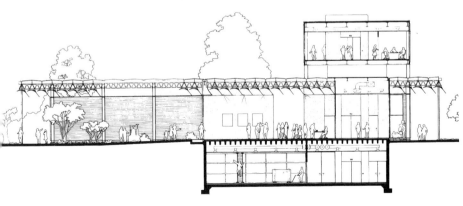

Louvre Pyramid

I.M. Pei

Location: Paris, France. **Date of completion**: 1987. **Architect**: I.M. Pei. **Scheme**: Construction of a glass pyramid as the new entrance to the Louvre Museum. **Photography**: Ana Quesada.

The project to modernize and extend the Louvre Museum, initiated by François Mitterand in 1981, envisaged a new underground building which would serve as a bridge between the three wings of the museum. The upper part of this building takes the shape of a huge glass pyramid, which rises up as the central feature of the huge courtyard, the center of gravity of the Louvre. The pyramid is now the new main entrance to the museum. Once inside, visitors find themselves in the Belvedere, shaped like a large triangular balcony, which overlooks the interior lobby and provides a view of the palace through the glass walls of the pyramid, providing a pleasing effect.

Museum of Rock Art

William P. Bruder

Location: Deer Valley, Phoenix, Arizona, USA. **Date of construction**: 1994–1995. **Architect**: William P. Bruder. **Associates**: Wendell Burnette, Bob Adams, Beau Dromiack, Rick Joy, Maryann Bloomfield. **Scheme**: Museum of Rock Art: reception, exhibition halls, archives, offices, lecture rooms and services. **Photography**: Bill Timmerman.

This museum was built over a watercourse: the building itself is designed as a funnel which channels visitor traffic from the parking lot to the mountain and the engravings of the Hohokam (native North Americans). The first floor is inserted in the angle formed by the mountain and a jetty, bringing civilization and nature into contact. The emotion produced by the architectural sweep helps to prepare one for contemplating the work of art. To make the space more cinema-like, there is a longitudinal area with two parallel stages at different heights: one continuous, for the public, where the museum itself is located, and the other more private, subdivided following the watercourse and housing the reception area, archives, offices, and lecture rooms. An opaque box was created with incisions which convert into light when any specific points or itineraries need to be emphasized. In this way the feeling of oppression is avoided, although the windows extend the gaze towards the rocks. The museum becomes a balcony over the jetty, and the visitor, as well as learning about the landscape, can enjoy it.

deer valley **rock art center**

Gagosian Gallery

Richard Gluckman

Location: Wooster Street, New York, USA. **Date of completion**: 1994. **Architect**: Richard Gluckman. **Scheme**: Conversion of an old garage into an art gallery. **Photography**: Paco Asensio.

The Gagosian is part of a New York trend for converting industrial premises into luxurious galleries. Designed by Richard Gluckman, it is the perfect venue for major exhibitions of contemporary sculpture. Conceived with the work of Richard Serra in mind, the building is a light, airy, and spacious design.

Gluckman believes that art should dominate the space, with the architect playing only a supporting role and merely creating a stage. Only the brick façade of the original garage remains intact although he added a new door in the original style as a historical tribute and a practical feature. This entrance remains open on summer afternoons, when the gallery glistens seductively, offering passers-by more than a glimpse of its contents. The interior was completely redesigned: the floor reinforced, the ceiling raised to its maximum height, and pillars built to increase the width. The smooth, polished floor contrasts with the brilliant white walls. Gluckman has left exposed beams, which match the original structure, visible in the new skylights, around which, in addition to natural light, industrial halogen lamps have been fixed.

Cultural Centers and Foundations

There is no substantial difference, in fact, between the projects included in this chapter and the other structures under the general Cultural Facilities heading. This distinction has been adopted to throw into relief a number of buildings that fall halfway between museum and art gallery, between exhibition hall and show space. This Cultural Centers and Foundations category embraces institutions that are normally private, often bringing together works of one particular artist, movement, or country. These projects celebrate the history or tradition of a place, or act as a perpetual record of something significant.

Chinati Foundation

Louis Jeantet Foundation

Cartier Foundation

Galician Center for Contemporary Art

Cracow Center for Japanese Art and
Technology

Stiklestad Cultural Center

Institute of the Arab World

Yerba Buena Visual Arts Center

Chinati Foundation

Donald Judd

Location: Marfa, Texas, USA. **Date of completion**: 1986. **Scheme**: Exhibition areas, offices, and services. **Photography**: Todd Eberle (also pp 302/303).

The Chinati Foundation is a museum of contemporary art founded and designed in 1986 by Donald Judd. It is located in Marfa, Texas, a small town of 2600 inhabitants in the southwest of the United States, near the Mexican border. The barren, arid countryside is part of the Chihuahua desert. The Foundation is located on a former military base, Fort D.A. Russell. The specific purpose of the Chinati Foundation is to exhibit large works by a few of the significant 20th-century artists.

Donald Judd himself was an architect who, when the military base was abandoned, renovated and adapted the buildings for their new purpose. Judd designed the windows, doors, and new access points, adding a new curved metal roof to the old warehouses and landscaping the grounds. He built new adobe walls and converted the barracks into exhibition halls.

Louis Jeantet Foundation

Domino Architects

Location: Geneva, Switzerland. **Date of construction**: 1996. **Architects**: Jean-Michel Landecy, Jean-Marc Anzévui and Nicolas Deville, Henri Bava, Michel Hoëssler and Olivier Philippe of Equipo Ter (landscape architects). **Scheme**: Garden and auditorium. **Photography**: Jean-Michel Landecy.

One of the issues the project team had to resolve was the imbalance in scale between the old neo-Renaissance building, with its grand front esplanade, the small space allowed for the project, and finally the extensive grounds surrounding the house.

Another problem was the distance between the two buildings, the house and the auditorium, and how they could be linked. The solution suggested by Domino was to optimize use of the garden area by breaking it down into two levels: a horizontal upper platform which occupied almost all the free space of the plot and which was on a level with the first floor of the house; and, cutting through the upper platform, a small patio garden acting as a common entrance to the house and auditorium.

The landscaping is inspired by Mogul gardens and the courtyards of Persian mosques, and, like them, uses natural elements to welcome visitors and prepare them for a new experience. The entrance walkway crosses the huge concrete wall which separates the courtyard from the street, and visitors suddenly find themselves in the small square courtyard on the inside.

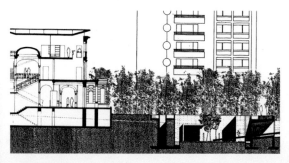

Cartier Foundation

Jean Nouvel

Location: Paris, France. **Date of construction**: 1991–1994. **Client**: Cartier S.A. **Architect**: Jean Nouvel. **Associates**: Didier Braoult (project architect); P.A. Bohnet, L. Ininguez, P. Mathieu, V. Morteau, G. Potel, S. Ray, S. Robert (associate architects), Ove Arup & Partners (structural engineers); Arnaud de Bussière et Associés (façade); Reidweg et Gendre (air-conditioning); Ingénieur et Paysage (landscaping). **Photography**: Christian Richters.

In the Cartier Foundation, the trees remain where they were, superimposing themselves on an architecture in which boundaries disappear and walls glide into space. The Chateaubriand cedar stands alone, between two enormous, unobstructed screens (only attached to the building by a few horizontal ties to counter wind pressure) which frame the entrance. Visitors walk under the cedar and enter an exhibition room in which the works of art intermingle with the trees and tall, stylized, evenly spaced pillars. As to materials, the whole expression of the building is given over to glass: a semireflective glass which avoids the emphasis and obstruction of completely transparent or totally reflective, mirror-like curtain walls. The vertical wall creates the impression of the Cartier Foundation as an ephemeral building on the verge of fading away. It belongs to an unspecified school of modern architecture.

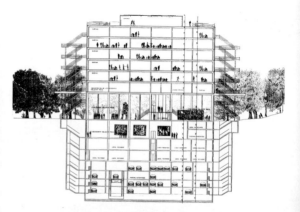

Galician Center for Contemporary Art

Alvaro Siza

Location : Santiago de Compostela, Spain. **Date of completion**: 1997. **Client**: Santiago City Hall. **Architect**: Alvaro Siza. **Scheme**: Exhibition halls, auditorium, library, documentation and administration centers, bookshop, cafeteria, service areas, administrative offices, management office, and viewing terrace. **Photography**: Tino Martínez.

The main issue with this project was its insertion in an area surrounded by buildings of quite different scale and significance. It was up to the Center to overcome these difficulties by transforming an agglomeration of spaces and buildings into a coherent fabric. The preservation/transformation criteria involved included the selection of cladding materials, so granite was chosen for the exterior, with color variations. The building consists of two L-shaped wings each of three floors, which converge in a north–south direction at a point on the southern end. The west wing houses the main entrance, distribution and reception areas, and access to the auditorium, the second floor, the library, and the documentation and administration centers. The basement of the east wing contains the exhibition halls, the bookshop, the cafeteria, the temporary exhibition halls (709 m², 7630 ft²), and the auditorium (367 m², 3950 ft²) are on the first floor. The triangular space between the two buildings is an overhead-lit transition area housing the entrance to the exhibition halls. The third floor internal service areas cover 1908 m² (20,500 ft²); on the second floor are the administration and management offices. The terrace areas (957 m², 10,300 ft²) are open to the public and can accommodate sculpture exhibitions. The terrace walls are 3.2 m (10.5 ft) high with the floor raised at the southern end, producing a viewing platform overlooking the city of Santiago.

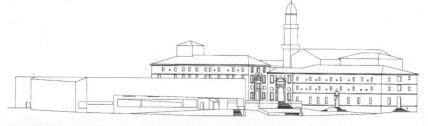

Cracow Center for Japanese Art and Technology

Arata Isozaki & Associates

Location: Cracow, Poland. **Date of completion**: 1994. **Client**: The Kyoto-Cracow Foundation. **Architect**: Arata Isozaki & Associates. **Associates**: Ghen Mizumo, Yusaku Imamura, Shigeru Hirabayashi, Dr. Jan Grabacki, EXIT engineers (structural engineers). **Plot area**: 0.49 ha (1.2 acres). **Net floor area**: 2120 m² (2280 ft²). **Gross floor area**: 3180 m² (3420 ft²). **Photography**: Yoshio Takase.

The building is on two floors: the main, upper floor to which direct access is provided; and the lower floor accommodating secondary offices and a large multipurpose room. With this layout, Isozaki is once again trying out a large undulating roof supported by a timber structure, designed by means of complex geometry. Thus, most of the perimeter of the building takes on a sinuous shape so that, at the intersection of the two planes, no part of the resulting arris has any straight lines. Moving down, floor by floor, towards the foundations, the building slowly acquires much more hybrid images: for example the bar terrace, or the access area, express idioms already tried and tested by modern tradition.

Stiklestad Cultural Center

Jens Petter Askim, Sven Hartvig

Location: Stiklestad, Norway. **Date project begun**: 1985. **Date of completion**: 1992. **Architects**: Jens Petter Askim, Sven Hartvig. **Scheme**: A museum to commemorate the Viking tradition. **Photography**: Bard Ginnes, Jens Petter Askim.

St. Olav is one of Scandinavia's most popular saints and Stiklestad is a place of pilgrimage. This museum therefore has a triple purpose: firstly, to commemorate the Battle of Stiklestad and St. Olav; secondly, to explain the significance and consequences of that historic event; and, thirdly, to demonstrate Viking culture prior to St. Olav, present scenes from and the remains of the battle, and provide information about the changes experienced by Norway since that date. Architecturally, the building is modern, carefully landscaped, and built with constant references to local architecture. The ridge roofs and the wall surrounding the courtyard on the southern side, the internal ridges, the slopes on which the building stands, and the structural design itself take their inspiration from simple, traditional elements. The architects had two intentions: that the building should harmonize with the landscape and that the architectural framework should visually prepare visitors for the archeological treasures and battle scenes they would find on the inside. Perhaps the main area of the museum is the courtyard, which is designed to accommodate all kinds of activities. The southern side is enclosed by a circular, concrete, windowless corridor, along which archeological items are displayed and scenes from the Battle of Stiklestad depicted.

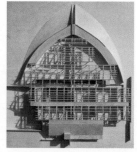

Institute of the Arab World

Jean Nouvel

Location: Paris, France. **Date of completion**: 1987. **Client**: Institut du Monde Arabe. **Architect**: Jean Nouvel. **Scheme**: Exhibition hall – Arab art and history museum. **Photography**: S.Couturier

The façade facing the Jussieu faculty at first sight looks like an ornament-decorated surface. Close up, however, we can see that this is not so, but a combination of the ancient art of controlling light and the use of the most modern technologies. Jean Nouvel himself explains: "This façade is not an imitation of ornamental decoration, but an interpretation of the tradition. More than that architectural form, what I wanted to reproduce is the play of light. To play with the system of its geometry, recover, and respect the principle of light filtration, of course adapted to the climate and the inconsistency of Parisian light. Because the most important thing about ornamental decoration is not its function per se but the way it adapts to the amount of light. It is a sensitive element. We could have achieved something similar with a venetian blind but, in line with tradition, I was able to use technology to instill the sensation rather than the function in this case."

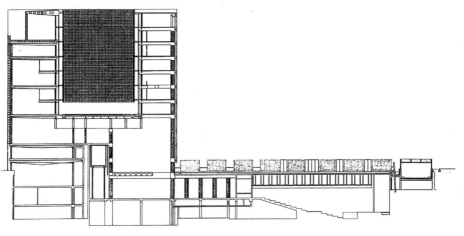

Yerba Buena Gardens Visual Arts Center

Maki & Associates

Location: San Francisco, California, USA. **Date of completion**: 1993. **Client**: San Francisco Redevelopment Agency. **Architect**: Maki & Associates. **Associates**: Fumikiho Maki & Maki & Associates; Robinson Mills + Williams; Structural Design Engineers (structural engineering); S.J. Engineers (mechanical engineering); F.W. Associates (electrical engineering); S. Leonard Auerbach & Ass. (lighting); Walsh & Norris (acoustics); Meachum O'Brien (landscaping). **Scheme**: Visual arts center, video projection room, exhibition rooms, and galleries; multipurpose forum; offices, and services. **Photography**: Paul Peck, Richard Barnes.

The San Francisco Visual Arts Center assumes a fundamental role in this cultural and commercial development, built in the city center, in the Market Street district. The building includes a video projection room seating 100 together with several exhibition galleries and a communal area in the form of a multifunctional forum. The internal and external areas have an informal flavor which contrasts with the usual serious and strict environments of museums and institutions. The projection room has a gallery, creating a more intimate area for small events, video screenings, and other related exhibitions. The rest of the areas are larger and can accommodate other activities. The forum accommodates avant-garde theater presentations as well as festivals, banquets, and concerts. Its L shape enables the building to be placed at a key point in this new urban development. The public square located at one of the corners of the complex acts as an open-air mall and an external extension of the internal facilities. Furthermore, some of the activities conducted in the building can be viewed from the outside through panels located in one of the two-floor façades. In this way, the building can be used as a single area to accommodate large-scale events where the public can move freely from one place to another.

Yerba Buena Gardens Visual Arts Center 319

Schools and universities

Design, drama, theater, economics, law, journalism, technology, geological sciences, astronomy, architecture...these are the subjects being studied today. The students of the last decade of the 20th century have significantly changed the traditional trends. The lack of job opportunities has forced international institutions to create new opportunities to allow young people to integrate better into the job market. This has also meant that large numbers of architects have been responding to competitive tenders for commissions from schools and universities, in which, until now, they had not been interested as this was not previously a field for innovative design.

Utrecht School of Design and Fashion

Erick van Egeraat

Location: Utrecht, The Netherlands. **Date of construction**: 1994–1997. **Client**: Utrecht Local Authority. **Architect**: Erick van Egeraat. **Associates**: Maartje Lammers, Ard Buijsen, Boris Zeisser. **Structural engineering**: Strukton Engineering b.v., Maarsen. **Fittings**: Sweegers & de Bruijn b.v., Den Bosch. **Façade subcontractor**: Rollecate, Staphorst. **Scheme**: High school for graphic design and fashion. **Photography**: Christian Richters.

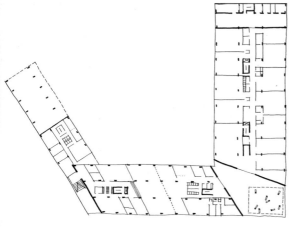

When Erick van Egeraat and his team were contracted for this project, the building had already been planned by another architect. In other words, they were not given a commission for a new building but were asked to take on an existing project in order to secure the approval of the regional Aesthetics Committee. The principal objective of the commission was to enliven the existing plans for the building and, as a secondary objective, to relocate the entrance hall. The architects decided to install a glass skin which would be superimposed completely independently on the existing façade. The building is thus enveloped by a kind of veil which reveals, and at the same time transforms, the perception of what lies behind it....

The redesigning of the entrance hall, located in one of the corners between two blocks, radically changed the whole concept of the space. Designed as a completely transparent building, the boundaries of which seem to disappear, the hall accommodates the lecture theater suspended on thin metal pillars, a reception area, and two connecting walkways between the two wings at the upper levels.

Glass is also used inside for the walkways, skylights, and façades, increasing the number of reflections from one surface to another.

School of Dramatic Art

TEN Architects

Location: Avenida Río Churubuscu, Mexico City. **Date completed**: 1994 **Developer**: National Council for Culture and the Arts. **Cost**: $12 million. **Architects**: Enrique Norten, Bernardo Gómez-Pimienta. **Associates**: Gustavo Espitia, Héctor L. Gámiz, Miguel Angel González, Armando Hashimoto, Carlos Valdez, Óscar Vargas (design team), Alonso-García + Miranda (structural engineers), Jaffe, Scarborough & Holden (acoustics), Tecnoproyectos (mechanical engineering), Francisco de Pablo, Jesús Estiva (directors of works), Department of the Federal District (contractor). **Scheme**: Classrooms, theater (300 seats), administrative offices, dressing rooms, and services. **Photography**: Luis Gordoa.

The School of Dramatic Art is at the west end of an area containing the various buildings of the National Arts Center, between highways and connecting roads at various levels. It is a setting dominated by constant traffic and noise.

There are no clear boundaries, no complex topography (the plot is practically flat), nothing natural to be respected, no defined façades: reference points are broken up and dispersed. However, as Enrique Norten himself says: "The site is subject to frictional and tensile forces created by speed and the urban energies of the setting." Although not a concrete point of reference, these forces do suggest a way of setting out the architectural components and a certain attitude towards composition.

The largest element is the large tubular metal roof. It is on an urban scale and is sufficiently abstract and monolithic that it can be recognized from a considerable distance and from a moving vehicle. Beneath the roof a collection of areas and planes contain and define the various facilities. All have their own expression according to their nature and particular conditions. They have been combined, apparently spontaneously and arbitrarily. But the virtual chaos nevertheless conceals a strict order derived from the specific function of each area and its complex inter-relationships, derived from the heterogeneity of the scheme as a whole.

New World School

Adolf Krischanitz

Location: Schwarzenstockallee, Vienna, Austria. **Date project begun**: 1993. **Date of completion**: 1994.
Architect: Adolf Krischanitz. **Associates**: Eric Red, Mark Gilbert (design team), Manfred Gmeiner, Martin
Haferl (structural engineers). **Scheme**: Classrooms, conference rooms, dining room, kitchen, and services.
Photography: Margherita Spiluttini.

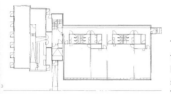

The project consists of, firstly, the conversion of a house into a school and, secondly, its extension. This is a small building: the house had two floors with a load-bearing wall structure and the extension is on a single floor. There is an entrance and staircase between the two parts of the building. The composition of the mirror-glass windows is completely abstract and regular: on the façade of the old house is a system of ten identical vertical rectangles set out in two lines, while in the new unit is an unbroken window at ground level. The external walls have been rendered in dark gray. Remnants of the countryside – mutilated trees, of which only the bases of the trunks are visible, are outlined on the dark, sealed walls.

High School of the Future

Architecture-Studio

Location: Jauney-Clan, France. **Date of completion**: 1987. **Architect**: Architecture-Studio: Martin Robain, J. François Galmiche, Rodo Tisnado, J. François Bonne. **Associates**: F.X. Desert, R.H. Arnaud, P. Balch. **Scheme**: Teaching and boarding buildings: classrooms, 34 rooms for boarders and teachers, communal services, laboratories, workshops, cafeteria, restaurant, sick bay, and communal garden. **Photography**: Stéphane Couturier.

Someone described this building, a boarding school for musicians, as "a UFO landed in the middle of a field." And this is undoubtedly a most appropriate description of the enormous, flat, inclined triangle of glass and metal, with an open, elliptical courtyard in its center and a sliding roof which runs along its longitudinal access until it leaves the building. It is an expression of technology, its potential evolution, its window on the future, and therefore it takes its aesthetic references from the imaginary world of science fiction, transformed into palpable reality.

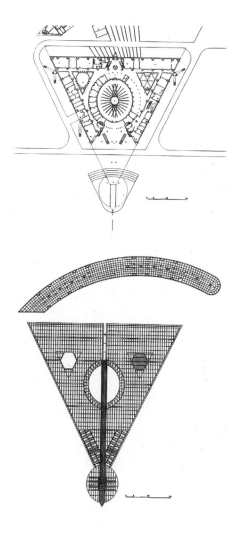

Faculty of Economics

Mecanoo

Location: Utrecht, The Netherlands. **Date project begun**: 1991–1992. **Date of construction**: September 1993–May 1995. **Client**: Foundation Financing Exploitation Accommodation Uithof, Utrecht. **Construction**: Hollandse Beton Maatschappij b.v., Utrecht. **Associated artists**: Gera van der Leun, Henk Metselaar, Linda Verkaaik. **Gross floor area**: 23,500 m² (253,000 ft²). **Scheme**: Classrooms, lecture theater, library, cafeteria, and administrative services. **Photography**: Christian Richters.

The new Faculty of Economics of the Polytechnic of Utrecht is located in an area of the "Uithof" campus known as the "kasbah." Like North African cities, the development of this area of the campus is characterized by its compactness, low buildings, and introspection, being built around internal courtyards. The 23,500 m² (253,000 ft²) of this center is built around three courtyards on only three floors.

Right from the start, it was intended to create a structure which not only fulfilled its requirements as an educational facility, but also tried to give students an opportunity to enjoy the building in a more complete way, providing a vast amount of undefined space for relationships between the student body, where they could chat, eat, and drink, on the understanding that these activities form as much a part of student life as does actual studying.

The layout of the faculty is clear and simple. On the north side, providing access, the lecture theaters,

multimedia library and cafeteria-restaurant are enveloped in a glossy skin of glass. From there, the outer sections of a comb-shaped series of wings accommodate the departments and the administration, while the central wings, grouped around the main courtyard, contain the classrooms. The courtyards in the center of the building give each area a different personality, each one creating its own characteristic ambience.

Faculty of Law, Cambridge

Sir Norman Foster & Partners

Location: University of Cambridge, UK. **Date of completion**: October 1995. **Client**: University of Cambridge. **Architect**: Norman Foster. **Structural engineers**: Anthony Hunt Associates. **Library capacity**: 120,000 volumes. **Gross floor area**: 9000 m² (97,000 ft²). **Scheme**: Auditoriums, classrooms, libraries, administrative offices, storerooms, and meeting rooms. **Photography**: Herman van Doorn (also pp 322/323).

The plot is in the middle of the Sidgwick campus, adjacent to the famous History Faculty building by James Stirling. It is surrounded by lawns and mature trees, which helps to minimize the impact of the buildings' size and retain as much as possible of the atmosphere of the garden in which it is located. The first floor contains various classrooms, and administrative and other staff offices. The underground floors consist of three large auditoriums, book stores, and student meeting rooms while, the top three floors are devoted to the library. The entrance opens onto a full height atrium providing access to all floors of the library building.

The library floors are terraced, tailored to the curved façade but not touching it.

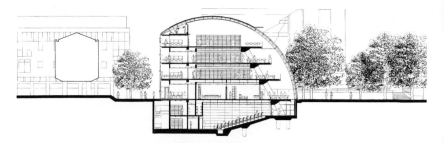

Faculty of Journalism

Ignacio Vicens/José Antonio Ramos

Location: Pamplona, Spain. **Date project begun**: 1994. **Date of completion**: 1996. **Architects**: Ignacio Vicens, José Antonio Ramos. **Associates**: Fernando Gil, Adam Blesnick. **Scheme**: Classrooms for theoretical and practical work, film studios, radio and television studios, conference rooms, offices, audio/video library, and services. **Photography**: Eugeni Pons (also pp 978/979).

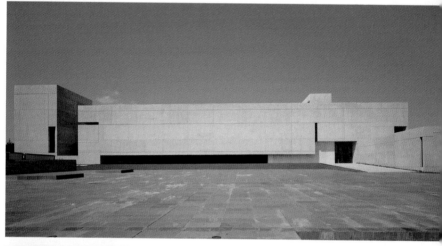

What gives the building its shape is the ratio between mass and space. The elements which stand out against the sky are just as important from the point of view of the skin, or image, as the spaces which penetrate the concrete to bring light to the interior. When the decision to adopt this shape, and not some other, was made, a dual strategy was at work. Firstly, the various functional areas are separated into different buildings. So, certain rooms, such as the main classroom on the first floor or the audio/video library block, with independent functions, tend to stand out as autonomous areas. Secondly, there is the desire to provide each area with a specific type of lighting and above all a special way of relating to the outside. Thus, regarding the building as a negative, looking down from above the exterior is built with holes and courtyard spaces.

Department of Geosciences, University of Aveiro

Eduardo Souto de Moura

Location: Aveiro, Portugal. **Date project begun**: 1991. **Date of completion**: 1995. **Architect**: Eduardo Souto de Moura. **Scheme**: Classrooms, laboratories, conference rooms, and services. **Photography**: Christian Richters.

The layout of the campus and conditions imposed by the university established clear guidelines: the gross floor area had to be 4314 m^2 (46,400 ft^2); the maximum height three floors; the length of the building 80 m (260 ft); the width 20 m (66 ft); the floor area given over to traffic approximately 20%; the material for the wall finishes, red brick. With

such clear planning provisions, who needed an architect, Souto de Moura must have thought: "With the rules of the game so clearly defined, the building took shape almost without discussion: a box divided by a central corridor." All you had to do was glance at the other buildings on the campus: straight blocks of brick, all with three floors, parallel and equidistant, the only difference being whether the windows were oblong or square, or the blinds white or dark.
In contrast, Souto de Moura's building is very austere: an obvious rejection of all architectural decoration; enormous attention to detail with the intention of minimizing its

effect on the final appearance of the building; the determination, in order to make the rules of construction of the building patently obvious, not to clad the structural elements; and an effort to abstract geometrically the component parts of the building. The rooms are devoid of superfluities, containing only essential furniture in each case.

School of Physical Sciences and Astronomy

Cesar Pelli & Associates Inc.

Location: Seattle, USA. **Date of completion**: 1994. **Architect**: Cesar Pelli & Associates Inc. **Scheme**: Building for the study of physical sciences and astronomy at the University of Seattle: classrooms, dormitories, study rooms, teachers' offices, cafeteria-restaurant, landscaping. **Photography**: C. Pelli.

The projects undertaken by Cesar Pelli have one distinctive feature in common: the lack of preconceived ideas. Every project is conducted according to its location, its climate, and its culture, in other words its position in the environment.

Using a wide range of solutions and materials, Pelli identifies and enhances the social value of the structures he designs, attempting to unite the aesthetic value with the social aspect in order to express the meaning of the buildings. Fully aware that buildings give shape to the city's skyline, he takes particular care with their design, making an extraordinary contribution to the quality of urban design in the 20th century with his public spaces, which provide social and cultural support for the dynamics of the city.

The design and construction of the School of Physical Sciences and Astronomy exemplifies all the differentiating qualities of this architect.

Faculty of Architecture, Genoa

Ignazio Gardella

Location: Stradone di San Agostino, Genoa, Italy. **Date of construction**: 1987–1990. **Client**: Faculty of Architecture, Genoa. **Architect**: Ignazio Gardella. **Associates**: Mario Valle Engineering SpA (construction plans), Angela Malaponti (assistant), Giampiero Peia (draughtsman), Piero Guerrini (works manager), SCI SpA Genoa (construction). **Scheme**: Lecture hall, subject classrooms, teachers' offices, gardens, cafeteria, and services. **Photography**: Federico Brunetti.

Planning a new headquarters for the Genoa School of Architecture was a clear exercise in urban remodeling which typified the dialogues between the old and the new, between historical/cultural heritage and new trends in building design.

On a difficult, uneven plot but on a special site,

where he could take advantage of some of the existing structures of the Church of San Silvestro, Ignazio Gardella designed an integrated building, using an architectural language full of serenity, devoid of excess, and a long way from even his most notorious works, such as his 1957 façade over the Giudecca canal in the city of Venice.

The materials providing this peaceful appearance are: slate, a typical Genoese material, which is used on the roof, the top of the eaves, the floor delineators and the frieze; the brick dust-clad plaster whose soft pink tones cover the whole of the wall; and the Akedal aluminum used in the building's partitioning.

Lyons School of Architecture

Jourda & Perraudin

Location: Lyons, France. **Date of completion**: 1989. **Architect**: Jourda & Perraudin. **Scheme**: Central building: classrooms, lecture hall, library, laboratories, exhibition rooms, cafeteria, teachers' offices, administrative offices, services, and gardens.

From the outside, the building looks like a compact block divided into two: a solid section like a frieze with large rectangular windows on one side and arched openings on the other; and an upper, much lighter section built of timber and glass. A secondary structure supports an awning which protects it from sunlight and acts as a horizontal finial to the building. The apse is a solid block with very narrow vertical openings which run the whole height of the building and are reminiscent of Romanesque apsidal windows in style.

The teaching areas (classrooms and library) and experimental areas (the laboratories) intercommunicate and form the first floor of the building. The areas set aside for project rooms are located in the large timber structure. The exhibition areas are spread throughout the building: along the central corridor and the apse or square. The formal distinction between the two floors is due to the contrast between the solid shape of the first floor and the vast upper structure. Thus, the first floor supports the workshops and is the anchor point for the lighter structure. The corridor is the central axis of the building, punctuated by the Café des Arts square and the library, which links the teaching areas with the hall of the semicylindrical building. This houses the administrative and teaching staff offices, which are kept away from the school in a separate, detached building.

Libraries

Libraries, places of study and reference *par excellence*, have not escaped the architectural revolution of the last few years. From gloomy, poorly lit, cold, and neutral places, architects have turned them into welcoming environments conducive to reading and concentration. These new buildings combine general-purpose study rooms with other more specific ones. Thus, in this section, we find a series of libraries dedicated to the study of very specific topics such as poetry, the Catholic religion, world literature, and child education.

La Bibliothèque Nationale

Dominique Perrault

Location: Paris, France. **Date of completion**: 1997. **Developer**: French government **Architects**: Dominique Perrault, Aude Perrault, Gaëlle Lauriot-Prévost. **Associates**: Danielle Allaire, Gabriel Choukroun, Guy Moriseau (director of studies), Pieffet-Corbin (economist), Séchaud & Bossuyt (structural engineers), Technip Seri Construction (fluids), Syseca (telecommunications and security), Sauveterre-Horizon (gardening), ACV (acoustics). **Photography**: Michel Denancé, George Fessy.

rectangular podium encompassing a central recreational park.

In this work, Perrault expresses two apparently opposed dimensions: monumentality, symbolized by the book towers, and the intimacy and calm of the garden next to the reading rooms. For its architect, the library embodies emotions based on the paradox between presence and absence, human scale and monumental, dark and light, opposing forces.

The Bibliothèque Nationale de France (French National Library) is located to the east of Paris, in Tolbiac, near the Seine, in accordance with the urban development plan of bringing more facilities and parks to this area. It is claimed that the city is expanding beyond its ring roads for the first time. This library was the last major commission of former president, the late François Mitterrand.

The new building, which has a capacity of more than three million visitors a year, has 3600 reading places, an exhibition center, an auditorium, conference rooms, and restaurants. It will also act as the hub of a computerized network of French libraries.

Four glass towers, lined with bookshelves, stand at the corners of a huge

La Mesa Public Library

Antoine Predock

Location: Los Alamos, New Mexico, USA. **Date of completion**: 1994. **Cost**: $5.1 million. **Architect**: Antoine Predock. **Associates**: Geoffrey Beebe (managing partner), Paul Gonzales, Breatt Oaks (design directors), Rebecca Ingram, George Newlands, Deborah Waldrip, Linda Christenson, John Brittingem, Cameron Erdmann, Geoff Adams, Mark Donahue (design team), Randy Holt & Associates (structural engineers), P2RS Group (mechanical engineers), Telcon Engineering (electricity), High-Point Schaer (construction management), Bradbury & Stamm Construction (construction). **Scheme**: Reading rooms, storage, administration, and services. **Photography**: Timothy Hursley.

The new library is halfway between abstract sculpture and integration into the natural surroundings. The library is a low, two-floor building. It is curved to enjoy the magnificent views to the north. A taller, pyramid-shaped tower cuts the library in two. This feature is reminiscent of the edges of the rock walls near Turfa close to Los Alamos. Where the tower intersects with the building, Antoine Predock has designed a courtyard over which access to the building is gained.

As with many of Antoine Predock's works, the main material used is concrete, both blocks and in situ shuttered concrete. Predock works with this material in a certain way, with the intention of achieving an image similar to that of the monumental constructions found in primitive villages.

Denver Central Library

Michael Graves

Location: Denver, Colorado, USA. **Date of completion**: January 1996. **Developer**: Denver City Council. **Cost**: $46.5 million. **Architect**: Michael Graves. **Associates**: Klipp Colussy Jenks DuBois Architects (managing), Hyman/Etkin Construction (management), S.A. Miro (structural engineers), The Ballard Group (mechanical engineers), Gambrell Engineering (electricity), Clanton Engineering (lighting), Engel/Kieding Design Associates (interior design), Badgett and Cover-Clark (landscaping), David L. Adams (acoustics). **Scheme**: Thematic reading rooms. **Photography**: Timothy Hursley.

Michael Graves built this extension to Denver's Central Library. The original building, designed by Burnham Hoyt in 1956, is listed in the National Register of Historic Places. The old library retains its institutional presence in the Civic Center Park, to the north, and its own identity as one element of a larger composition. The extension is to the south, at the back, with a strong, new public image. With its signature round, south-facing façade, it is destined to become a focal point of Thirteenth Avenue.

Scale, color, and variety of shape synthesize with the surroundings. The downtown image is an authentic geometric composition of prisms of different sizes and colors which overlap in a horizontal plane. Michael Graves in turn works with absolute, known shapes: cylinders, prisms, cones, pyramids, etc.

Graves in some way applies to an individual design the ratios which the buildings establish with each other within the overall cityscape.

However, the Indianapolis architect is not only seeking to integrate the design into the city but also for it to carry a symbolic and meaningful charge. In other words, Graves is trying to give architecture a quality which is absent from the modern movement: monumentality. Especially in the case of public buildings, Graves believes that architects have an obligation to translate into their work the significance of every institution in society.

Phoenix Central Library

bruderDWLarchitects

Location: Phoenix, Arizona, USA **Date of construction**: 1994. **Architects**: bruderDWLarchitects. **Consultants**: Ove Arup (structural engineers), Baltes/Valentino (construction engineering), Lighting Dynamics (lighting), Tait Solar (natural lighting), FTL/Happold (fabric structure), Construction Consultants Southwest (cost control), Steve Martino (landscaping). **Scheme**: Reading rooms, book storage, small research rooms, conference rooms, lobby, offices, and services. **Floor area**: 26,000 m² (280,000 ft²). **Photography**: Bill Timmerman.

BruderDWLarchitects are used to working with metaphors of the countryside and the rural and mining constructions of Arizona. In this case, the new Phoenix Central Library is reminiscent of the rocky formations of the amazing Monument Valley. Inside, they have sought maximum flexibility due to the difficulty in forecasting changes in the structure of the library within a few decades of completion. The structure consists of a network of 10 m (33 ft) pillars. The east and west façades consist of a series of horizontal copper sheets, while the north and south façades are pure glass. The south façade includes several vertical stretched canvas elements which act as sunshades.

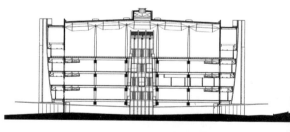

Kuhmo Library

Jyrki Tasa

Location: Kuhmo, Finland. **Date of completion**: 1990. **Client**: Kuhmo, Finland. **Architect**: Jyrki Tasa. **Scheme**: Central public library: reading rooms, music room, cafeteria, and other services. **Photography**: Antii Luutonen.

The most important functions of the library are located on a single floor, thus establishing between them a firm connection which will gradually integrate them into the common floor area. This connection is thematic and is achieved in what could be called the "library road," which, starting at the entrance, runs parallel to the main wall and all round the center, with all the library services organized around it. This center also has other unique features: including the music room, located opposite the café, and the grand hall, with spectacular views of the lake, which hosts all library activities. The selection of materials was also determined by the desire to create a friendly atmosphere. For the floor, pillars, and features in the wall facing the lake, reinforced concrete was used. For the roofs, Jyrki Tasa settled for timber and steel materials.

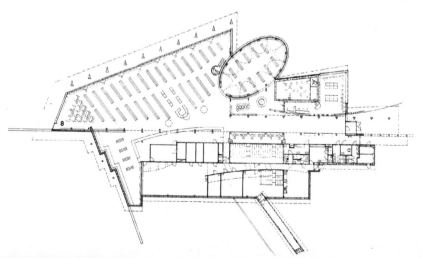

Eichstätt Library

Günter Behnisch & Partners

Location: Eichstätt, Germany. **Date of completion**: 1988. **Client**: German Catholic University. **Architect**: Günter Behnisch & Partners. **Scheme**: New central library and faculties of sociology, languages, and literature: classrooms, library and administration department, conference room, periodicals and newspaper library, shop, reference department and lending library, cloakrooms, cafeteria, and services. **Photography**: Christian Kandzia.

The city of Eichstätt has the only Catholic university in Germany. The university needed to expand its facilities to accommodate a new central library and the faculties of sociology, languages, and literature. The whole building is arranged around a central lobby which is subdivided into several areas: the library administration department, a conference room, a periodicals and newspaper library, a shop, the reference department and lending library, and the cloakrooms and cafeteria. The two upper floors are reserved solely for books.

Monterrey Central Library

Legorreta Architects

Location: San Nicolás de los Ganza, Nuevo León, Mexico. **Date of completion**: 1994. **Client**: Universidad Autónoma de Nuevo León. **Architect**: Legorreta Arquitectos. **Associates**: Armando Chávez, José Vigil. **Interior design**: Legorreta Arquitectos, Chávez Vigil Arquitectos Asociados. **Photography**: Lourdes Legorreta, (also pp 348/349).

traditional Mexican architecture appear in a totally contemporary form. The focal points of intense color and light filtered through courtyards and latticework remind us of the country's popular architecture, which the library incorporates in its essence, referring to the context through its reworking, but not quoting the forms literally.

The main section of the library consists of two large structures: a central cube within an embracing cylinder. The cylindrical corona opens towards the lake, terminating in triangular buttresses, the largest of which spills directly into the water. The central cube, hidden from the rest of the perimeter by the cylinder, can be seen through these two wedges. The reading areas are located in the cylindrical corona, offering panoramic views over the park.

Externally, the building impresses by the roundness and simplicity of the geometric twins, which, despite their size, harmoniously integrate themselves into the surrounding park. Only two materials are used for the walls: the brick of the imposing cylinder, in perfect harmony with the visible concrete of the rest of the buildings, with the exception of the tower and access corridor, which are also made of open brickwork. Elements of

Monterrey Central Library 363

Children's library

Paula Santos

Location: Oporto, Portugal. **Date of completion**: 1996. **Architect**: Paula Santos. **Associates**: Rui Ramos, Joaquin Santana. **Photography**: Luis Ferreira Alves, Paula Santos.

The little pavilion located among the trees in the garden has a dual height lobby and two floors intercommunicating via a wooden staircase. The library has the appearance of an *objet trouvé* in the wild, part of the hazardous nature of the countryside. The light, welcoming

building looks like a railroad car slightly raised off the ground. It gives the impression that it has been carefully placed there without damaging or altering the surroundings. The materials used in its construction respect and adapt to the countryside following the textures and colors of nature.

The structure and wall panels are of timber and the windows are strips of transparent polycarbonate, located at a child's height, with excellent views over the garden. The idea of a toy box met with such approval that the local authority decided to build another pavilion in Oporto City Park, now in use, to

serve as a children's library and toy library.

A few modifications have been introduced in this second building to make the walls able to withstand the cold of an Oporto winter. Wood has been used as it is a versatile material which is suitable for various building systems and because it is very expressive. Wood is also perfect for parks.

Religious buildings

Of all the sections of *The World of Architecture*, this one features projects that have probably recently undergone the greatest change in concept and design. This is the main reason that we decided to allocate these buildings a separate section. Edifices dedicated to keeping the faith and developing the spirit always used to be very old structures which had endured up to the present. Many of the projects presented here are, of course, from countries with strong religious traditions. However, there are many major international architects who have decided to take the risk involved in merging architecture and spirituality in a building. We have included the most recent works by Siza, Maki, Holl, Fuksas and others.

Männistö Church and Parochial Center

Juha Leiviskä

Location: Kuopio, Finland. **Date of completion**: 1993. **Client**: Kuopio Lutheran Evangelical Parish. **Architect**: Juha Leiviskä. **Associates**: Pekka Kivisalo (urban development), Parkku Pääkkönen, Mirja Arias (plastic arts), Harry Dunkel (structural engineer), Markkanen & Tiirikainen (mechanical engineering), E. Pitkänen & K (electricity). **Photography**: Arno de la Chapelle, Jussi Tiainen.

The church, parochial center, and local authority social center are located on a slope, on a strip of land between tall 1960s apartment blocks and a recreational park.

The entrance is on the lower level. The church has an undefined profile: light enters through its many folds. The inner spaces are built around the natural lighting of the building.

"I have tried to ensure that all the component parts, the walls (with their respective works of art), the ceiling, the first floor amphitheatre, the organ… form a whole. My intention is to provide vital interaction between the large and the small, the open and the closed, the high and the low, spaces as instruments to interpret the light, the veil woven by the reflections and their continual changes." Its proximity to the baroque world (Lutheran asceticism, but not the suffering and punishment of the Counter-reformation) is not so much aesthetic as epistemological.

Leiviskä identifies artistic experience with religion and mysticism. Therefore, it is acceptable to say that his work transcends architecture, because space is not the end-purpose of the work but rather seeing reality as a revelation.

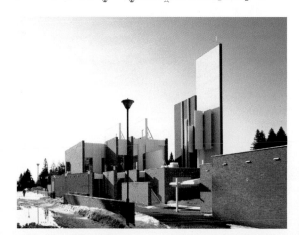

Kol Ami Temple

William P. Bruder

Location: Scottsdale, Arizona, USA. **Date of completion**: 1994. **Client**: Temple Kol Ami. **Architect**: William P. Bruder. **Associates**: Wendell Burnette, Eric Robinson, Beau Dromiack, Maryann Bloomfield, Tim Wert (design team). **Photography**: Bill Timmerman.

The architecture of the Kol Ami Temple provides Spartan spaces which acquire their definitive value from the precise entry of the light. William P. Bruder summons all the significance of natural lighting: its physical reality, its spiritual feeling, and its emotive capacity. At the same time, he juxtaposes that which is rightfully the opposite of light: matter (texture, earth, and place). The project provides a center of religion and of learning in the form of an archaic settlement, in the image of the ancient communities of Masada and Jerusalem. The Jewish temple and school are like a fortified village which continues the tradition of those desert communities, 2000 years later, on another continent and in another desert.

With the restrictions imposed by an extraordinarily small budget and the aspiration to encompass a strong symbolic presence, the emphasis of this center's design lies in the employment of concrete blocks as an essential building material. They have been used as a finish, both internally and externally; they have not been covered and the expressive possibilities of their texture have been carefully studied. This has created a special impression, with dry, irregular surfaces, deliberately weathered by sandblasting, conjuring up an image of thousand-year-old stone walls and forming a strong link to the ground underneath them.

Kaze-no-Oka Crematorium

Maki & Associates

Location: Nakatsu, Japan. **Date of design**: 1993–1994. **Date of construction**: 1995–1997. **Client**: Nakatsu Local Authority. **Architect**: Fumihiko Maki. **Associates**: Sasaki Environment Design Office. **Scheme**: Park, parking, crematorium, private chapel, chapel, and offices. **Total area of the park**: 3.3 ha (8.2 acres). **Photography**: Nacasa & Partners Inc.

The crematorium is built on a single floor, on an obviously large scale, so that its outline, visible from the park, is one of the outstanding features of the area. The building is basically in three sections: the sloping chapel (the tallest of the buildings), a blank, sloping, crowning wall which encloses some of the functional areas, and a gateway opening onto the park which links the other two sections.

Behind this screen lie the facilities of the crematorium, which are generous in terms of size and scrupulously arranged according to the functional requirements of the cremation service.

The interior, however, is in itself a precise form of landscaping: by painstaking control of the entry of light, the layout of courtyards, openings, pools, screens, etc. Proceeding through the interior has all the qualities of a walk in the countryside areas of Japan.

1. Parking lot
2. Court yard
3. Porch at the entrance
4. Oratory
5. Crematorium
6. Mortuary
7. Court yard
8. Waiting hall
9. Offices
10. Chapel
11. Park

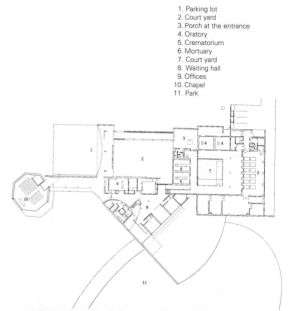

Cemetery and place of worship

Bernard Desmoulin

Location: Fréjus, France. **Date of construction**: 1997. **Architect**: Bernard Desmoulin. **Scheme**: Cemetery, museum, and place of prayer. **Photography**: Michel Denancé, Hervé Abbadie.

On the site of the former encampment from where French soldiers set sail for Indo-China, Bernard Desmoulin has created a cemetery, a garden, a small museum, and a place of quiet meditation for Christians, Buddhists, Jews, and Muslims. Desmoulin's intention is for Mediterranean plants (mimosa, olives, lavender) to cover entirely the concrete walls surrounding the circular garden and the cemetery itself, located along its center line. On one side, set slightly away from the cemetery, a small copper pergola encloses the four prayer houses, one for each religion. The museum is at the entrance to the precinct.

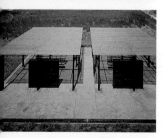

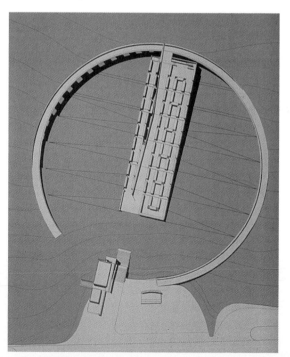

Church of Christ, Tokyo

Maki & Associates

Location: 1-30-17 Tomigaya, Shibuya-ku, Tokyo, Japan. **Date of completion**: 1995. **Architect**: Maki & Associates. **Associates**: Kimura Structural Engineers; Sogo Consultants (furniture, lighting, etc.), Takenaka Corporation (contractor). **Photography**: Toshiharu Kitajima.

The building is divided vertically: the first level, a dense and complex layer, houses all the ancillary facilities of the church (offices, dining room, kitchen etc.). Above this is the main area, designed as an extensive, diaphanous space, which occupies the whole of the second floor of the building, where the community meets to worship. The shape of the building expresses the idea of placing on a complex base a single area which is open to the sky and the light. The side walls are slightly inclined so that the building expands as it rises; and the roof is designed like a thin, plain dome, imitating the dome of the heavens. The front wall is designed as a huge screen of light to flood the inside of the church with diffused, filtered, magical, intense light.

The curtain wall consists of two layers of glass with an 80 cm (30 in) gap which provides excellent soundproofing, as well as a current of air between the two layers, which reduces overheating due to the rays of the sun.

Chapel of St. Ignatius

Steven Holl

Location: University of Seattle, Washington, USA. **Date of construction**: 1997. **Client**: University of Seattle. **Architect**: Steven Holl. **Associates**: Olson/Sundber Architects (associate architects), Baugh Construction (general contractor). **Area**: 790 m² (8500 ft²). **Photography**: Paul Warchol (also pp 368/369).

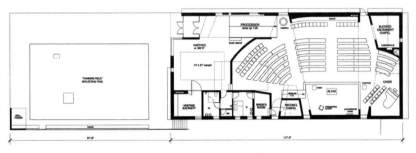

The Chapel of St. Ignatius serves the Catholic Jesuit community of the University of Seattle and is therefore designed to meet their religious requirements.

It has a rectangular floor plan, whose first roof (from which all the others start) is a basic horizontal plane which gives rise to a prism whose subsequent changes define each of the dimensions of the chapel. Insofar as the bell tower, the highest structure, is located on the opposite side of the pool, the whole of the religious area strictly speaking is confined within the larger rectangle which runs from the bell tower to the opposite end, including the location of the pool. For the interior, Holl uses very deliberate devices for lighting purposes. Each area has its own skylight. In defining the quality and significance of the light for each area, Holl talks about a "field," which is where the internal dividing walls of each area are located, and "lenses," which specify the color of the light filter of each opening. Thus, the code can be defined as follows:

– Processional entrance and narthex: natural daylight
– Nave: yellow field with blue lenses (east); blue field with yellow lenses (west)
– Holy Sacrament: orange field with purple lenses
– Choir: green field with red lenses
– Reconciliation : purple field with orange lenses
– Bell tower and pool: projected and reflected nocturnal light.

Catholic Church of Paks

Imre Markovecz

Location: Paks, Hungary. **Date of completion**: 1988. **Architect**: Imre Markovecz. **Scheme**: Design and construction of a Catholic church in pine. **Photography**: Miklos Csak.

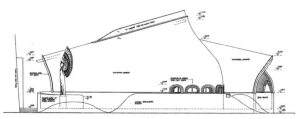

The design consists of a building with an ogee arch over which rises a sleek tower capped off by three pinnacles each about 25 m (80 ft) tall. The church also has a noticeable dimorphic character, both in the configuration of the floor plan and the layout of the various elements it contains. The central nave is vaguely triangular and is accessed from the southwest. The structure of the church has been made entirely of pine, which is a very soft and highly malleable material. The role played by light is highly symbolic: a dark area, the lower part of the nave, represents the mundane; the middle section, halfway between heaven and earth; and the highest part of the church, a celestial canopy with an almost supernatural quality to its design.

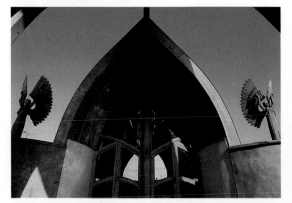

Cività Castellana Cemetery

Massimiliano Fuksas, Anna Maria Sacconi

Location: Cività Castellana, Viterbo, Italy. **Date of completion**: 1987. **Architects**: Massimiliano Fuksas, Anna Maria Sacconi. **Area**: 1.6 ha (4 acres). **Photography**: Doriana O. Mandrelli.

with a common formal line: all of them have been built several meters off the ground and, like the house outside, are raised on pillars as if in an attempt to get spiritually closer to the life after death.

The circular shape seems to encompass the whole atmosphere of the surroundings. Only the railway track breaks this continuity by breaching the wall and, after crossing the whole of the cemetery, it exits through the second opening to finish its run in a tunnel outside. Those who wish to access the cemetery can only do so across this track.
What at first sight seems to

be a warehouse is the chapel, and the water tank has been converted into an ossuary. The niches inside the wall which runs round the site have been disguised so that it is impossible to identify them from the outside. The track runs into the consecrated ground as far as the covered square, the church, and finally the ossuary. Three completely different structures, but

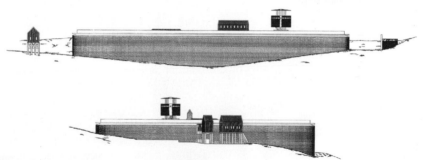

Church of Santa Maria-Marco de Canaveses

Alvaro Siza

Location: Marco de Canaveses, Portugal. **Date completed**: 1999. **Architect**: Alvaro Siza. **Scheme**: New Church of Santa Maria: entrance door, font, embrasure, presbytery, altar, pulpit, sacristy, and furniture. **Photography**: Luis Ferreira Alves, Rosina Ramirez.

On entering the town, the first aspect of the church you see is its northeast façade, less stark and more airy than the main façade due to its curvilinear shape and the different heights of its various sections. The main façade opens onto a pedestrian area, houses, a school, a nursery school, and a nearby parochial center. The building is completed by two further façades: to the southeast, a huge rectangular white wall with a narrow horizontal opening at the bottom; and, to the northwest, another wall, with five enormous upper windows through which sunlight enters at the top. It is controlled illumination, filtered by its direction to prevent the nave being flooded with too much light. Before entering the church we find ourselves before the tall, dignified, extremely heavy main entrance door in the façade of the building. Once inside, the interior seems like an "empty box" full of order and light, in which a curvilinear wall with a huge visual impact stands out. This wall gives depth to the three large windows. The presbytery stands on an area slightly raised above the nave by means of three steps. The light, transparent design of the nave requires complementary furniture. The seats are light, simple, functional and safe. Their shape discreetly imitates kneeling to pray.

Leisure facilities

All the buildings presented here are the result of both the application of the particular style of each architect and their attention to the specific requirements of the projects. In fact, a leisure facility is an example of the ability to combine creative freedom (expressed in the morphology of the building, construction techniques, and finishes) with existing regulations (which determine dimensions, public access, safety, and the functioning of facilities). On the other hand, holding sports events unfailingly goes hand in hand with significant quantitative and qualitative changes in the urban scene, from which the city and its inhabitants benefit. The analysis of the projects in this section covers these favorable repercussions and other design-related issues resulting from the desire for integration. This philosophy rejects the concept of the architectural design as an independent and self-sufficient entity. Even in the most isolated situation, there are still factors conditioning the shape of the building in relation to the countryside and the configuration of the site. The location also, to a large extent, determines the design decisions: the selection of materials, specific matters of form, and access systems, which differ according to the degree of integration of the building into the urban framework. Finally, a review of the projects included here reveals the importance of certain aspects of construction such as lighting technology, paving, and roofs.

Auditoriums

Theaters and Cinemas

Sports facilities

Theme parks and attractions

Bars, discotheques, and games rooms

Shopping malls

Stores and showrooms

Restaurants

Auditoriums

The design of auditoriums is undoubtedly
conditioned by their functional
requirements. Acoustic demands
determine the final shape of the concert
hall. Materials and finishes have specific
sound reverberation qualities and thus also
influence the acoustic behavior of the hall.
Architects, assisted by specialists, must
ensure that the building works correctly
from both the technical point of view and
in relation to its patrons: travel
connections, auxiliary services, external
connections, etc. The examples given here
achieve a perfect balance between
functionality and aesthetic harmony; they
are emblematic buildings which are
regarded as unique, virtually essential to
the city which houses them.

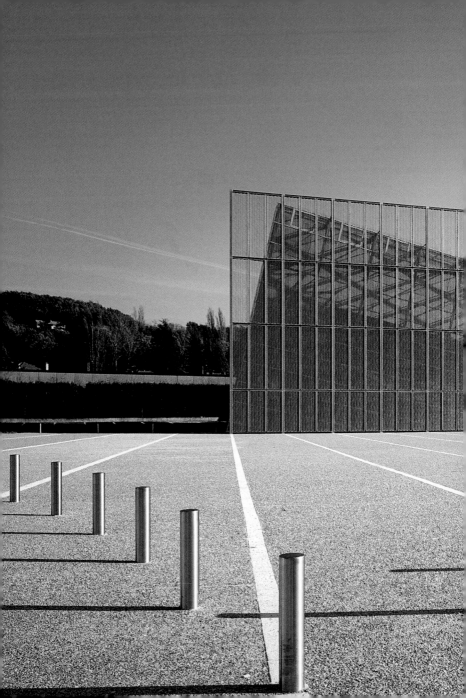

Auditorium in Nagaoka

Toyo Ito

Location: Nagaoka, Niigata, Japan. **Date of design:** 1993-1994. **Date of construction:** 1994–1997. **Architect:** Toyo Ito. **Structural engineers:** KSP- Hanawa Structural Engineers Co, Ltd. **Scheme:** Concert hall (700 seats), theater (450 seats), studios. **Gross floor area:** 9700 m² (104,000 ft²). **Photography:** Nacása + Partner.

On the outskirts of the Japanese city of Nagaoka, on the banks of the river Shinano, in a place with distant views of the Echigo mountains, this building put the finishing touch to an extensive cultural area. The building creates its own topography. Running in an east–west direction, it offers four main facilities: theater, a concert hall, some studios, and an administrative area.

The corridor acts as a foyer, social area, and cafeteria, It extends under a curved roof of concrete slabs which covers the whole of the building and from which the two main sections, which are the theater stage housing and the concert hall, project.

Le Sémaphore

Christian Drevet

Location: Roussillon, France. **Date of completion**: September 1994. **Developer**: City of Roussillon (Isère). **Cost**: Fr 11.2 million **Architects**: Christian Drevet Architectures, Nicolas Guillot. **Associates**: Bruno Bossard, Jean-Christian Cheze (assistants), Bernard Thaon (acoustics), Alain Ranvier (metal structure), Guy Poulain (concrete structure), Jean-Pierre Chailleux (fluids), Robert Blanpain (economist). **Scheme**: Seating area (250), stage, dressing rooms, workshops, store rooms, banqueting suites, kitchen, bar, services. **Photography**: Eric Saillet (also pp 392/393).

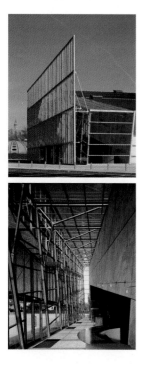

Le Sémaphore is a multipurpose complex designed for shows, concerts, parties, and banquets. Because of this, the use and shape of the space does not follow the traditional layout of a theater as there are obvious differences, especially in the stage and ancillary rooms, as these areas are used for eating or for dancing.

Le Sémaphore is located on the outskirts of the city of Roussillon, alongside the freeway to the south (Autoroute du Sud), next to several factories. It is therefore a typical suburban landscape: factors of scale, use, and speed all combined. Responding to these various issues, the project has three elements: a light mast, a metal screen, and a parallelepiped.

Behind the metal screen of the façade is a second skin of glass and behind that a wall which folds like a curtain. Each of these successive skins creates a scenic plane. The spectacularly inclined camera obscura interprets the heights of the various areas: higher in the auditorium and lower in the party and banqueting hall. Inserted between these two areas is the 9 x 12 m (30 x 40 ft) and 8 m (26 ft) high stage. This layout enables the stage to use the banqueting hall as an additional space or conversely large parties to use the stage. The whole space can thus be used.

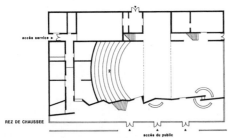

Kyoto Concert Hall

Arata Izozaki & Associates

Location: Kitayama district, Kioto, Japan. **Date of construction**: 1995. **Architect**: Arata Izozaki & Associates. **Photography**: Katsuaki Furudate, Yoshio Takase.

The building of the Kyoto Concert Hall is in commemoration of the 1200 years since the foundation of this Japanese city. The layout of the project is emphasized by two main factors: on the one hand the size of the complex, in relation to the more immediate urban surroundings, as the plot is in a central area of Kyoto; and, on the other, its dimensions, its spatial configuration, and the layout of the seating in the two main halls, one accommodating 1800 people and another smaller one with 500 seats.

The final choice was to design the facility as a complex of three buildings, each of a different shape: the main hall is housed in a rectangular building at right angles to the façade; the smaller hall is circular in shape, slightly conical, without any apparent orientation, although its interior configuration faces northwest; and the third building, which houses the cloakrooms and areas outside the halls, faces in the same direction as the buildings located on neighboring plots.

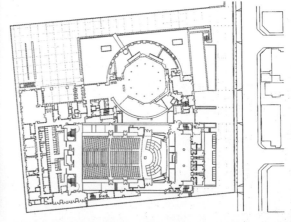

Barcelona Auditorium

Rafael Moneo

Location: Barcelona, Spain. **Date of construction**: 1999 **Architect**: Rafael Moneo. **Client**: Barcelona Local Authority. **Scheme**: Two concert halls, practice rooms, museum of music, library, recording rooms, restaurant, offices, and services. **Photography**: Ana Quesada.

The Barcelona Auditorium is located on an unattractive plot which did not offer the architect any inspiration. The compelling, forceful autonomy of the building can be seen in the contained and compact architecture, which must nevertheless accommodate and house highly complex and extensive facilities: two concert halls, one with seating for an audience of 2500 and the other for 700, with all the services that accompany such halls; practice rooms for orchestras and soloists, a museum of music, library, recording rooms, restaurants, store rooms, and other facilities.

Faced with such elaborate demands, the design opted for compactness, imposed by the strict size dictates of the structure. The fabric of the building is a network of reinforced concrete complemented by stainless steel panels on the outside and oak panels on the inside. Compactness also requires empty spaces which establish distances and define contiguities.

Galicia Auditorium

Julio Cano Lasso and Diego Cano Pintos

Location: Santiago de Compostela, La Coruña, Spain. **Date of completion:** 1989. **Client:** Santiago Local Authority. **Architects:** Julio Cano Lasso and Diego Cano Pintos. **Scheme:** Concert hall, theater, and conference halls, exterior landscaping, cafeteria-restaurant, meeting rooms, administrative offices, and services. **Photography:** Francesc Tur.

The auditorium has been designed with the intention of combining local architectural heritage with modern formality. This symbiosis is achieved by the use of a material which exalts the timeless values of tradition: stone, in its monumental appearance, becomes the leitmotif of this construction. The building also sought to bring order to a district which at that time was under development.

The project took advantage of the existence of a stream, which was used to form a small artificial lake below the building, in order to make a feature of reflections in the water.

The strategic use of vegetation, which includes local trees, helps to give the complex a wholly natural appearance.

The building looks like a huge set of granite chairs which are grouped to form simple shapes; the use of glass galleries superimposed over the walls highlights the contrast between the weight of the stone and the fragility and brilliance of the glass panels.

Copper is used as the third material for the exterior, especially for the roof and the lining of the large arch which dominates the stage.

Le Corum

Claude Vasconi

Location: Montpellier, France. **Date of completion**: 1990. **Architect**: Claude Vasconi. **Scheme**: Auditorium, meeting room, committee room, exhibition room, bars, restaurants, rehearsal rooms, shopping complex, administrative center, three-floor parking lot, and services. **Photography**: S. Couturier. Archipress.

The Regional Opera House/Conference Center, Le Corum (located on the Charles de Gaulle Esplanade in Montpellier) was a step in a new direction for its French-born architect. The brief given to Claude Vasconi was to build a huge facility to the

following specification: a total floor area of 70,000 m² (750,000 ft²) housing a 2000-seat auditorium with a sound system in front of the stage and service areas, a large hall seating 800, a committee room for 300, 4000 m² (43,000 ft²) of exhibition space, bars and restaurants, rehearsal rooms, a shopping complex, administrative centers, and finally a three-floor underground parking lot with capacity for around 500 vehicles. The interior of the building is arranged using a four-floor hall as a reference point. This receives direct natural light thanks to a huge glass roof which can be opened or closed.

Another characteristic of the inside of Le Corum is the presence of a series of fixed stairs and escalators providing access to the various parts of the building and at the same time optimal internal distribution.

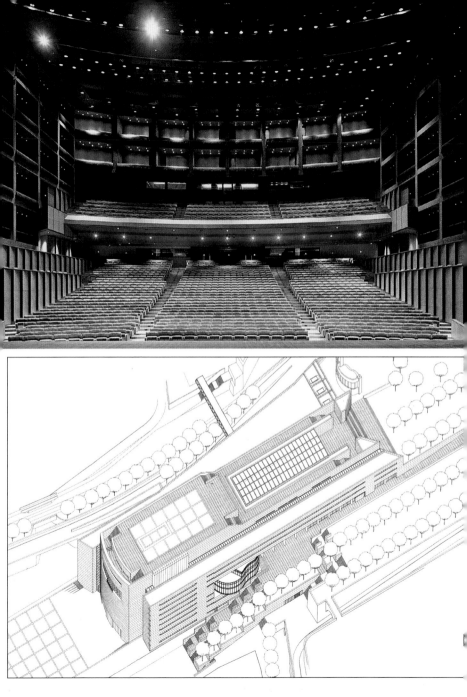

Stadthalle Bielefeld

Meinhard von Gerkan

Location: Herdorfer Str. Bielefeld, Germany. **Date of design:** 1980. **Date of completion:** 1990. **Architect:** Meinhard von Gerkan. **Scheme:** Multipurpose cultural center: two multipurpose rooms, interior gallery, lobby with mobile units for temporary exhibitions, cloakrooms, offices, services, and outside garden. **Photography:** Richard Bryant.

In 1990 Bielefeld opened a new cultural venue, called the Stadthalle, designed as a multipurpose center for musical and theatrical activities, exhibitions, conferences, and symposia.

The solitary Stadthalle now sails like a big ship on the recently designed Bahnhofspark. Both in its shape and the choice of materials and colors, the building is designed simply. Its elements are laid out following the structure's geometric plan. The façade encompassing the building consists of two layers between which are the stairs connecting the lobby with the first floor cloakrooms, the hall level, and the second floor gallery. The two halls of this facility, the larger of which holds a maximum of 2300 people, and the smaller 700, are located opposite each other. They are joined by their stages and follow the central line of symmetry of the building in such a way that, by removing the partition between them, the two spaces can be used as a single entity.

Theaters and cinemas

The theater can be a sacred ceremony or
simply entertainment, a show of three acts
or a spontaneous production, the actors
can declaim from the stage or mix with the
audience.... Although they may come in
many shapes, theaters do not vary much
because in the end the problem to be
solved is always the same: lots of
spectators looking at a few actors. But
what has changed, and it is different in
every project, is the way in which this
isolated space relates to the rest of the
world, both inside and out.
The external appearance of the building,
the method of access to the reception area,
the stairs, the lobbies... as well as the
finishes, colors, materials, fabrics, and
decorations. In other words, everything
which exists before the actors start to
speak, before the lights go down, before
the band begins to play.

Pathé Cinemas

Kosmos UFA-Palast

City of Arts Cinema-Planetarium

La Géode

American Conservatory Theater

Chassé Theater

Cultural center in Tapiola

Theater Arts Center

The Hague Dance Theater

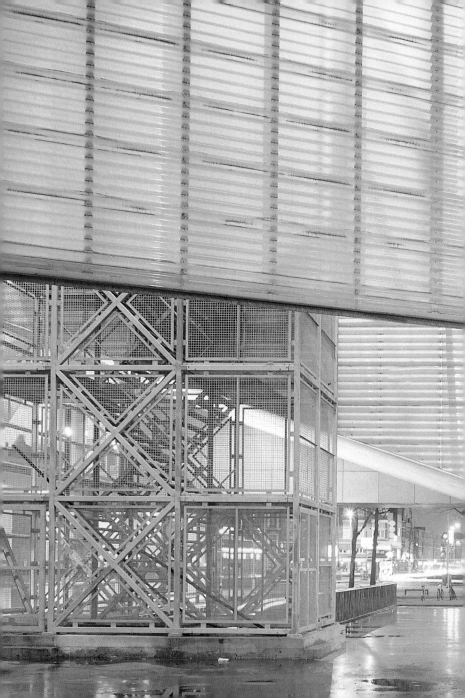

Pathe Multiplex Cinema

Koen van Velsen

Location: Rotterdam, The Netherlands. **Construction dates**: July 1994 - December 1995. **Client**: Pathé Cinemas. **Architect**: Koen van Velsen. **Collaborators**: Gero Rutten, Marcel Steeghs, Lars Zwant, Okko van der Kam. **Acoustical engineering**: van Dorsser. **Scheme**: A seven-screen cinema center, a restaurant and a café. **Gross floor surface**: 8473 m². **Photography**: Kim Zwartz (also pp 410/411).

Pathé Cinema's new cinema center adds to the variety of cultural activities offered in Rotterdam's central Schouwburgplein (Shouwburg Square). The complex contains seven screens with a total seating capacity of 2700.

Much of the project has been conditioned by technical factors. The building rests on a preexisting underground parking garage, part of which has been removed to allow space for the restaurant, or Grand Café. A metallic structure is wrapped in a thin translucent skin, lightening the building both in physical weight and in visual presence.

Each cinema hall is an isolated box separated from the other halls by corridors and restrooms. The façade of undulating polycarbonate cladding has a structure independent from the rest of the building but which wraps around it in free form. The translucent polycarbonate cladding covers both the inside and outside of the surrounding independent wall so that air pipes and fire escapes are partially hidden. The undulating sheets lend the construction an industrial appearance during the day, and at night transform it into a softly glowing light bulb, becoming the center of attention on the plaza.

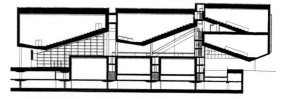

Kosmos UFA - Palast

Rhode Kellermann Wawrowsky

Location: Berlin, Germany. **Date of construction**: 1997. **Design team**: Andrew Barley, Stefanie Bode, Daniel Bush, Hans Feyerabend, Kathleen King, Matthius Pfeiffer, Katharina Riedel, Willi Robens, Michael Ross, Brigitte Treutner, Marc Ulrich, Walter Wernecke. **Floor area**: 9000 m² (97,000 ft²). **Photography**: Christian Gahl, Florian Protitlich.

The Kosmos cinema was built in 1962 by Josef Kaiser as part of the monumental Karl-Marx-Allee in the Friedrichshain district of East Berlin. It was a detached building surrounded by enormous apartment blocks, set back from the road behind a parking lot.

After reunification, it was purchased by a private company which decided to modernize and extend it. As it was a listed building, RKW decided to restrict themselves to restoring the original building and to place the new buildings around it. The old and new sections are connected by

an elliptical corridor lit from above in the daytime by means of a skylight. The surface parking lot has been replaced by an underground one and a square created in front of the cinema.

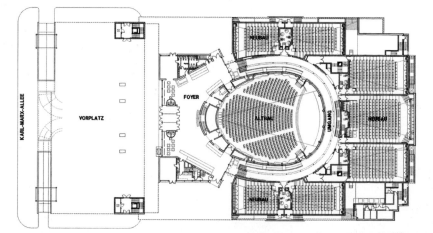

City of Arts Cinema-Planetarium

Santiago Calatrava

Location: Valencia, Spain. **Date of construction**: 1999. **Architect**: Santiago Calatrava **Scheme**: Cinema-planetarium, exhibition hall, bar, offices, and services. **Photography**: Paco Asensio.

The City of Arts & Sciences is the beacon project of a culture/leisure complex built on the dry bed of the river Turia in the city of Valencia which includes, in addition to the cinema-planetarium, an art gallery, science museum and oceanographic center. Virtually all the buildings were designed by the Valencia-based engineer and architect Santiago Calatrava.

The cinema-planetarium is designed for showing Omnimax films as well as regular flat projections in a planetarium. The cinema itself is a white sphere. However, Santiago Calatrava built a second roof on it which protects the lobby and access areas. A system of telescopic arms on the sides enables a huge area of glass to be closed or made into a protective canopy.

La Géode

Adrien Fainsilber

Location: La Villete, Paris, France. **Date of completion:** 1988. **Client:** Paris Municipality. **Architect:** Adrien Fainsilber. **Scheme:** Museum of science and technology, cinema. **Photography:** Charlie Abad.

La Géode is the result of an urban development project by the Parisian authorities to reconstruct some old buildings, previously used as abattoirs, and convert them into a major science museum known as the City of Science and Industry. The whole of the museum is designed as a surprise for the visitor, who enters an unknown world where the latest advances in scientific and technological innovation are revealed. One of the main attractions of the complex is the Géode, a huge steel sphere, somewhere between a building and a monument, which houses a high-tech cinema whose audiences are bombarded with spectacular images. Like a crystal ball, the circular geometry of La Géode makes a striking visual contrast to the straight lines of the museum's main building. From a distance, this compact steel ball seems to float gently on a platform of water, giving a surreal impression.

American Conservatory Theater

Gensler & Associates

Location: San Francisco. USA. **Date of completion**: 1997. **Client**: City of San Francisco. **Architects**: Gensler & Associates. **Scheme**: Refurbishment of the old City Hall, new annex. **Photography**: M. Lorenzetti.

seats and the distance between rows has been increased. New elevators to all floors have been installed and disabled access improved.
New dressing rooms, offices, and costume maintenance workshops have been built in an annex to the main building.

After the damage suffered by the 82-year-old building from an earthquake in 1989, the authorities decided to appoint Esherick Hornsey & Davis to produce an initial scheme for its refurbishment. Gensler was later commissioned to revise the design and take it through to the construction stage. Appropriate permits were obtained from local and national institutions to work on the remains of a protected building of historical importance.
The Geary Theater, as it is currently called, now has a larger reception area after the removal of several walls located at the rear of the auditorium. The acoustics, which previously suffered from outside traffic noise, have been improved. Space on the upper floors has also been expanded and used to build additional boxes, areas for use during intermissions, and new restrooms. Although the seating capacity has been reduced by 400 seats, the size of the remaining 1035

Chassé Theater

Herman Hertzberger

Location: Breda, The Netherlands. **Date of construction**: 1992–1995. **Client**: Breda Local Authority. **Architect**: Herman Hertzberger. **Associates**: Willem van Winsen, Folkert Stropsma, Ariënne Matser, Patrick Fransen, Marijke Teijsse-Braat. **Scheme**: Main auditorium for 1200 spectators, hall for 500 spectators, two cinemas, small multipurpose room, offices, and ancillary facilities.

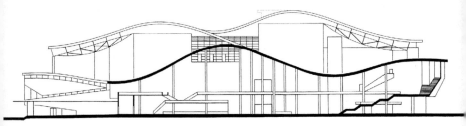

The exterior of the building is notable for its undulating roof, which adapts to the varying size requirements of its component parts and unifies the complex.

The layout of the main auditorium follows the traditional stage/audience pattern but not as far as the seating layout is concerned, where asymmetry follows the visual and acoustic asymmetry of the presentation itself, appearing in the design as a result of the linear structure of the foyer. Access to each level is by various staircases running along the rear walls and enjoying panoramic views of the outside.

The medium-sized auditorium is designed like a "black box," a theater with retractable seats offering immense versatility for shows. Between the two large stages, raised above the level of the foyer lies the third theater, a small area also suitable for various uses, above which is the complex's office suite. Structurally, the theaters are three concrete boxes 30 cm (1 ft) thick, which provide sound insulation; in the roof, prefabricated concrete profiles support all the machinery and equipment located in the spaces created by the undulations in the design of the roof.

Tapiola Cultural Center

Arto Sipinen

Location: Tapiola, Finland. **Date of completion**: 1991. **Client**: Tapiola Local Authority. **Architect**: Arto Sipinen. **Facilities**: Public cultural center: auditorium, exhibition halls, café-restaurant, library, workers' music institute. **Photography**: Arto Kivienemi.

The factors which the design had to consider can be summarized as: a large building which faces the presence and complexity of an artificial lake and a hotel, at the same time that it has to take on a horizontal layout that enhances the verticality of the neighboring office complex. The large central buildings of the Center accommodate the two auditoriums, while behind the glass façades lie the cloakrooms, reception area, exhibition halls, and the café-restaurant.

The south wing of the complex is a more layered structure which houses various cultural activities:

the library and the workers' music institute.

The external finishes consist of large blocks of quartz sandstone, tiled floors, and glass. Inside, the building is characterized by the use of see-through partitions, birch cladding, and decorative plants.

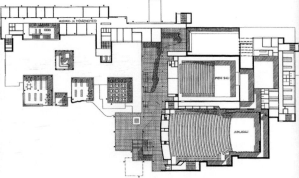

Theatre Arts Center

James Stirling & Michael Wilford Ass.

Location: London, UK. **Date of completion**: 1990. **Architects**: James Stirling & Michael Wilford Ass. **Scheme**: Theater and visual arts center: dance studios, mini-theaters, and outside courtyard. **Photography**: Richard Bryant/Arcaid.

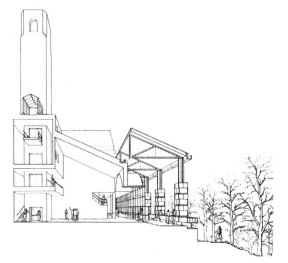

The PAC module consists of an 80 m² (860 ft²) octagonal pavilion which acts as an information center and a shelter for the nearby bus stop. The unit consists of an upper floor with premises belonging to the Theatre Arts Department which can be adapted for touring companies. A smooth cylindrical body, arranged on the roof of the prism, exercises an expressive counterpoint of geometry and color.

On the faces of the basic building there are various openings complemented on their upper section by a series of circular windows. Next to the pavilion is an open space which can be accessed from College Avenue. This area is designed as a meeting and recreational area for students, and various items of street furniture, such as seats and a pergola, have been installed. The pergola is made of five visually strong prism-shaped pillars on which sit wooden structures supported by two back-to-back triangles. The most expressive elements which make up the image of the façade are a large circular opening, located asymmetrically at one end, and a large central arch from which emerges a glass prism, which is the main dance studio in the complex.

The Hague Dance Theater

Rem Koolhaas

Location: The Hague, The Netherlands. **Date of completion**: 1984. **Architect**: Rem Koolhaas. **Associates**: Jeroen Thomas, Willem-Jan Neutelings, Frank Roodbeen, Jaap van Heest, Ron Steiner, Dirk Hendriks, Frans Vogelaar, Wim Kloosterboer, Hans Werlemann, BOA, Petra Blaisse. **Scheme**: The Hague Dance Theater: auditorium, box office, cafeteria, offices, and services. **Photography**: Peter Aaron, Esto Photographics.

The site intended for the Koolhaas project leads into a pedestrian area which shares space with other new buildings: a hotel, a concert hall and the town hall and its offices. This physical proximity issue was resolved by instituting a shared area, located in the tinted glass lobby, where the access doors to the respective buildings are placed side by side. The building looks more like a "nave," in industrial terminology, than a compact, monumental theater complex.

The structure is designed in three individual yet integrated components: an inverted conical building, glazed at the top with a golden finish, which houses the box office and cafeteria; the sinuous, undulating profile of the auditorium roof; and finally the vast cube of the gridiron tower, presided over by a magnificent mural by Madelon Vriesendorp (Koolhaas' wife), which suggests pictorially what happens inside the theater. The sobriety of the background and minimalist rationality of the interior design turns the Dutch dance theater into a lucid example of a new way of understanding architecture in the 20th century.

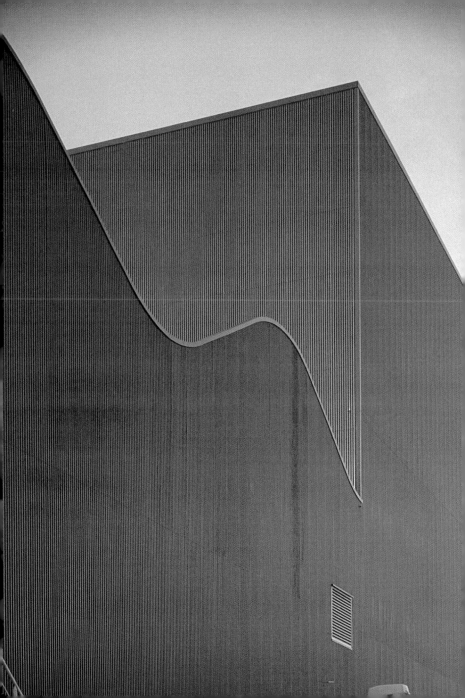

Sports facilities

Designing sports facilities is a fascinating
challenge, from which have emerged
magnificent buildings that successfully
resolve aesthetic and pragmatic issues, at
the same time balancing the individual
style of the architect with the various
demands of the natural environment, the
regulations of the sport in question, or the
requirements of the developer.
This chapter aims to summarize trends in
international architecture in recent years.
The projects included clearly demonstrate
wide diversity, a direct consequence of
evolution in sporting practice.

Tobu Golf Club

Masayuki Kurokawa

Location: Yubari-gun, Hokkaido, Japan. **Date of completion**: July 1983. **Architect**: Masayuki Kurokawa Architect & Associates. **Associates**: Sasaki Structural Consultants and Nishida Engineering Equipment, Kankyo Engineering Inc. (structural engineers), Matsushita Electric Works Ltd. **Scheme**: Club room, restaurants, cloakrooms, gymnasium, meeting rooms, administration, and services. **Photography**: Nacasa & Partners Inc (also pp 432/433).

The club consists of a main building and an annex. The main building is rectangular in shape with another rectangular open space at the center. The annex roof continues the slope of the main building so that they seem to be joined. The building attempts to blend into the scenery. However, when the door is opened and the lobby is accessed, the building's image changes completely. The central courtyard contains a large pond; the areas around the pond, the lounge and a corridor, take light from the courtyard. In other words, the empty space becomes the heart of the building. It works like a trap which ensnares nature, to the benefit of the members.

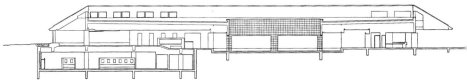

Fuji Chuo Golf Club

Desmond Muirhead

Location: Mount Fuji, Japan. **Date of construction**: 1995. **Architect**: Desmond Muirhead.

Muirhead based the layout of the 18 holes on the wood engravings of the Japanese artist Hokusai. They are laid out exactly like a hundred different readings of Mount Fuji, the most famous of which is "The Great Wave," which is the 17th hole. Thus from a list in which each of the 18 holes was assigned an engraving by Hokusai, with its own title and theme, Muirhead independently designed each of the holes, giving the theme shape through the very design instruments of golf courses themselves: bunkers, lakes, wooded areas, slopes, etc.

The various changes that the landscape undergoes during the day and the seasons (changes in light, presence or absence of snow, fog or other elements which alter the appearance of the mountain) are taken into account in Muirhead's project as factors of a landscape in constant metamorphosis, reflecting the passage of time and the special feeling of every hour of the day or time of the year.

Le Stadium

Rudy Ricciotti

Location : Vitrolles, France. **Date of completion**: 1995. **Architect**: Rudy Ricciotti. **Scheme**: Sports track, bleachers, ticket offices, offices, bar, foyer, and services. **Photography**: Philippe Ruault.

Le Stadium is a kind of enormous monolith that breaks up the countryside, a completely hermetically sealed building, such that its purpose cannot be distinguished from the outside. The inside of the building has a much clearer layout. Bleachers are laid out on one side only because the stadium is primarily for rock concerts and to a lesser extent for sports meetings. The ground plan is almost a perfect square: 58 x 56 m (190 x 184 ft). The foyer is just underneath the bleachers. The restrooms are located on both sides, with the stages just opposite them.

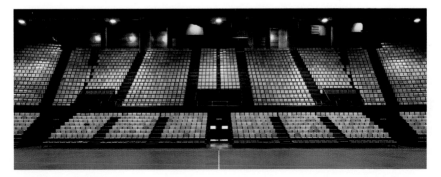

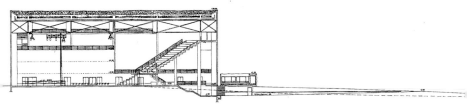

Melbourne Cricket Stadium

Tompkins, Shaw & Evans/Daryl, Jackson Pty.Ltd.

Location: Melbourne, Australia. **Date of completion**: 1992. **Client**: The Melbourne Cricket Club. **Architects**: Tompkins, Shaw & Evans/Daryl, Jackson Pty.Ltd. **Scheme**: Remodeling of the grandstand of an old cricket ground, restaurants, bars, and food and drink stands. **Gross area**: 81,300 m² (875,000 ft²). **Photography**: Melbourne Cricket Collection.

The main feature of the stadium renovation is the design of the remodeled south stand in a new elliptical shape. Components had to be prefabricated or pre-cast and made lighter so as to avoid on-site operations. The pedestrian walkway runs around the south, north, and northeast slopes of the stadium.

The south stand is approached via a gentle slope which joins a nearby park to the stadium. In this way, the main arterial road which runs alongside the building is in fact 5.5 m (18 ft) below the level of the building.

One of the most notable features of the stadium's new image is its impressive floodlighting arrangement. Another of the more significant features is the vast array of services it offers, in particular 73

corporate hospitality boxes, each holding 16 people, from where the match can be seen through stylish glazing. Also worthy of mention are seven new restaurants, two bars and 23 food and drink stands.

Bari Stadium

Renzo Piano

Location: Bari, Italy. **Date of completion**: 1989. **Architect**: Renzo Piano. **Associates**: L.Pellini, T.Carfrae, M.Milan, A.Vitone, T.Vitone, V.Matarrese, N.Andidero, J.Zucker, M.Belviso. **Scheme**: Multidisciplinary sports stadium. **Photography**: Peter Cook.

Puglia region, which are reminiscent of classical times when problems of scale and proportion were freely approached.
Piano created an artificial mound from which he excavated the first row of bleachers, making the field of play lower than the surrounding land.
In this way he created a type of crater from which the building could be erected in any direction.

Of all the stadiums erected for the 1990 World Cup in Italy, Bari's is undoubtedly the most interesting due to the spectacular way it is built into the landscape. The shape of the stadium, with capacity for 60,000 spectators, took its inspiration from the characteristics of the land around it: the peaceful, undulating lines of the

Lord's Cricket Ground

Michael Hopkins

Location: London, UK. **Date of completion**: 1988. **Architect**: Michael Hopkins. **Associate**: Ove Arup. **Photography**: Richard Bryant.

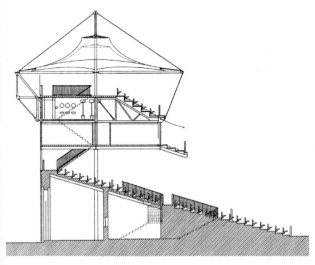

Michael Hopkins surrendered to tradition in the reconstruction of the Mound Stand of Lord's Cricket Ground. The materials are modern and the structure innovative, but the base is a restored 19th century brick arcade and a suspended roof reminiscent of traditional protective awnings.

The challenge was to keep the existing public seating capacity and add 27 boxes, eight private dining rooms, kitchens, and seating for members. A new structure with traditional seating had to be suspended over the lower bleachers causing the minimum disturbance. The existing wall around the façade of the Mound Stand was replaced with an extension of the colonnade with new brick arches, which continued the original arches as far as the field. This new structure enabled the boxes to be supported by means of six steel columns and buttresses placed along the outer line of the colonnade. A mezzanine floor was built between the second and third floors with restrooms and storage areas. Above this was seating for members and the bars. The boxes, dining rooms, and kitchens are located on the second floor. In those places where it was necessary to see out, light concrete blocks were used with sliding glass, both functional and attractive.

Utopia Pavilion

Regino Cruz – Arquitectos e Consultores, S.A. and S.O.M.

Location: Lisbon, Portugal. **Date of completion**: 1998. **Client**: Lisbon Municipality. **Architect**: Regino Cruz – Arquitectos e Consultores, S.A. and SOM – Skidmore, Owings & Merill Inc. **Scheme**: Multifunction stadium. **Photography**: Paco Asensio.

The Utopia Pavilion is the result of collaboration between the US team S.O.M. and Regino Cruz. Beneath the metal roof with sawtooth skylights, the huge laminated timber beams which support an opening of 114 m (375 ft), make the inside of the pavilion seem like the hull of a ship. Externally, the building consists of a metal casing, something like a seashell, which provides access for the public via a glazed façade. The texture of the casing is broken only where ventilation shafts or projections housing services appear. The appearance of the pavilion is the result of a complex paradox: though the external shape is very organic, very natural, the metal and glass finish gives it a markedly futuristic appearance. This unusual combination, and the fact that it stands free and clear on the plot, distinguishes the building and makes it one of the flagships of the architectural and urban development work carried out for Expo '98.

Palau Sant Jordi

Arata Isozaki & Associates

Location: Montjuïc, Barcelona, Spain. **Date of construction**: August 1985–1990. **Clients**: Barcelona Municipality, COOB'92, Institute for Energy Saving and Diversification (IDEA), and HOLSA. **Architect**: Arata Isozaki & Associates. **Scheme**: Multisports pavilion for the 1992 Olympic Games. **Photography**: Fransesc Tur.

The invitation to tender specified a sports arena which would comply with the requirements of senior competition and at the same time meet the requirements of Barcelona, which needed a covered area also able to accommodate major non-sporting cultural events. The construction design was based on three factors: firstly, formal integration with the contours of the mountain, resulting in the Palau being built as a set of low buildings covered by a vast roof whose undulations were suggestive of the curves of the landscape. Size,

smoothness, and balance were the essential guidelines followed by the Japanese architect. The second factor was the use of the most advanced building techniques, especially for the roof, a spatial mesh which combines architecture and technological processes. Finally, the new building had to be integrated into its cultural environment, using traditional materials and those most closely related to the architecture of Barcelona.

The most interesting construction feature is undoubtedly the impressive cupola which

covers the main arena. In a structure of such vast dimensions (128 x 106 m, 420 x 350 ft), the design and its implementation must be the result of a deep dialectic process in which very diverse factors are at work. Furthermore, despite its irregular shape, the cupola must act as a roof to an approximately rectangular floor. All these features place the Palau Sant Jordi in a well-deserved position among the major works of current world architecture.

Tokyo Municipal Gymnasium

Fumihiko Maki

Location: Tokyo, Japan. **Date of completion**: 1988. **Client**: Tokyo Municipality. **Architect**: Fumihiko Maki.
Scheme: Public gymnasium/sports center: gymnasium, swimming pool, tennis courts, changing rooms, cafeteria, equipment store. **Photography**: Toshiaru Kitajima.

The importance of the Tokyo Gymnasium lies in the relationship between the structure and the location. The most outstanding feature is a roof which rests on a pair of parallel arches; these form a triangular structure which covers a distance of

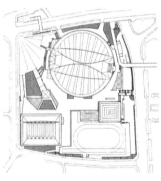

about 80 m (260 ft) on the north-south axis and reaches a maximum height of 23 m (75 ft) at the apex. The extensions of these arches are made of reinforced concrete. The basic framework of the roof runs over both arches in a transverse direction. By contrast, the side structures, which copy the same spatial design, describe a slope which starts at the arches and terminates at the pillars of the bleachers, and are made of pre-stressed concrete. In an effort to make the volatile quality of the roof apparent, it is separated from the base of the structure. In this way the roof is erected as a

structure capable of determining the layout of the inner space and also contributing to the creation of the productive tension between the various areas. Another of the features which makes the Gymnasium an outstanding architectural structure is its asymmetry. Fumihiko Maki decided to encircle the multiple apparent symmetries by rotating the axis of the secondary area, the oblique structure of the stairs and the extensions emanating from the main hall area.

Hamar Olympic Hall

Niels Torp AS Arkitekter Mnal

Location: 2300 Hamar. Norway. **Date of completion:** 1992. **Client:** Hamar Olympiske Anlegg AS (HOA). **Architect:** Niels Torp AS Arkitekter Mnal. **Associates:** Biong & Biong Arkitektfirma AS; Bjorbekk & Lindhem AS (landscaping). **Gross floor area:** 25,000 m² (270,000 ft²). **Cost:** NKr 230 million. **Scheme:** Olympic ice stadium. **Photography:** Jiri Havran.

The concept for the special design of this Olympic complex started with the team of architects coming up with an idea for the roof, which is undoubtedly the building's most outstanding feature. The architects managed to give it essential flexibility and luminosity by releasing it from the unattractive structure of the rest of the building. Its vastness and design made the selection of materials and colors a secondary issue.

With regard to the general layout, it was difficult to get away from the traditional dull lines of this type of sports facility, and so the team concentrated on producing this attractive roof completely separate from the rest of the building proper.

The team thus decided to adopt the structure of 1000-year-old Norwegian ships, which still retain the beauty of the original designs. They were careful to show the detail of the old wooden arches and joints where steel is now joined to concrete. In this way they managed to make the finishes look both simple and attractive.

Another important factor that had to be taken into consideration was how to bring natural light inside the building. This was achieved with self-illuminating glass.

All details were simplified as far as possible, which enabled the traditionally low budget for this type of construction to be met.

Olympic Archery Stadium

Enric Miralles, Carme Pinós

Location: Hebron Valley Olympic Park, Barcelona, Spain. **Implementation phase**: 1990–1992. **Client**: Olympic Committee. **Architect**: Enric Miralles, Carme Pin(s. **Associates**: A. Ferr(, E. Prats, R Prats, S. Mart(nez, A. Obiols, R. Brufau (structures). **Scheme**: Archery training and competition stadium, changing rooms, and storage facilities. **Photography**: David Cardel(s.

The scheme, situated at the foot of the Collserola massif, is divided into two areas – one for training, the other for competition. Each has its own archery fields, as well as athletes' buildings, including toilets and changing rooms. The gradient of the site and its terracing have been turned into the principal feature of the buildings. The structures seem to vanish into the ground and support the soil of the terrace immediately above. They therefore have only one façade connected with the shooting, over which they display an unobtrusive dominance. In the training enclosure, it is the movement of the containing wall that defines the limits of the building. The tectonic dynamism of its concave lines generates a series of curved, flat, vertical and horizontal surfaces with an array of pitches serving to close off, cover, separate, and protect. By contrast, the competition enclosure was designed with accessibility in mind. Here, the movements of the earth form traverses, including the spectator in the landscape. The building emerges from the repetition of changing room and shower units, each of which is a block closed off at the front by concrete screens. In the words of the architects themselves, they built a tectonic fault and a hole, with concavities in the containing wall.

Theme parks and attractions

In an era in which virtuality and fiction are gaining an increasing presence in our daily lives, reality is continually breaking down. It is no surprise that the places where adventures and fantasies are lived out have ended up by surpassing even the wildest dreams and have crystallized into actual cities. The sites are being used to weave a network of venues whose sole function is recreation and entertainment. These leisure and theme parks are characterized by the way in which they take on the form of isolated "cities" surrounded by nature, with a landscape completely at odds with the traditional. Alongside these have appeared another type of center within an enclosed domain. Here, adventures are no longer played out in real space but, for example, behind a computer screen.

Sydney International Aquatic Centre

Philip Cox

Location: Sydney, Australia. **Year of opening**: 1994. **Client**: Kaiser Bautechnik. **Associates**: Reinhold Meyer (structural engineering), Kaiser Bautechnik (works supervision), Roger Preston (mechanical and electrical engineering). **Photography**: Ralph Richter/architekturphoto.

The Sydney International Aquatic Centre was one of the key elements in the success of Australia's bid to host the Olympic Games in the year 2000. This complex will house the main water sports events, but is also intended as a major leisure center. It combines the functions of a specialized facility capable of staging top class sporting events and a recreational center.

The huge arch supporting the roof has the greatest visual impact and can be seen for miles around. A talus, like a fold in the landscape next to the building, reduces the architectural impact. Access is at intermediate level. Passing through the entrance, the visitor reaches one of the walkways beneath the rows of seats. A bridge crosses to connect the side tiers, separating the competition side from the recreation and entertainment area. This is an elevated walkway for the public with views to both sides, which breaks up the area's continuity without separating the two zones completely. It also has a false corrugated ceiling, which helps the transition to be made between the different roof heights from one zone to the following one.

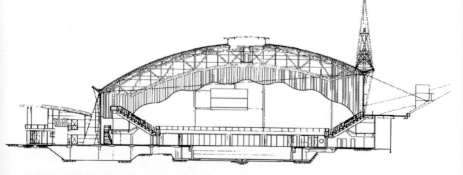

Duisburg-North Park

Latz & Partner

Location: Duisburg, North Rhine-Westphalia, Germany. **Date of project**: 1990 (competitive tender). **Date of construction**: 1991–2000. **Client:** Development Company of North Rhine-Westphalia and the City of Duisburg. **Architects:** Latz & Partner. **Associates:** IBA (Internationale Bauausstellung), IG Nordpark, Society for Industrial Culture and Duisburg City Gardens Department. **Scheme:** Recreational, sporting, and cultural park. **Area:** 230 ha (570 acres). **Photography:** Latz & Partner, Christa Panick, Peter Wilde, Michael Latz, Angus Parker.

The Duisburg-North Park project is part of an enormous green belt area in the Emscher region. The German state of North Rhine-Westphalia, along with cities in the Emscher region, have implemented several projects aimed at regenerating former industrial areas in the Ruhr river basin.

Duisburg-North Park is located in an area of heavy industry centered on coal and steel between the urban districts of Duisburg and Oberhausen. Disused plant is still to be found on the site of the former Thyssen foundry – boilers, storage sheds, furnaces, and railway installations. An international competition, won by the Latz & Partner team, planned to regenerate the area completely. The aim was to provide the region's dense population with recreational, sporting, and cultural venues in the context of the regeneration of old industrial plant, exhibiting an awareness of its enormous value, not only as a memorial to the site, but also as a genuine act of research into industrial archeology. Wherever possible, materials found in the area have been used, either directly or as recycled products, such as the iron for the walkways, platforms, or gates.

Port Aventura

Peckham, Guytin Albers & Viets, Inc.

Location: Salou, Tarragona, Spain. **Date of completion:** 1995. **Architect:** Peckham, Guyton Albers & Viets, Inc. **Scheme:** Theme park. **Photography:** David Cardelús (also pp 458/459).

To visit Port Aventura is to become immersed in the seductive charms of the far-off and the unknown. Visitors become the main protagonists in five fascinating adventures:

they are moved by the quiet, unobtrusive charm of the Mediterranean coast, discover the exuberance of tropical Polynesian vegetation, move on to China ruled by mandarins and emperors, get to know Mexico, both in its pre-Columbian days and during the heights of its colonial era, and even play the boldest cowboy in the Wild West. The single element that unifies the park and, at the same time, allows such distinct landscapes to coexist within a limited space, is water. The construction of a giant artificial lake in the middle of the site affects the project in a variety of ways and is of fundamental importance to its internal organization. The fact that the center is inaccessible creates a circular sequence between spaces, making it easier for each sector to

become an isolated unit. A perspective view emerges of each setting, from one side of the lake to the other, giving visitors a general view of each area and of the park as a whole, which enables them to control the pace of their visit and decide on their priorities. Crossings from one zone to another can be made by boat or steam train. Water is also the main ingredient of some of the park's most exciting rides, such as the Rapids, the Wild River Ride or the Tutuki Splash. The park's vegetation has been another of its major successes, with the importation of native species and the use of other indigenous varieties similar to those found in the countries represented on the site.

Disneyland Paris

Derek Lovejoy Partnership

Location: Marne-La-Valle, France. **Date of completion:** 1990. **Client/Developer:** Disney Corporation. **Architect:** Derek Lovejoy Partnership. **Associate:** Imagineering. **Scheme:** Leisure and theme park. **Photography:** David Blackwood Murray, Clive McDonnell.

This park, situated in Marne-La-Valle, 32 km (20 miles) from Paris, marks Europe's introduction to the concept of the theme park and recreational center created by the Walt Disney Corporation, which has already enjoyed 40 years of success in the United States and Japan. The project involved the commissioning of the Derek Lovejoy Partnership to complete the general background scenery and landscape design in the five zones and service areas. The generous dimensions of the site of this magical kingdom (2000 ha, 4800 acres) are bounded by a bank rising to a height of 20 m (65 ft), which transforms the park into a landmark, standing out against the plane of this French plateau. This acreage is in turn subdivided into the five main attractions or "worlds." The elements used to create this subdivision are secondary banks planted with vegetation – trees and shrubs, which are strategically placed to create an individual backdrop for each of the five zones.

The use of the company's CAD system in the final design phase also helped to achieve the theoretical objectives and demonstrate that landscape design, like art, can be skillfully used to combine reality and fantasy in such a park.

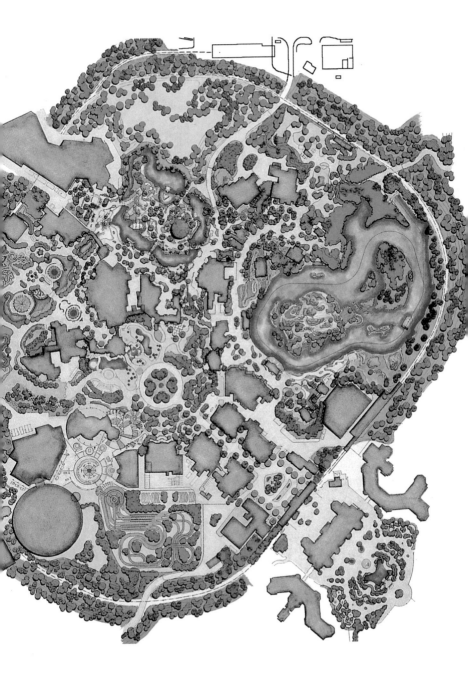

Parque Nasu Highland

Swa Group

Location: Naju, Japan. **Date of completion:** 1996. **Client:** Towa Real Estate Development Company. **Architect:** SWA Group. **Photography:** Tom Fox.

This project has been developed over successive phases, in view of its magnitude and the nature of each of its attractions. The first of these is the rock 'n' roll neighborhood, where the main street has a distinctly '50s feel, with its neon signs and parked-up Cadillacs: music is the main theme of this area. The second phase is the 38 m (120 ft) high carousel. The third phase consists of the House of Cards and Toyland. The inspiration here is the world of toys, making visitors feel as though they are walking through a child's playroom, strewn with toys and brimming with imagination. Another of the zones has a galaxy theme: an area with three roundabouts and blue paving, situated alongside one of the park's most impressive Russian mountains. Waterplay, where the paving is in the form of indigo-colored metal palm trees and waves, is one of the latest of the many new projects under way in this park. Apart from the rides and attractions found at Fantasy Point, Nasu Highland Park also includes hotels, tennis courts, and golf clubs.

Asahikawa Shunkodai Park

Mitsuro Man Senda

Location: Asahikawa, Japan. **Date of completion:** 1994. **Architect:** Mitsuro Man Senda. **Scheme:** Children's adventure park in an urban setting. **Photography:** Fujitsuka Mitsumara.

Touch and smell are in no way alien to the games played out by children in the park. Touching, jumping, chasing, feeling their way, climbing, and sliding. Using all their senses. Adapting their bodies to each of the different situations as they emerge, one after the other, along the length of the course, which is constructed using wood, rope, netting, mesh, sheet metal, lights, shade, and ramps.

There is no single path, but a whole complex of to's and fro's, crossroads, discoveries and encounters. Play is intermingled with nature, creating a sort of partnership. It is no coincidence that the park in this project is located on a site affording the maximum contact with nature.

In the words of the architect, Mitsuro Man Senda, play can involve nature as its friend. In an attraction aimed at children, it is their height and, more particularly, their height of vision, that must be the determining factor when considering the project and its design. The details must also be studied meticulously, as must the materials, to ensure they are both harmless and suitable, no matter how the children choose to use the play area and whatever whim overtakes them at any given moment.

Ski Dome

Kajima Design

Location: Funabashi-Shi, Japan. **Date of completion:** 1993. **Architect:** Kajima Design. **Construction area:** 87,300 m² (940,000 ft²). **Scheme:** Ski dome with restaurants, equipment hire shops, shopping center, changing rooms, gymnasium, sauna, and swimming pool. **Photography:** Satshi Asakawa.

The main Ski Dome building is a steel structure supporting a sloping concrete slab foundation which is 500 m (1640 ft) long and has a maximum height of 100 m (325 ft). There are three different grades of piste – beginners, intermediates and advanced, with gradients of between 7 and 20. The chair lift takes a minute and a half to travel from the bottom of the piste to the top. Connected to the main complex via its lower level, another four-story building houses the ski-related services and leisure facilities (restaurants, shops, equipment hire, ticket offices, gymnasium, sauna, and swimming pool). The inside temperature varies between 2 and 6°C and is primarily maintained thanks to an efficient insulation system that prevents any air from escaping outside. The shape of the structure is dictated by the building's response to earthquakes, which are commonplace in Japan. A variable height structure may be affected by different vibrational frequencies during the same seismic movement, which can prove extremely dangerous. In order to alleviate this situation, the architects decided to divide the building into six parts separated by joints, each with an independent structure, so giving scope for movement.

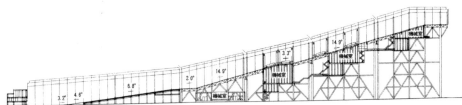

Florida Aquarium

Hellmut, Obata, Kassabaum, Inc.

Location: Tampa, Florida, USA. **Date of completion:** 1995. **Architect:** Helmut, Obata, Kassabaum, Inc. **Associates:** Joseph Wetzel, Gyo Obata. **Photography:** George Cott.

The aim of this project is to give visitors the sensation of being submerged in a marine environment. The immersion begins in a sort of cavern next to the stairs. Here, visitors can learn about the origins of Florida's water, while walking under a course of fresh water flowing above their heads. A winding path then takes them through the various habitats of the swamplands, a journey of light, passing between vegetation beneath a magnificent glass roof shaped like a seashell and designed by Gyo Obata. The last stage of the journey marks the start of Florida's bays and beaches, moving from a sunny environment to shade and grottoes, where visitors can see the fish moving about on the same level. The second section of the aquarium is devoted to an extraordinary habitat found off the Florida coast – the coral reef. The final stage is an enormous window opening onto the seabed for viewing the reef.

Oceanarium

Peter Chermayeff

Location: Lisbon, Portugal. **Date of completion:** 1998. **Client:** Expo '98 Lisbon. **Architect:** Peter Chermayeff. **Scheme:** Oceanarium. **Photography:** Paco Asensio.

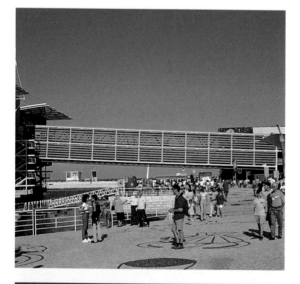

One of the most symbolic elements of Expo '98 is the Oceanarium, designed by Peter Chermayeff, which proved the greatest daytime attraction.

This huge nautical-style structure anchored in the harbor waters consists of a main tank housing marine species, around which the other exhibition areas are carefully arranged.

Access to the Oceanarium is by way of a metal grid ramp, which leads the visitor to the upper level. The building, which takes the form of a sophisticated oil production platform, is made up of a solid base of rocky materials and a glass covered upper section with views of the sea and Expo. The awnings create wings and afford protection from direct sunlight. They are hung from cables suspended from metal pillars standing at the edges of a cross on the floor, which delineates the structural rhythm.

This pavilion was one of the most remarkable buildings at the Lisbon Expo in 1998.

Itäkeskus

Hyvämäki, Karhunen & Parkkinen

Location: Helsinki, Finland. **Date of completion:** 1993. **Architect:** Hyvämäki, Karhunen & Parkkinen.
Scheme: Public baths and swimming pool complex. **Photography:** Jussi Tiainen.

In the years leading up to the disintegration of the Soviet Union, Helsinki's eastern suburbs needed an emergency shelter while at the same time planners were looking at the possibility of building a public baths and swimming pool complex within the environs of a central park area. By making use of an easily excavated rocky hill situated in the forest, developers were able to fuse the two ideas into a single project. This enabled them to save on the cost of two independent projects and, at the same time, prevent the park from being developed.

The only area not underground is the entrance, designed as a semicircular glass arch, which seems to emerge from inside the earth, like a transparent phalanx proclaiming a crystalline secret within.

Beneath an enormous white dome, a wide ranging program of functions includes an Olympic swimming pool with a separate diving area, fun, leisure, and children's pools, plunge pools,

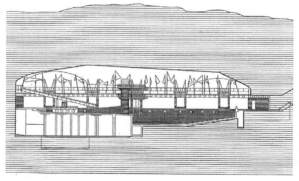

Turkish baths and steam rooms, saunas, solariums, a gymnasium, treatment rooms, and two cafeterias. Accompanying all this is a series of individual tableaux, linked by music and brought together by sound screens, which enable visitors to remember each area and find their way around an originally mystifying enclosed environment.

Mad River Trips

William P. Bruder

Location: Jackson, Wyoming, USA. **Date of completion:** 1997. **Architect:** William P. Bruder. **Associates:** Wendell Burnette, Tim Christ, Jack De Bartolo III, Leah Schneider (design team). **Photography:** Bill Timmerman.

The Arizona desert is one of the few places where architecture retains both an artistic and a symbolic function. This is where William Bruder has been designing structures since the end of the 1970s. His work creates a continuous dialog with the landscape – the mountains, water, dryness, color, and also the indigenous architecture of Arizona – old rural buildings, mines, barns, etc… His buildings try to evoke lyrical images of Arizona and, at the same time, endeavor to salvage the simplest building materials, reusing them exquisitely. The Mad River Trips building houses both the offices and storeroom and the home of the owners of this small company, which organizes river-rafting trips.

Shonandai Cultural Center

Itsuko Hasegawa

Location: Fujisawa, Kanawaga, Japan. **Date of completion:** 1990. **Client:** Kanawaga City Hall. **Architect:** Itsuko Hasegawa. **Associate:** Architectural Design Studio. **Scheme:** Cultural center, public square and theater, panoramic cinema, children's museum, and services. **Photography:** Shuji Yamada.

This is a Cultural Center with ambitious pretensions. It includes a public theater, a panoramic cinema, a children's museum, and a division of the city hall's administrative services. All the Center's units embody the design philosophy of the Japanese architect, as is reflected in the formal diversity of the pavilions and the way in which sunlight penetrates the offices at midday. However, the feature that most accurately embraces Hasegawa's creative doctrine is the square, whose proportions determine those of the structures rising so majestically from around its surface. The square was conceived as a backdrop for a multiplicity of events, a vessel for the entire universe, with spherical objects dotted within its boundaries to represent the cosmos, the earth, and the moon. These, on the other hand, act as the architectural hallmark of this magnificent Cultural Center, with all its attractive buildings.

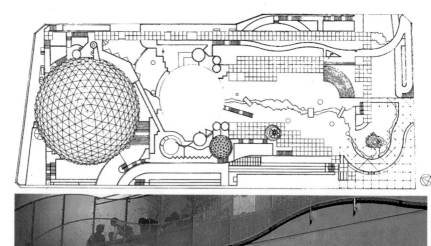

Planetarium of the Northern Lights

John Kristoffersen

Location: Tromso, Norway. **Date of completion:** 1988. **Architect:** John Kristoffersen. **Scheme:** Construction of a planetarium, telescope, tower, laboratory, and spectators' module. **Photography:** John Kristoffersen.

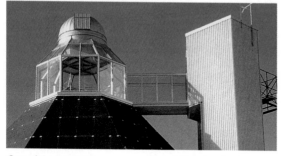

One of the principal attractions of this planetarium is the way it recreates for the visitor the marvelous spectacle of the Northern Lights, projected onto the immense semispherical screen erected inside the building. At the same time, in the knowledge that the recreated phenomenon is a long way from reality, the building has been clad in gray glass, which acts as a mirror, reflecting the surrounding countryside. A telescope positioned in the equatorial cupola, which crowns the structure, evokes the investigative aspect, albeit intended for teaching purposes. The complex is made up of a tower in which elevators travel to the laboratory above, the bridge linking up to this, and the large octagonal building where spectators are welcomed beneath the 12 m (39 ft) diameter screen. The structure is made from reinforced concrete, chosen principally to insulate against the aircraft noise from outside. The outside of the octagonal building is clad in 8 mm (¼ inch) thick gray glass, the tower in gray steel panels, which provide protection from the elements.

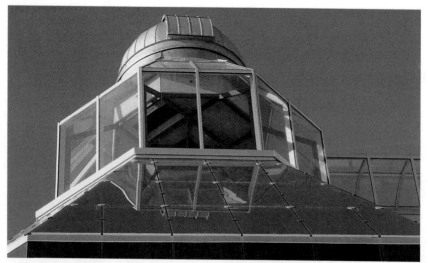

Bars, disco-theques, and games rooms

The projects presented here serve a surprising variety of different functions. This collection of interior public spaces constitutes a broad and at the same time ambiguous category. However, all these restaurants, bars, discotheques, and night clubs are part of the leisure culture, a concept that is both frivolous and vital to human existence, and, like all activities, subject to constant change. Nevertheless, the individuals responsible for these projects have met these challenges energetically, their work combining their own creative experience with the demands of the consumer.

Pachinko Parlor

Kazuyo Sejima

Location: Hitachiohta, Ibaraki, Japan. **Date of completion**: 1996. **Architect**: Kazuyo Sejima. **Structural engineers**: Matsui Gengo & O.R.S. **Scheme**: Games room, rest area, and office. **Gross floor area**: 800 m² (8600 ft²). **Photography**: Nacasa & Partners Inc (also pp 488/489).

Pachinko Parlor is a very popular game in Japan, combining recreation and skill. Games rooms are to be found across the length and breadth of the country, each offering similar facilities – simply rows of individual pachinko games machines.

Situated in the provincial city of Hitachiohta, Pachinko Parlor occupies a large site overlooking a busy freeway.

The curve of the façade and the use of light and materials are a sufficient advertisement in themselves, with only a modest sign being required to indicate the name of the establishment. On the façade, shiny black strips frame apertures of colored glass. While during the day it is the black that softly reflects the light, at night the interior light makes these strips disappear, giving the façade a disjointed air.

On the ground floor there is a typical pachinko room with rows of games machines, a prize collection corner, as well as a rest area. The office is separate from the rest of the facilities in the design.

Stop Line

Studio Archea

Location: Curno, Bergamo, Italy. **Date of completion**: 1996. **Architects**: Laura Andreini, Marco Casamonti, Giovanni Polazzi (Studio Archea). **Associates**: Antonella Dini, Paolo Frongia, Michael Heffernan, Claudia Sandoval, Andrea Sensoli (architects), Silvia Fabi, Nicola Santini, Giuseppe Fioroni, Pier Paolo Taddei (design team), Studio Myallonnier (structural engineers), Studio Armondi (layout), Kreon (lighting), Martin (scenic lighting), Outline (audio), Alessandro Trezzi, Antonio Falduto (video). **Scheme**: Discotheque, bowling alley, ice rink, billiards, games rooms, and restaurants. **Photography**: Pietro Savorelli, Saverio Lombardi Vallauri.

Stop Line is located on the outskirts of the city of Bergamo, in an industrial landscape where it coexists with large factory buildings, traffic signals, and billboards. The building is actually an old warehouse with a total area of 5400 m² (58,000 ft²).This is perhaps why during the day the building, with its façade measuring almost 60 m (200 ft) overlooking the freeway, is a plain yet impressive giant of a structure. A single, hermetically sealed wall clad in Corten steel gives no clue as to the activities within the building.

At night, a series of holes drilled in the steel plate turn into an array of points of light, creating an intangible wall in the darkness. The lights are reflected in the pond at the foot of the façade.

Stop Line houses a discotheque, ice rink, billiard tables, restaurants, video screenings, computer games rooms, and more.... It is a huge center created for entertainment, but at the same time capable of being turned into a venue for fashion shows, conferences, and business presentations. The main corridor, running parallel to the main façade, consists of a module on three levels, one of which is underground. The rest of the building is a single space, an enormous hall with free-standing structures here and there, which are reached by stairs or ramps.

Belgo Centraal

Ron Arad Associates

Location: Covent Garden, London, UK. **Date of completion**: April 1995. **Client**: Belgo Centraal. **Architects**: Ron Arad, Allison Brooks. **Associates**: Shaun Fernandes, Oliver Salway, Sarah Low, Kai Stania (design team), WSP Consulting Engineers (structural engineers), Gleeds (section supervisor), Delcon Construction Ltd (construction), Parsley in Time (kitchen), Daconair (mechanical), Jets Electrical (electrical), Chroma (painting), Noto (seating, stools). **Scheme**: Bar, cafeteria, and office. **Photography**: F. Busam/architekturphoto.

At the start of the 1980s, Ron Arad and other young Londoners revitalized the design scene in England. They concerned themselves with the regeneration of industrial objects, obtaining images that, in the words of one critic, would not be out of place in *Mad Max*. Nevertheless, this industrial archeology is surprisingly appropriate in the case of this former wine cellar. The outside walls painted a vivid red at entrance height, the original design of the chairs and tables, the repeated steel accessories, the provocatively arranged decorative features: these are just some of the elements inherent in the defiant and aggressive signature of Ron Arad's work. This project, as with all Arad's design, is the result of his special vision of the creative process, which, although undoubtedly part of an entirely contemporary approach, is at the same time far removed from the most stereotypical modern trends. Arad breaks with convention and his search for beauty through new forms gives his work a special elegance unaffected by precept.

Taxim Nightpark

Branson Coates Architecture

Location: Istanbul, Turkey. **Date of construction**: 1990–1991. **Client**: Metin Fadillioglu. **Architect**: Branson Coates Architecture. **Associates**: Cathi du Toit (architectural work), Dewhurst McFarlane (structural enginee-ring), Lightworks Ltd (lighting). **Scheme**: Conversion of an old factory into a restaurant/discotheque. **Photography**: Valerie Bennet.

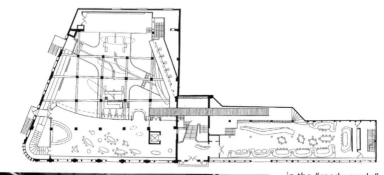

The Taxim Nightpark project in the Turkish capital emerged from a desire to convert a former dye factory into an up-to-date venue with an elegant restaurant, dance studios, and a huge discotheque. Firstly, the building's original structure was retained to support the idea of a building within a building, establishing a peculiar distinction between the container and the contained. As part of this, the factory's revamped structure became an outer skin. The second key to this project lies within the sphere of artistic theory. This involves the earlier structure being treated as an object. In this way, the façade assumes a double function (providing a face for a new reality within and reclaiming an old building in the "ready-made" tradition), which means the project represents an exceptional challenge to current design laws.

The strips running vertically down the windows have been treated using a characteristic Turkish method, involving a system of glass engraving by sandblasting, following a printed textile pattern. Inside the building, the plan was to create new areas and through routes, making space and movement the essential constituents of the project. All these components combine to make Taxim Nightpark – and especially its entrance – a masterly demonstration of bold, daring design.

Towers of Ávila

Alfredo Arribas, Miguel Morte

Location: Pueblo Español, Barcelona, Spain. **Date of completion**: 1990. **Architects**: Alfredo Arribas, Miguel Morte. **Associate**: Javier Mariscal. **Photography**: Francesc Tur.

The entire project was intended to represent a contrast of opposites – two towers facing one another representing day and night, sun and moon. The space in between is transformed into a communicating element between the two originally disconnected bodies. The real motivating force behind the project involved giving each of the towers a sort of stage setting that would evoke suggestions loaded with meaning. Each structure is divided into five stories interconnected by staircases and metal landings; these are separated by glass galleries, which act as viewing points, enabling visitors to enjoy the spectacular view. The circular platforms in the Moon Tower, on the left of the entrance to the site, culminate in a star-studded cupola symbolizing a planetarium. The Sun Tower, on the right, defines its position by way of a contrast of alternating light and shade, the main attraction being an artificial sun that rises from the upper lantern. There is also a place for conjuring up the past, with the preservation of the old battlements, the access drawbridge, esoteric symbols, and the concept of the towers as a suggestion of a past recovered via a blend of respect and imagination.

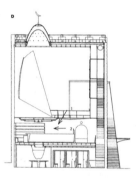

Iridium Restaurant

Jordan Mozer

Location: New York, USA. **Date of completion**: 1994. **Architect**: Jordan Mozer. **Photography**: Mihail Moldoveanu.

The Iridium is situated between Columbus Avenue and Broadway, right next to New York's Lincoln Center Complex. Jordan Mozer conceived a place where the furniture and the columns, the doors and the roof, all the elements, had to dance. Although the forms used in the Iridium may appear random, almost all of them transform into architecture images from the world of music and dance. Each architectural detail, each piece of furniture, each lamp, has been individually designed. The sequence of the work is extraordinarily direct and specific. Otherwise, it would have been almost impossible to complete such an outstanding and personal project and bring it to fruition successfully.

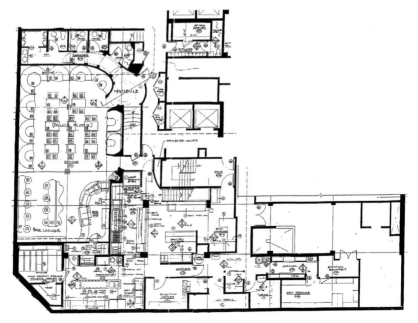

Caroline's Theater and Comedy Club

Paul Haigh, Barbara H. Haigh

Location: Manhattan, New York, USA. **Date of completion**: 1993. **Client**: Caroline Hirsch. **Architects**: Paul Haigh, Barbara H. Haigh. **Associates**: Nicholas Macri, Miriana Donaya, Justin Bologna, Karla Kuperc; CMA Enterprises (construction). **Scheme**: Club for staging theater and comedy performances. **Photography**: Elliot Kaufman.

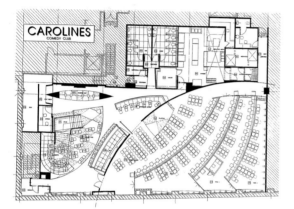

In this theater especially designed for comedy performances, the architects tried to create a closeness between audience and performers.

Inside the club, the visitor encounters a neomedieval world of harlequins, pantomime, and jokers. This iconography extends throughout the club, in different colors, forms, and scales. Paul Haigh has used velvet wall coverings, varnished woods, terrazzo flooring, and moquette for the finishes. The basement is divided into two by a curved wall. On one side is the theater, with three rows of continuous, curved seats at different levels. On the other is the restaurant/bar, which also acts as a foyer and a venue for occasional performances; it is made up of a series of small separate areas, with wide corridors running between them, providing easy access.

Obslomova

Shiro Kuramata

Location: Hotel Il Palazzo, Fukuoka, Japan. **Date of completion**: 1991. **Architect**: Shiro Kuramata. **Scheme**: Design of a restaurant/bar within the Hotel Il Palazzo. **Photography**: Nacasa & Partner.

Within the Hotel Il Palazzo complex there are four venues situated in the two parallel modules making up the central building. These are restaurant/bars, each of them designed by a great name of international repute: four bars commissioned for a genuinely international project, endorsed by the creativity of top class designers. Each bar has a totally different ambience. The Obslomova is a bar with an intimate atmosphere where soft colors and light forms suffuse both the furnishings and the actual structure of the space.

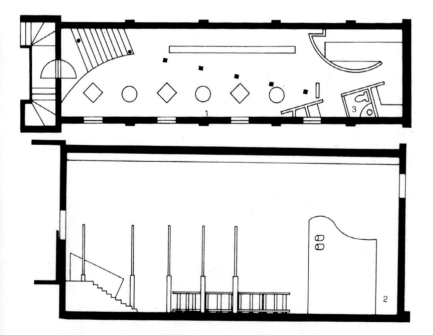

Circus Theater

Sjoerd Saeters

Location: Zandvoort, The Netherlands. **Date of construction**: 1996. **Architect**: Sjoerd Saeters. **Scheme**: Amusement arcade in the old town of Zandvoort. **Photography**: Koo Boji.

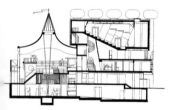

Sjoerd Soeters was commissioned to construct an amusement arcade and cinema in the old town of Zandvoort. The building had to be both attractive and colorful.

The result is a showy structure of stimulating façades, with giant banners in every color imaginable, enormous orange painted pillars, and a curved roof like a circus tent, supported by three posts. Soeters designed the games room as a genuine labyrinth, with numerous islands at different levels and ramps connecting them, mirrors that doubled the space, and every conceivable type of staircase – all painted in striking, vivid colors. The site is roughly L-shaped. The longest leg is divided into three circles corresponding to three imaginary circus rings; this strip leads onto a pedestrian walkway that joins a busy shopping street. The short leg of the L leads off to a quiet square. On the first floor there is a bar and the cinema foyer. Above this are the offices and services necessary to manage the establishment, and on the top floor is the cinema. The building is clearly divided into two wings, in terms of both space and form. On the one side is the games area located within a large, double-sized continuous space and, on the other, are the quieter areas, separated by different floor levels.

Shopping malls

The importance acquired by large
shopping malls is due to a number of
sociocultural and economic factors that
can be broadly divided into two main
groups for analytical purposes. Firstly,
there is the supremacy of the concepts of
commerce and the marketplace as pillars
of the macroeconomic structure that
governs today's society and, secondly, the
profound interrelationship established
between leisure and consumerism.
Due to the vast number of shopping mall
projects, it is impossible to make
generalizations about them.
Consequently, this section aims to reflect
the great variety of shopping mall
schemes that can be found today within
the field of commercial architecture.

Emmen Shopping Mall

Galeries Lafayette

Triangle des Gares, Euralille

L'Illa Diagonal

Bercy 2 Shopping Mall

Nordwest-Zentrum

Stockmann

Haas Haus

Saar Galerie

Rio Shopping Center

Centro Torri

Emmen Shopping Mall

Ben van Berkel

Location: Emmen, The Netherlands. **Date of construction**: 1994–1996. **Client**: Multi Vastgoed bv, Gouda. **Architect**: Ben van Berkel. **Construction**: IHN Noord bv, Groningen. **Project coordinator**: René Bouman, Harrie Pappot. **Project manager**: Wilbert Swinkels. **Glass**: HuMa-glas bv. **Scheme**: Shopping center and apartments. **Photography**: Christian Richters.

The building housing the new Vroom & Dreesmann stores is the result of a large-scale remodeling of an old building dating back to the 1960s, which was used for the same purpose then. Van Berkel's project adds an apartment building, reorganizes the entire complex, and completely changes the façade, replacing it with an all-enveloping skin. The project intelligently recognizes the impossibility of achieving a strict style for the building's remodeling. The shopping mall complex consists, from the point of view of space, of a large number of elements, forming a system. There is the base on the first floor, some of its stores with direct access from the street; the sheer size of the second floor, which van Berkel has converted into an enormous, squat, glass-covered unit; a five-story tower situated in one of the corners, which will house the apartments; a three-floor prism, which has received special treatment in terms of its strictly cubic nature; and an intermediate structure that projects above the large, glass-covered element.

Galeries Lafayette

Jean Nouvel

Location: Friedrichstadt Passagen Block 207, Friedrichstrasse-Französischestrasse, Berlin, Germany. **Competitive tender**: March 1991. **Date works commenced**: September 1992. **Date of completion**: March 1996. **Client**: Euro-Projekt Entwicklungs GmbH. **Architect**: Jean Nouvel. **Project managers**: Barbara Salin (tender phase), Laurence Daude (execution phase), Judith Simon, Viviane Morteau (works management). **Net floor area**: 39,585 m² (426, 000 ft²). **Scheme**: Shopping mall, offices, apartments, and parking. **Photography**: Philippe Ruault.

This is a building with a fairly diverse composition, including store space for Galeries Lafayette, as well as offices, shops,

apartments, and parking. As shown in the photograph, the chosen site occupies a little over half a block in Berlin, next to the Schinkel Schauspielhaus.

The size of the block will enable up to seven floors to be constructed, as well as four underground levels. Nouvel plans to have the four sides of the building (including the roof) completely covered with glass, so that the play between the natural light

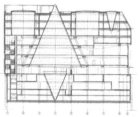

penetrating from outside, the artificial light produced by the building itself, and, finally, the various reflections generated by all these creates an atmosphere that is both spectacular and at the same time clearly has a functional element.

In order to achieve these objectives, and given the dimensional characteristics of the building, Nouvel resorted to the strategy of drilling holes from the roof through the entire glass structure, so that the light penetrates at numerous points, all of them different and organized in hierarchical fashion.

Triangle des Gares, Euralille

Jean Nouvel

Location: Lille, France. **Date of completion**: September 1994. **Client**: Shopping mall: SNC (Société du Centre Commercial du Centre Euralille). **Architects**: Jean Nouvel, Emmanuel Cattani & Associés. **Associates**: Patrick Cosmao, Cyril Ruiz (planning team), OTH NORD PROJETUD (engineering), Sophie Berthelier, Isabelle Guillauic (project managers). **Scheme**: Shopping mall, offices, hotel, apartments, and parking. **Photography**: Philippe Ruault, Ralph Richter/architekturphoto.

Situated at the junction between the Paris-London high speed rail (TGV) link and the future Paris—Brussels-Amsterdam-Cologne line, Lille is the city that has experienced the greatest transformation due to the opening of the Channel Tunnel. It was a major protagonist in this enormously ambitious project, aiming to become a major center in a new "borderless" Europe.

As part of the remodeling of Euralille, Nouvel was entrusted with the Triangle des Gares project, an extensive shopping mall crowned by a row of office blocks to the south, and flanked by a line of apartments and a hotel on the west side.

The project has been planned as a single unit, with simple, understated forms; yet the treatment of materials and colors, and the incorporation of symbols and images as elements of the architectural composition succeed in transmitting, with subtlety, the building's overall complexity.

L'Illa Diagonal

Rafael Moneo/Manuel de Solà-Morales

Location: Barcelona, Spain. **Date of construction**: 1994–1997. **Developer**: Winterthur. **Architects**: Rafael Moneo Vallés, Manuel de Solà-Morales i Rubió. **Associates**: Lluís Tobella, Antón María Pàmies, Andrea Casiraghi, Francesc Santacana, Lucho Marcial, Félix Wettstein, Román Cisneros, Isabel Pericas, René Hochuli, Kate Webb, Toni Casamor, Oriol Mateu (design), Mariano Moreno (structural engineer), Sereland (mechanical), SECOTEC (supervision), AGROMAN (construction). **Scheme**: Offices, shopping mall, auditorium, discotheque, parking, and services. **Photography**: Ramón Camprubí, Ivan Bercedo.

L'Illa Diagonal is not strictly speaking a building, but a chunk of city designed on the basis of a single project. The complex includes offices, a hotel, various shopping malls, small shops, squares and pedestrian precincts, a public park, parking levels, a discotheque, and an auditorium. Now, when we talk about L'Illa Diagonal being a chunk of city, we are not referring to its size, nor to the concentration of activities, nor to the fact that it is a complex of different buildings. On the contrary, L'Illa Diagonal is a single building which, nevertheless, is not designed as such, but as a segment of a major thoroughfare or part of a neighborhood that includes alleys, a square, a small park – that is what makes it a chunk of city. In other words, the play of forms conceived by Manuel de Solà Morales and Rafael Moneo is not designed to produce an architectural image, but rather a specifically urban one.

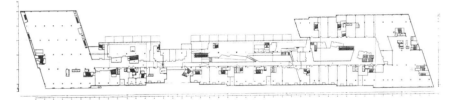

Bercy 2 Shopping Mall

Renzo Piano

Location: Charenton-le-Pont, Paris, France. **Date of construction**: 1987–1990. **Client**: Emin, J. Renault. **Architect**: Renzo Piano. **Associates**: Noriaki Okalie. **Gross floor area**: 100,000 m² (1.08 million ft²). **Photography**: Anne Fauret, Archipress.

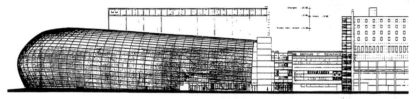

Growing from within, the building's ovoid form is repeated with different radii until it merges with the outer shell, ceiling and façade, since the roof presents no break in continuity along its curvilinear course.

The monumental roof was designed by superimposing three circular matrices with varying radii and cladding them in a vast metal skin. As to the building's internal articulation, the height of 25 m (81 ft) is distributed between six floors, with the three lower ones – two of which are underground – being devoted to the creation of 2118 parking spaces, occupying an area of some 50,000 m² (538,000 ft). The three remaining levels, each of which is 10 m (33 ft) wide and 100 m (325 ft) long, accommodate the sales areas, covering an actual space of 34,000 m² (366,000 ft).

Renzo Piano imagined the internal space as a valley. In the center, from the first underground parking level to the second shopping mall floor, is a 1000 m² (10,100 ft) garden area, with trees growing to heights of up to 12 m (39

ft). A waterfall cascading down from above through an inclined plane introduces the symbol of a watercourse flanked by two banks. The entire site is fragmented by long, gently sloping moving walkways, which link the different floor levels.

Nordwest-Zentrum

Estudio RKW

Location: Frankfurt, Germany. **Date of conversion**: 1990. **Architect**: Estudio RKW (Rhode, Kellerman, Wawrowsky & Partner). **Scheme**: Conversion of a former shopping mall: stores, pedestrian area, kindergarten, social center, library, banks, police station, fire station, and census center.

This shopping mall and leisure center is the result of the renovation and redesign of a multifunctional center opened in 1968, whose structure had become outdated. The main aspects of the conversion involved covering over the pedestrian walkways, reorganizing the shopping and leisure facilities, improving internal communications and accessibility, and creating a new, more attractive, and up-to-date overall design. Some 10,000 m² (108,000 ft) of glass were used to cover the two existing shopping streets and the different interconnecting sections. A total of 5200 glass panels rise to a height of over 17 m (55 ft), spread across a pedestrian area of 9200 m² (100,000 ft). Another feature has been the planned combination of types of activity, with the addition of 18 medical practices, a veterinary surgeon, a pharmacy, and various auxiliary facilities. All this is rounded off by the municipal infrastructure – a children's park, centers for the young and old, a library, post office, banks, a police station, fire station, and census center.

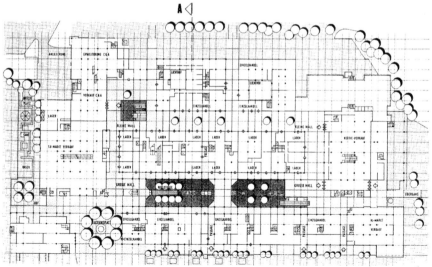

Stockmann

Gullichsen, Kairamo & Vormala

Location: Helsinki, Finland. **Date of completion**: 1989. **Architect**: Gullichsen, Kairamo & Vormala. **Scheme**: Shopping mall, warehouse area, parking, offices, beauty salon, and cafeteria.

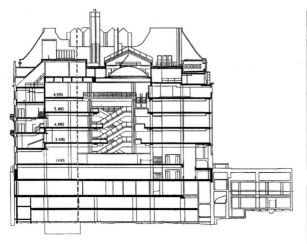

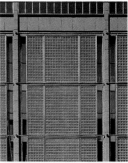

The functional scheme adopted for the project is characterized by its schematic simplicity, as well as its spatial clarity. The building is on various levels, starting with the underground, basement level, where there is parking, storage, and one of the sales floors. The four floors above this function as shopping areas.
On the fifth floor is an extensive exhibition room, from which there is an escalator access to the restaurant on the floor above.
A small offices area and all the technical equipment are housed at the top of the building. There is also a beauty salon and a cafeteria on this floor. The highest point of the structure is crowned by a large dome, which is completely covered in glass. This has a dual function, creating a system of natural lighting from outside and adding great aesthetic value, encouraging visitors to keep going until they reach the upper floor levels of the building.

Haas Haus

Hans Hollein

Location: Vienna, Austria. **Date of completion**: 1989. **Architect**: Hans Hollein. **Scheme**: Design and construction of a new shopping mall with parking. **Photography**: Albert Worm.

The new building presents itself as a series of adjacent, superimposed cylindrical shapes – a sort of visual collage, whose variety is one of its most important characteristics. The structure appears to be dominated by curved lines, forming an undulating outline, which increasingly gains space towards the outside walls.

The significance of the exterior lies essentially in the plurality and expressiveness of the complex, contrasting radically with the surrounding environment, but coexisting in complete harmony. Inside, the need to introduce a broad, varied scheme called for considered planning, distinguishing between functional spaces, and strategic location of the communication systems. To ensure optimum selling space, the technical installations were located on two underground levels; on the first of these levels is a cafeteria, visually linked to the shopping area as a whole.

The method used to make this connection involved organizing the four public access areas around an enormous central atrium, in the form of an inverted cone, in which the stairs connecting the different levels were arranged.

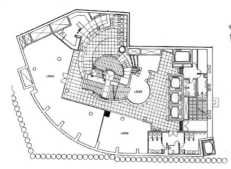

Saar Galerie

Volkwin Marg

Location: Saarbrücken, Germany. **Date of completion**: 1991. **Architect**: Volkwin Marg. **Scheme**: Shopping galleria with store and parking. **Photography**: W. Giencke.

The galleria, over 100 m (325 ft) long and 12 m (39 ft) wide, and divided into six floors, is surmounted by a 38 m (125 ft) high octagon, which is clearly visible and is now a famous landmark on the Saarbrücken skyline. The main entrance, in the form of a wide, open portal, looks onto the busy Reichstrasse. The body of

the building, which houses local stores and offices, is connected to a four-story parking lot by a series of panoramic elevators, serving all the floors and supported by an independent steel structure. Inside the galleria, the stores are spread over two levels and the appropriate arrangement of entrances and stores ensures optimum circulation of customers between them. The external perspective of the Saar Galerie is articulated by caesuras in the structure, designed in the form of recesses housing the lightweight steel emergency exit staircases. As it approaches the Reichstrasse, the galleria reverts to the classical motif of its porticoes.

Above, the external walls are clad between pillar axes in light-permeable concrete elements, in the form of a huge lattice in square modules with staggered relief. To achieve the façade's vertical structure, the galleria's mezzanine level is framed with laminated steel profiles.

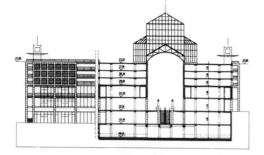

Rio Shopping Center

Martha Schwartz

Location: Atlanta, Georgia, USA. **Date of completion**: 1988. **Client**: Ackerman and Co. **Architect**: Martha Schwartz. **Associates**: Arquitectonica Architects. **Scheme**: Incorporation of landscaping in a shopping mall. **Photography**: Rion Rizzo.

The artificial hedges of the Whitehead Institute are perhaps the best example of visual interest done economically, as demonstrated by Martha Schwartz. These features have pop connotations, with the use of synthetic accessories, the sort of everyday objects found in the popular landscape, a theme also undeniably represented in the golden frogs that stake out the black fishpond of the Rio Shopping Center, symbols of the purest suburban American kitsch.

The Rio Shopping Center, with its relatively modest dimensions, was designed to accommodate specialist stores. Visualized as a small urban nucleus, with separate, defined structures, the complex planned by the Arquitectonica International Corporation enables the visitor to stroll from the interior patio to the parking area outside. The objectives of the landscaping project were to create a highly visible space that would encourage a high level of activity, to make the transition from the road running about 3 m (10 ft) above the first level of stores, and to create an image in the adjacent crossroads, jammed with traffic, an image that would be at once striking and memorable, and would incorporate the energy of the nearby intersection as a further element of the shopping mall.

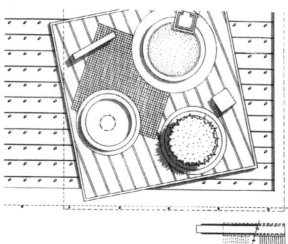

Centro Torri

Aldo Rossi

Location: Parma, Italy. **Date of completion**: 1988. **Architect**: Aldo Rossi. **Associates**: G. Braghieri, M. Baracco, P. Digiuni. **Scheme**: Shopping mall: home improvement center, supermarket, specialist stores, parking, and community and support services. **Photography**: Federico Brunetti.

The new Torri Center is made up of three units, which combine to create the shopping galleria. The most characteristic features of the complex are the ten brick towers, rising up to indicate the entrance door and main foyer. Inside the building are a home improvement center, the IPERCOOP supermarket, and a further 31 specialist stores. Community and support services are also included. The structure is built almost entirely on the same level, except for the towers, the central section housing the home improvement center offices, and an elevated room within the supermarket. The towers have exposed brickwork and are finished with a profiled cornice and copper plate. Just under the cornice, the bricks are clad in ceramic tiles, a decorative motif repeated on all the towers. The shopping galleria is clad in copper plate and underpinned by a supporting green iron structure.

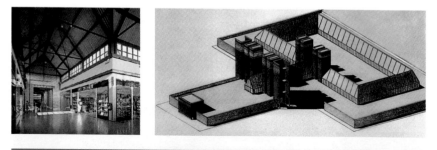

Stores and showrooms

The design of the setting in which any sort of sale takes place is of prime importance. Aesthetic considerations are not the sole preserve of garment or perfume bottle design, but extend to the architecture of chain and flagship stores. This chapter aims to bring together a selection of recent projects that have proved internationally outstanding, due to both their interior and exterior architecture – Calvin Klein, Armani, Ralph Lauren, Jil Sander, Carita... the big brands are investing increasingly in the designs and architecture of famous names (John Pawson, Peter Marino, Shigeru Ban, Ron Arad, Andrée Putman...) when opening stores and showrooms in the world's major cities.

Calvin Klein Madison Avenue

John Pawson

Location: New York, USA. **Date project begun**: 1995. **Date of completion**: 1996. **Architect**: John Pawson. **Scheme**: Men's and women's fashion and accessories store. **Photography**: Kristoph Kicherer.

The similarity between this store and an art gallery is no accident – it is both intentional and merited. The interior uses none of the usual sales strategies, instead inviting the shopper to stroll through an environment expressing a personal idea of elegance and luxury.

The store is situated within four floors of a building with classical façades, which once housed the J.P. Morgan bank.

Inside, the defining features are the stone floor, white walls, and, above all, the careful placement of objects. No attempt is made to guide, lead, or direct the customer, as is the case in most stores. On the contrary, visitors are intended to move serenely, unhurriedly, with a sense of privilege, soaking up the atmosphere. The arrangement of the establishment itself provides them with their reference point.

The store has a total floor space of 1860 m² (20,000 ft), with ceilings up to 6 m (19 ft) high. The first floor is devoted to women's accessories, the next two floors to women's and men's fashion, respectively. In the basement, household items are exhibited room by room, with accessories for the bathroom, kitchen, and dining room.

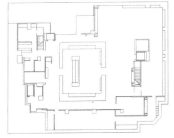

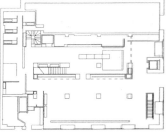

Giorgio Armani store

Peter Marino

Location: New York, USA. **Date of completion**: 1996. **Architect**: Peter Marino. **Associates**: James Carron, Kevin Wingate, Stephen Moser, Sarah Marsh, Osamu Mochizuki, Arturo Padilla, Philip Cozzi. **Scheme**: Men's and women's fashion and accessories. **Photography**: David Cardelús (also pp 536/537).

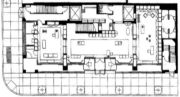

Criticized for its apparent contempt and disinterest in the urban context, this structure, located on the northeast corner of Madison Avenue and 65th Street, is a "white box" that stands out against a dark backdrop of old, brick-built factories. The Armani building opts for introversion, for withdrawal, for asceticism, as a reaction to the aggressiveness and disorder dominating the city environment: a structure created to oppose the excess of objects and saturation of symbols. Marino seeks unity in his formal language as a guarantee of the quality of the architectural work. Color disappears because it distracts and disturbs. In a certain way, the "Armani style" also pursues a sort of asceticism and abstraction in a world of overabundance, sensationalism, and excessive ornamentation. As a result, and without this being its sole and ultimate objective, Peter Marino's building is representative of the style that it contains.

Ralph Lauren showroom

Jeffrey Beers Architects

Location: New York, USA. **Date of completion**: 1996. **Client**: The Schwab Company. **Architect**: Jeffrey Beers Architects. **Associates**: Timothy Schollaert, Seung Jae Lee, Excel Inc. (contractor). **Scheme**: Small showroom for children's clothing. **Photography**: Paul Warchol.

Little Me, an American company based in Cumberland, Maryland, has just signed a contract with Ralph Lauren for the manufacture of its children's clothing and plans to move from its small 1000 m² (10,800 ft) showroom in New York to a full floor area of 7000 m² (75,300 ft) in the Childrenswear building. In the entrance hall, Beers establishes for the first time the dual nature of the showroom. The floor is an expanse of ceramic tiles with drawings of green leaves, surrounded by pine flooring and sponge painted walls. There are Plexiglas panels in the ceiling for lighting. At one end is the Ralph Lauren entrance, very understated, decorated in pine with white walls. At the other is the entrance to Little Me, with a curved, wooden reception counter and accentuated joints with amusing pictures and clothing samples. There are strange sculpted icons, such as birds or trains, placed on pedestals against the wall. The showroom contains furniture designed by Beers himself and items from the company. In extremely characteristic form, all the spaces are defined by moving wooden pieces with a grid system at the back, where the graphics elements are strategically positioned.

Jil Sander

Michael Gabellini

Location: Paris, France. **Date of completion**: 1995. **Architect**: Michael Gabellini. **Associate**: Johnson Schwinghammer. **Photography**: Paul Warchol.

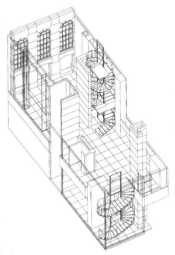

Gabellini has introduced a new genre, establishing a dialogue between the building's architectural inheritance and its new transformed state. The most important decision was to eliminate 40% of the wrought iron on the second floor to create a double entrance space, like a courtyard, opening onto the street. When one walks in, two columns made from the same white marble as the floor rise up against the side walls, defining the majestic entrance area.

A system of sensors fitted to the building's façade monitors the daylight and adjusts the interior lighting to different levels, accordingly. Low down in the side walls are recesses containing shelving or clothes hangers.

These recesses create a mysterious illuminated background for exhibiting stock in the store.

Dr. Baeltz

Shigeru Uchida

Location: Kitazawa y Hiroo, Tokyo, Japan. **Date of construction**: 1995. **Architect**: Shigeru Uchida. **Scheme**: Small cosmetics store; warehouse/office. **Photography**: Nácasa & Partners.

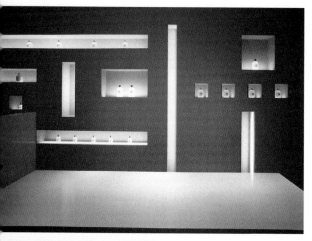

The cosmetics store designed by Shigeru Uchida for Dr. Baeltz represents the adaptation of an atypical functional scheme to small-scale commercial premises. This has involved the components being minimized right down to their fundamental characteristics, as part of an analytical process resulting in their complete integration in a unitary design combining aesthetic and functional features. The premises are limited in size (29.80 m² and 38 m², 320 ft and 409 ft) and rectangular in shape, with the entrance incorporated in a continuous glass wall, which forms part of the façade towards the shopping mall and gives a complete view of the interior. The area is divided into three sections: the store, a client consultation counter, and facial treatment area at the back. The counter, running along the length of the store, with steel chairs upholstered in blue, is the only element to invade the empty space. The merchandise has been positioned close to the peripheral walls and the facial treatment area is separated from the rest by a panel stopping short of the ceiling and permitting the physical and visual continuity of the space. The composition of openings in the walls is reinforced by their own individual lighting, which provides a dramatic backdrop for the products being displayed in a small number of packaging combinations. The use of beige as the predominant color is aimed at giving the premises a more spacious feel.

One Studio Off

Ron Arad Associates Ltd.

Location: London, UK. **Date of completion**: 1995. **Architect**: Ron Arad Associates Ltd. **Scheme**: Workshop/ studio and showroom for the architect and designer Ron Arad. **Photography**: F. Bisam/architekturphoto, C. Kicherer.

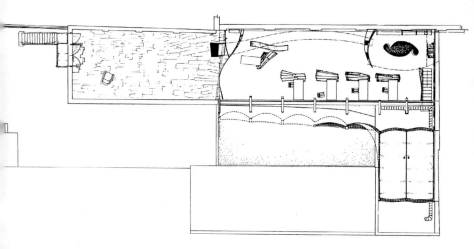

In 1989 the Ron Arad studio of architecture and design decided to bring its premises together under one roof at the One Studio Off workshop and showroom. A derelict building in northwest London was chosen for this project. Furniture production began in the ramshackle building, measuring 50 m (165 ft) deep by 5 m (16 ft) wide, at the same time as the new workshop/studio were being designed from the same interior.

In order to create a division between the furniture showroom and the design area without constructing a wall between them, the designers explored the possibilities of the floor being transformed topographically. As a result, at a given point the floor, made up of irregular pieces of different woods, starts to rise like a hill, enabling a view of the design area to be gained from its peak. From the top, a narrow blue bridge crosses towards an attic area, where there is a screened office.

The calligraphic pillars are structures designed to act as a skeleton for the swing windows, which are made from 8 mm (1/4 in) thick PVC and have their ends mounted in a metal frame.

Bottega Veneta

François de Menil

Location: Bloomingdale's, New York, USA. **Date of construction**: 1996. **Architect**: François de Menil. **Associates**: Jan Greben, James Moustafellos, Viken Arslanian. **Photography**: David Cardelús.

The architecture of François de Menil departs from geometry, color, and space and attempts to take the aesthetic experience to its very limit. This is an architecture that declares its presence through the strict physical aspect of its volumes and materials. De Menil uses a double strategy for organizing the objects on display. On the one hand, leather articles appear like jewels in the display cabinets, dream objects in the wall recesses... the traditional store window disappears and the area it once occupied becomes a space through which we are able to observe the interior. These are new store windows – the entire domain is easily recognizable from the street, with both the product and the customer being exhibited likewise. The architecture and methods of displaying merchandise work together to create a strong visual identity. Horizontal show windows and light are used to manipulate the relationship between the floor, ceiling, and walls, breaching all preconceived barriers.

La Bottega de San Valentino

Luigi Lanaro, Massimo Cocco

Location: Lugano, Italy. **Date of conversion**: 1989–1990. **Architects**: Luigi Lanaro, Massimo Cocco. **Scheme**: Renovation of a former religious building for conversion into a showroom. **Photography**: Tapparo, T Vicenza.

Following an exercise in sensitive, respectful restoration, this religious building now houses within its ancestral walls not only a store, but also a modern, pragmatic cultural center. The building's original architecture was simple – a rectangular floor with an entrance atrium above a triple arcade of decorated vaults. A wooden dividing structure was erected, creating a double height that enabled an intermediate iron platform to be located between this and the floor. The roof was modified to enable as much natural light as possible to be captured from the upper arches. All the materials were used in their natural state, in order to preserve the historic feel of the building. Making use of soft, diffuse natural light is one of the key factors in the creation of a meaningful atmosphere, offering an ambience that is at once sober and fascinating, in accordance with the general spirit of the project.

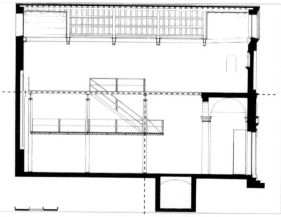

Carita

Andrée Putman

Location: Paris, France. **Date of completion**: 1986. **Architect**: Andrée Putman. **Associate**: Bruno Moinard. **Photography**: Archipress.

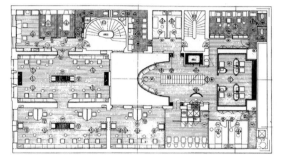

In Carita, the display cases where the establishment's exclusive products are exhibited are to be found, eventually, in the corridor leading to the lounge. They occupy a single narrow strip running at eye level in a linear showcase built in between neutral gray panels. Carita has a first floor and three further floors arranged by theme. The first floor houses the reception, a skin diagnosis cubicle, Christophe Carita's studio, the point of sale for the products on offer, a video room, the cloakroom, and a cash desk.
The first floor focuses on hair treatments, while the hair salon, with all the usual associated services, is located on the second floor. The third floor is divided into one area for women's beauty treatments and one for men's. The staircase is the

heart of the establishment. The designers preferred to opt for neutral finishes, offering tranquillity and elegance, rather than excessively innovative elements that would have a jarring effect on the clients or could become outmoded.

Restaurants

Restaurants, perhaps more than any other business establishments, are places most closely connected to our personal experience. They are intimately linked to the memory of a date, a celebration, a journey, a city where we used to live, or an era. Not all restaurants, however, seek this complicity with the user. There are others with a more pragmatic spirit that try simply to fulfill their essential function; they are perhaps integrated, as in a museum, concert hall, or station. The selection described here is intended to illustrate a range of very different restaurant concepts: intimate spaces and mass purveyors, establishments situated within a company, a government body, a viewing tower... none of these projects remotely resembles any other. On the contrary, the aim is to demonstrate the various ways of approaching an architectural project: with different sensibilities, but with equally valid results.

Oxo Tower

One Happy Cloud

Brindley Place Café

Restaurante Théatron

Río Florida

Wagamama

Gagnaire

Restaurant at the Department of Foreign Affairs

Petrofina Restaurant

Televisa Restaurant

Oxo Tower

Lifschutz Davidson

Location: London, UK. **Date of completion**: 1997. **Client**: Harvey Nichols. **Architect**: Lifschutz Davidson.
Scheme: Lifschutz Davidson. **Associates**: John Sisk & Sons (construction), Buro Happold/WSP (structural engineers), Mecserve/How Engineering (construction services), Equation Lighting Design (lighting), ECHarris and Partners (quality control). **Photography**: Chris Gascoigne/VIEW.

Since 1930 the Oxo Tower has been one of the landmarks on the banks of the Thames. In recent years the building has been renovated to house a diverse range of activities.

The first three levels are used for commercial purposes, the five intermediate floors are occupied by 78 apartments, and, finally, on the ninth floor there are two places to eat (a restaurant and a brasserie) and the Harvey Nichols bar. Aware of the exceptional panoramic view offered by the restaurant, the architects have constructed a light ceiling supported by a latticework of beams in the form of a bobbin, which rests on two pillars situated in the center of the building. The glass skin has virtually no uprights or carpentry. A few ties attached to the ceiling support the intermediate anchors of the plate glass. The first 3 m (10 ft) of the façade are therefore completely transparent.

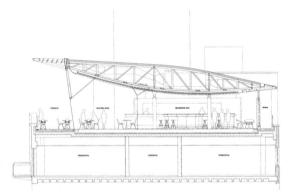

One Happy Cloud

Marten Claesson, Eero Koivisto, Ola Rune

Location: Karlavägen 15, Stockholm, Sweden. **Date of completion**: 1997. **Client**: Masao Mochizuki. **Architects**: Marten Claesson, Eero Koivisto, Ola Rune. **Associates**: Christiane Bosse, Mattias Stahlbom (assistants), New World Inredning AB (construction), Ralambshovs Snikerier AB (carpentry), Nybergs Glas AB (glass). **Photography**: Patrick Engquist (also pp 558/559).

The developer of One Happy Cloud, a Japanese restaurant situated in Stockholm, wanted to convert his establishment into a point of integration between the Japanese and Scandinavian cultures, both from a gastronomic and an aesthetic point of view. The result is a space of extraordinary simplicity and elegance, without direct references to Japanese culture, but with subtle allusions to the atmosphere and tranquillity found in that country's traditional architecture.

The restaurant takes up an area of approximately 150 m² (1600 ft), with an almost square floor plan. The eating area is organized into two narrow rooms, which form an L shape. The rest of the space is occupied by the rest rooms and kitchen. All the walls are plastered and painted white, except for the one behind the bar, where there are drawings by graphic designer Nill Svensson.

Brindley Place Café

CZWG Architects

Location: Brindley Place, Birmingham, UK. **Date of completion**: 1997. **Client**: Argent Development Consortium. **Architect**: CZWG Architects. **Associates**: Adams Kara Taylor (structural engineers), Townsend Landscape Architects (landscape design), Silk & Frazier (monitoring), Kyle Stewart (contractor). **Photography**: Chris Gascoigne.

The Rouge restaurant-bar, now the Brindley Place Café, is a small eatery on a square in the city of Birmingham; it re-creates the spirit of old pavilions – minimal buildings falling halfway between urban fixtures and sculpture. CZWG Architects felt that the project should not only satisfy the scheme's functional requirements and the relationship with the urban environment, but it should, above all, constitute a significant piece of work in itself. In this sense, it is far removed from the typical hermetically sealed structures that normally occupy the streets, and both the façade looking onto the square and the roof are constructed using glass and steel. This means that, although the pavilion is an element of the square, from the inside it seems that the relationship of dependence is reversed, with the square becoming the bar's terrace.

Restaurante Théatron

Philippe Starck

Location: Mexico. **Date of completion**: 1996. **Architect**: Philippe Starck. **Associates**: Baltasar Vez (project management), Cardona y Asociados (electricity), Electro Media (special installations). **Photography**: Alfredo Jacob Vilalta.

Beyond its immediate function, the restaurant Théatron has a scenographic side, in which customers become leading characters in their own plays.

One room is lit by an antique chandelier, the next by a bare bulb hanging from the ceiling by a flex. Guests ascend a disproportionate, monumental staircase and then pass through a dark,

narrow corridor. The restaurant itself is submerged in a misty atmosphere. Light, airy curtains adorn the room, meandering their way down from the ceiling to chair height, so that they only half divide the space. Although it covers an area of over 300 m² (3200 ft²), the lobby displays only three decorative elements: a huge picture frame approximately 10 m (32 ft)

high by 6 m (19 ft) wide, containing a photograph by Richard Avedon, a large staircase, and a gray velvet curtain backed with scarlet silk, which is over 12 m (39 ft) high by 16 m (52 ft) wide, and very striking.

Río Florida

Roberto Ercilla, Miguel Ángel Campo

Location: Florida Park, Vitoria, Spain. **Date of completion**: 1995. **Client**: Pablo Calvo Aguriano. **Architects**: Roberto Ercilla, Miguel Angel Campo. **Associates**: Javier Valdivieso (foreman), Eduardo Martín (structure), Javier Bárcena. **Photography**: César San Millán.

There is not much of a modern tradition for the building of stalls and kiosks in the middle of large parks or public spaces. The difficulty involved in positioning this structure here led the designers to split the building into three interconnected pavilions. Each of these has an associated function: restaurant, bar, and terrace. The whole building was envisaged as a complex of prefabricated units, subsequently assembled on site. The sectional structure of the three elements is made entirely from Oregon pine, assembled using galvanized steel parts. The flooring, wall facing, and furniture are of the same material. Glass envelops the two closed, transparent units. The aim of the project is to create for guests the sustained illusion that they are eating in the middle of a forest. Architectural expression is minimized in favor of the landscape, so as not to dominate it.

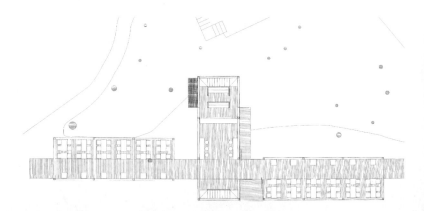

Wagamama

David Chipperfield, Victoria Pike, Pablo Gallego-Picard

Location: 10 Lexington Street, London, UK. **Date of completion**: 1996. **Architects**: David Chipperfield, Victoria Pike, Pablo Gallego-Picard. **Associates**: Overbury Interiors Ltd. (contractor), Chan Associates (structural engineers), BSC Consulting Engineers (service engineers), Tim Gatehouse Associates (section supervisor). **Photography**: Richard Davies.

Wagamama, a Japanese restaurant in London's Soho district, occupies the first floor and basement of a low yet wide-fronted building. The dining room is situated in the basement, while the kitchen is on the first floor. Inside, diners wait to be seated in a long corridor from which they can see into the kitchen and therefore follow the preparation of the different dishes. On the other side of the corridor, an acid etched glass screen separates the customers from the double space and the street. At night, diners waiting for their tables can be seen from outside silhouetted against the glass of the screen. Dishes prepared in the kitchen are delivered to the basement by a system of anodized aluminum service lifts, from where they are distributed to the tables. A series of counters lined up against the back wall of the basement display the desserts, juices, and drinks on offer to diners. There is also another counter just below the staircase, with items for sale to the restaurant's customers.

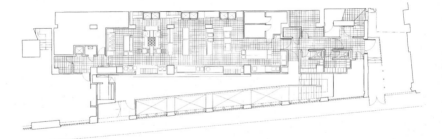

Gagnaire

Studio Naço

Location: Saint Etienne, France. **Year of opening**: 1992. **Client**: Pierre Gagnaire. **Architect**: Studio Naço (Alain Renk, Marcelo Joulia). **Associates**: Jean-François Pasqualini, Allard Kuyken, Beatrice Berin (architects), Muriel Quintanilla (designer), Olivier Dubos (graphic designer). **Scheme**: Conversion of a former country house into a restaurant. **Photography**: Mario Pignata-Monti.

Pierre Gagnaire is one of the world's best-known chefs. He chose a country house built in the 1930s as the place to start up his own business as an independent restaurateur. The conversion project bestows equal importance on the cooking areas and cellars and the rooms reserved for guests. Each of the former rooms has been turned into a dining room.

Studio Naço uses systems of sliding doors, engraved glass screens, and large wall hangings painted in different colors to establish a relationship of variation, repetition, continuity, and isolation between the different rooms in the building.

Restaurant at the Department of Foreign Affairs

Bernard Desmoulin

Location: Paris, France. **Date of completion**: 1995. **Client**: Department of Foreign Affairs. **Architect**: Bernard Desmoulin. **Associates**: MAE (master of works), Serete Constructions, Novorest (studies), Bouygues TEP, La Felletinoise (construction), Christian Granvelle (basement fresco). **Photography**: Hervé Abbadie.

The project endeavors to explore the potential of a privileged space by re-creating the conditions that turn these small and often concealed courtyards into almost magical places. Only a partially underground structure (see section diagram) could satisfy all the scheme's requirements and, at the same time, restore the garden. The first floor's glass façade is continued by the ground surface in the garden and becomes the roof/skylight of the restaurant's basement. It is, therefore, a glass square through which natural light enters the two dining room levels.

A bridge made from wooden planks crosses the bed of a stream, leading to the orchard with its rows of

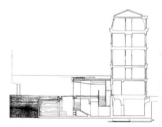

apple and pear trees. Metal guides have been fitted to the dining room roof, enabling an awning to be released on very sunny days if required.

Petrofina Restaurant

Samyn et Associés

Location: Brussels, Belgium. **Date of construction**: 1994-1995. **Client**: Petrofina S.A. **Architect**: Samyn et Associés. **Scheme**: Construction of a restaurant in the head offices of an oil company. **Approximate area**: 2086 m² (22,450 ft²). **Photography**: J. Bauters, Ch. Bastin, J. Evrard.

The building, constructed in 1851, is typical of the mansions of this period still remaining in the district. The scheme expresses the oil company's objectives for its image – transparency, openness, and humanity. The space at the back of the building has been replaced by a large glass canopy suspended between the back of the mansion and the small office building. This canopy

covers the staff dining room, creating a garden-like atmosphere. A second restaurant is to be found on a second floor terrace, running along the mansion's rear, north facing façade, above the food service area of the first floor restaurant. A large lobby unites the curved ceiling area with the main office infrastructure, which houses the restaurant's cleaning and storage facilities.

Televisa Restaurant

Ten Arquitectos

Location: Mexico City. **Date of completion**: 1993. **Client**: Televisa S.A. **Architects**: Enrique Norten, Bernardo Gómez-Pimienta (TEN Arquitectos). **Associates**: Roberto Scheimberg (project manager), Gustavo Espitia, Rebeca Golden, Héctor Gámiz, Javier Presas, Leonardo Saldívar (design team), Ove Arup + Partners NY, Salvador Aguilar (structural engineering), Electroinstalaciones Industriales (electromechanical engineering), Inrasa (drainage), Eclisa (air-conditioning), Guma Gas (gas), Inseurban, David Serur (works management). **Photography**: Luis Gordoa.

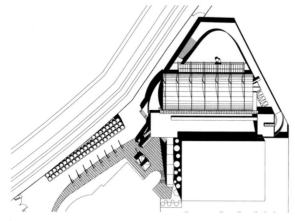

This project has two essential characteristics. Firstly, it is a space designed on the basis of an existing structure and, secondly, it is a building that is difficult to see, since it is concealed by another construction and, above all, the adjacent street layout means it is only possible to catch partial glimpses of it. Perhaps the most important decision was the choice of a light roof for the restaurant itself, since the existing structure could not support a greater load. Yet this solution, of purely technical origins, became the most important formal proposal of the entire project. The roof and façade constitute a unit and are defined by a single outline. The project is made up of three independent roofing sections, of which only the largest (and central one) is curved. The other two, the one covering the kitchen and the canopy above the square, are slightly inclined, adapting to the dynamism of the curved roof. This discontinuity also enables natural light to enter, through skylights located at the junctions between the three sections.

Public buildings, institutions, and offices

Among the virtues of contemporary architecture it is worth highlighting the notable efforts made to reconcile the urban and natural environments. This issue occupies a place of special importance for the subjects under analysis in this chapter – public buildings, institutions, and offices. These constitute one of the most interesting areas of architecture, combining fundamental elements of design, construction, and landscaping. The principal characteristic of the projects included here, apart from their indispensable aesthetic and pragmatic values, is their relationship to the world of work. The major corporations and multinationals have finally recognized the need to harmonize architecture with the landscape, not only as a sign of respect for environmental conditions, but also as a means of achieving an attractive corporate image and a suitable working environment. As a result, the design of all these recent buildings has been based on two fundamental parameters – the construction of a meaningful, identifying image and the creation of a working environment that is pleasant, harmonious, and, above all, respectful of the all-important human dimension.

In fact, the importance today's society attaches to image is reflected in the headquarters of the major corporations and in many public buildings, where top class architectural design has become the best way of expressing a philosophy, whether corporate or governmental. In some cases, the emphasis has been placed on tradition and perpetuity; in others, on innovation and creativity. The common thread running through all the projects, however, is their attempt to present an image that accords with a philosophy of work.

Public bodies

Public institutions at international level have been caught up in the general trend for updating and reviewing the architectural principles of their buildings. There is a clear desire to dispel the myths surrounding the role of public bodies in the personal life of the individual and what better than a change of image and structure to try to create a friendlier face? But this is not simply a question of redesign. The idea goes much further than this. It also involves the inclusion of environmental considerations in the construction of these buildings, which house anything from the parliaments of major countries to city halls, law courts, embassies, and courts of human rights. In following this new direction, landscaping and environmental activities place these new buildings on the threshold of a fresh, intensely ecological millennium.

Court of Human Rights

Richard Rogers

Location: Strasbourg, France. **Date of completion**: December 1995. **Client**: Council of Europe. **Cost**: FFr 455 million. **Architects**: Sir Richard Rogers (Rogers Partnership Ltd.), Claude Bucher. **Associates**: Ove Arup, Ominium Technique Européen (engineering and structures), Thorne Wheatley Associates (work sections supervision), David Jarvis Associates, Dan Kiley (landscape design), Lighting Design Partnership (lighting), Sound Research Laboratories, Commins Ingemansson (acoustics). **Scheme**: Court and Commission rooms and administrative services. **Photography**: F. Busam/Architekturphoto.

The building claims to be the symbolic and mechanical representation of the tasks undertaken by the internal organs of the Court of Human Rights: it is an open, transparent structure. According to Richard Rogers, it is an articulated complex of head and body: the two parts are linked by a vertical communications nucleus. The head is the public part, where the working rooms used by the Court and Commission are to be found; the lower section or body, by contrast, contains the administrative divisions. As in almost all of Richard Rogers' buildings, there is an extraordinary precision in the expression of details. His architecture always exhibits the desire for transparency and lightness. Rogers does not try to conceal the structure, but elevates it through the use of high tech.

Deutscher Bundestag

Günter Behnisch

Location: Bonn, Germany. **Date of completion**: 1993. **Developer**: Bundestag (German Parliament). **Architects**: Günter Behnisch, Winfried Büxel, Manfred Sabatke, Erhard Tränkner. **Associates**: Gerald Staib, Hubert Burkart, Eberhard Pritzer, Alexander von Salmuth, Ernst Tillmanns (project architects), Ulrich Liebert, Heinz Schröder, Bernd Troske (contract architects), Schlaich, Bergermann and Partner (structural engineers), S.H. Keppler (air-conditioning and installations), Zimmermann + Schrage (electricity), Graner + Partner (acoustics), Lichtdesign Ingenieurgesellschaft, Lichtplanung Bartenbach (lighting), Berthold Mack (façade consultants), Hans Luz + Partner (landscape design). **Scheme**: Parliament, presidential offices, administrative offices, lobbies, restaurant, visitors' area, and services. **Photography**: Christian Kandzia (also pp 584/585).

The Bundestag (German Parliament) occupies a privileged position – close to the Rhine and next to a long riverside avenue. In view of its considerable size, it was felt necessary to make doubly sure that it did not distort the landscape. The roof is virtually transparent. Beneath the skylight, the hall is transformed into a miniature valley in the midst of a forest, into which the light filters through the branches of the trees. Day and night, sunsets, seasons, snow in winter, the leaden skies of fall, the color of flowers in spring - they all penetrate the building. This metaphor naturally demands great technological application, not only in matters of climate control, but also problems of security. Nevertheless, the transparency motif has endured: it is always possible to see through the building. From the chamber floor, trees can be seen, from the lobby the chamber of deputies, and from the staircases the river Rhine....

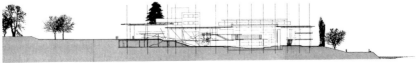

Finnish Embassy in Washington D.C.

Mikko Heikkinen and Markku Komonen

Location: Washington D.C, USA. **Architects**: Mikko Heikkinen and Markku Komonen. **Date of completion**: 1994. **Associates**: Sarlotta Narjus, Angelous Demetriou & Associates, Eric Morrison (architects); Lee & Liu Associates (landscape design); Chas. H. Tompkins Co. (contractor). **Scheme**: Offices, conference rooms, meeting rooms, and services. **Photography**: Jussi Tiainen.

The Finnish Embassy in the United States is situated on Massachusetts Avenue, in the heart of embassy land. It is an area of low density, populated by noble buildings, isolated from one another by hundreds of different types of trees. The building combines the rational, coherent distribution of its office areas and studies in two parallel rectangular blocks, with a Piranesian central space four stories high, in which walkways interrupted above the void, sections of circular staircases, and volumes suspended in the air are interwoven.

By contrast to such innate exuberance, the outside of the building seems to reject the introduction of bold forms. On the side façades, the green granite reflects the branches and foliage of the trees. The front façades are constructed using blocks of translucent glass with a soft, greenish hue, echoing the structural elements and metal panels, which have been painted with a patina of the same color.

Finnish Embassy in Washington D.C. 591

European Free Trade Association

Samyn and Partners

Location: Brussels, Belgium. **Date of construction**: 1993. **Architects**: Y. Azizollahof, W. Azou, J. Ceyssens, A. Charon, P. de Neyer, H. Dossin, L. Finet, S. Finet, D. Gelhausen, T. Hac, T. Khayati, P. Mandel, P. Mayeur, A. Mestiri, N. Milo, Ph. Samyn, B. Selfslagh, V. Van Dijk, D. Verboven, B. Bleurick. **Scheme**: Offices, meeting rooms, parking, and services. **Area**: 11,000 m² (118,000 ft²). **Photography**: Ch. Bastin & J. Evrard, J.M. Byl.

The European Free Trade Association (EFTA) building is in the heart of the Léopold district, Brussels' financial quarter. The building can accommodate any sort of office, from individual rooms to full floor, open plan designs.

The structure is divided up by two rows of separate pillars measuring 10.8 m (35 ft), which provides a great deal of flexibility in the arrangement of desks. The façade consists of a double glass skin with a perimeter corridor.

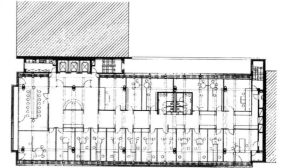

Reichstag

Foster & Partners

Location: Berlin, Germany. **Date of construction**: 1999. **Client**: Federal Republic of Germany. **Architects**: Foster & Partners. **Associates**: David Nelson, Mark Braun, Dieter Muller, Ingo Pott. **Photography**: Dennis Gilbert, Nigel Young.

This project emerged from the initiative to transfer the German Parliament from Bonn to Berlin and rehouse it in the Reichstag building. In 1992 a competitive tender was issued for the construction of an area measuring 33,000 m² (355,000 ft²), almost double the size that could be contained by the Reichstag building. The total area was later reduced to a realistic 9000 m² (97,000 ft²).

The scheme involved reopening a chamber within the Reichstag building – a structure that had been opened in 1894, set on fire in 1933, partially destroyed in 1945, restored during the 1960s and "wrapped up" in 1995. The complexity of the architectural planning was heightened by the desire to review the building's design from an environmental viewpoint. This involved designing an energy efficient structure, with ambient heating inside and, associated with this, self-generation of heat and energy production and a reduction in waste emissions from it.

The new glass dome is the point of departure for the interior work and enables the building to be opened up to natural light and views. It acts as an essential component in energy saving and natural lighting strategies. The dome was envisaged as a "lantern," with the broad interpretations implied by this description.

Federal building on Foley Square

Hellmuth, Obata & Kassabaum

Location: New York, USA. **Date of construction**: 1995. **Architects**: Hellmuth, Obata & Kassabaum.
Associates: Tishman Foley Partners (contractor), Linpro NY Realty (developer), Israel A. Seinuk (engineer).
Area: 87,300 m² (939,000) ft²). **Cost**: $276 million. **Scheme**: US Federal Government office building.
Photography: Paco Asensio.

This building's steel structure began to emerge even before the final contract designs had been completed. The architects were responsible for each of the design details on every floor and for making the most cost effective use of the space available. The result is a high rise, but not aggressive, building which combines authoritarian architecture with some softer finishes. These create an extremely dignified structure, highlighted by the circular section towards the top of the building, which was inspired by skyscraper designs from the 1920s. Decorative elements in the form of cornices and pilasters give form to the façade. Building work on the entrance hall had to be suspended following the discovery of Afro-American remains during the excavation work. This building is currently protected as an area of historical interest.

Court building on Foley Square

Kohn Pedersen Fox Associates

Location: New York, USA. **Date of construction**: 1995. **Architects**: Kohn Pedersen Fox Associates.
Associates: Lehrer McGovern Bovis (contractor), Structure Tone (interiors), BPT Properties (developer).
Photography: Paco Asensio.

This is one of the greatest Federal buildings in the United States, situated in an area of large-scale urban development. The designers had difficulties with the scale of the project during the initial phase, due to the problems involved in incorporating this skyscraper in a district in which civic centers and residential buildings coexist. A square at the front of the building minimizes the visual and spatial impact of a structure of this height. The building's west wing includes a first floor gallery, which creates a sensation of continuity and connection between the different public buildings. Neoclassical in style, it takes its design reference from the earlier 1936 court building here.

Inside, an effort has been made to situate the large courtrooms and the judges' chambers in the most accessible areas. This has been achieved by situating these rooms within an oval space connected to the main tower. The judges have their own access route and move around within an independent domain, which includes private elevators, enabling them to be completely isolated from the defendants, who enter and leave the building through specially constructed tunnels. The public access area includes a reception area and the gallery connected to the square at the front.

Government offices for the Department of Bouches-du-Rhône

Alsop & Störmer

Location: Marseilles, France. **Date of construction**: 1994. Architect: Alsop & Störmer. **Associates**: Ove Arup (structural engineering and fittings), Hanscomb (sectional supervision). **Scheme**: Offices, meeting and conference rooms, cafeteria, and services. **Area**: 44,500 m² (479,00 ft²). **Photography**: Roderick Coyne.

After Alsop & Störmer were awarded this contract, the construction of the building in Marseilles marked a point of departure in their career. The importance of the structure in the building's image and its intense blue color make it a highly unusual piece of work. It is a powerful, futuristic construction reminiscent of Archigram images in its overall effect.

The scheme is divided between two parallel rectangular blocks containing the offices and a cigarette-shaped structure housing the assembly and conference rooms. Between these is an atrium with a network of suspended passageways and bridges.

Tokyo City Hall

Kenzo Tange

Location: Tokyo, Japan. **Date of construction**: 1986–1991. **Client**: Tokyo Municipality. **Architect**: Kenzo Tange. **Photography**: Osamu Murai, Shinkenchiku Shashinien.

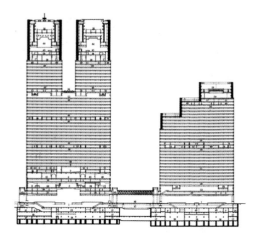

Two aligned towers face the central park of Shinjuku, forming a complex together with the Assembly Building and the square lying between them. Tower I, located between the square and the park, contains the office of the governor, the most important of the administrative departments, conference rooms, and a disaster control center. From floor 33 the building divides into two twin towers, reaching a height of 243 m (800 ft). Tower II, 163 m (535 ft high), accommodates a number of agencies, public corporations, and other departments. The upper part progressively decreases in size, in a stepped arrangement in relation to Tower I, to form a combined profile at the summit of the buildings. The floors develop from a reticular network of 6.4 m (21 ft). In order to achieve flexibility and free space for the working areas, a superstructure was conceived for each tower, formed by eight large nuclei of 6.4 x 6.4 m (21 x 21 ft), supported on some floors to form "superbeams." The result, with lights of 19.2 m (63 ft), is a spatial distribution which opens to the outside with a sense of total freedom, exceeding the virtual perimeter defined by the nuclei. The façade, in modular design with panels measuring 3.2 x 4 m (10.5 x 13), reflects the superstructure and acquires a certain traditional character in its latticework design element.

City Hall, The Hague

Richard Meier

Location: The Hague, The Netherlands. **Date of completion**: 1998. **Client**: City of The Hague. **Architect**: Richard Meier. **Scheme**: Construction of the City Hall of The Hague, Central Library for public use, administrative rooms, and services. **Photography**: Anna Tiessler.

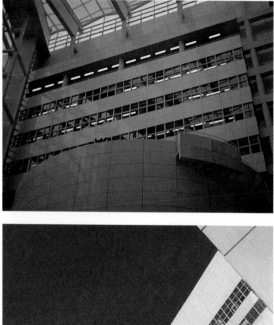

In one single project, the City Hall harmonizes with the spatial complexity of the centre of the city in which it is located. This is a theme which is encountered in many of Richard Meier's buildings: urban and rural situations are expressed in the same buildings, which in this way are converted into the natural epicentre of their location. The spatial composition of the axes of perspective, lines, and throughways creates an image of the building and its surroundings which is complex yet balanced. At street level, the building is open on all sides; the interior and exterior have a natural flow, and at each corner subtle relationships are created between open and enclosed spaces, access routes, and lines of perspective. This is clearly seen on the two glazed sides of the entrance atrium, a space of intense use and direct access, and the focus of attention from the working areas. Essentially, the project is a large, empty, covered square, which the population of The Hague must take it upon themselves to fill.

Rezé-le-Nantes City Hall

Alessandro Anselmi

Location: Rezé-le-Nantes, France. **Date of completion**: 1988. **Architect**: Alessandro Anselmi. **Scheme**: Construction of a new City Hall which encompasses the two existing old buildings. **Photography**: Philippe Ruault.

The task was to construct a modern City Hall which would function as a means of rejuvenating the municipal administration and act as a dynamic source of development for Rezé. Anselmi designed the new project by concentrating the structures on the east and west of the site, leaving a vast amount of free space. The result is that this area, treated as a garden amenity, provides the image of the whole of the architectural complex, in the form of a thoroughfare running north to south, which surmounts the hill and extends into the extraordinary residential estate of Le Corbusier. The municipal technical services are accommodated in the west part of the building, and are connected at the entrance level by means of a vertical traverse in the form of stairways and elevators. Finally, the politico-administrative functions, the municipal council chamber, the offices of the mayor, the secretariat, the finance department, and the information center are all located in the eastern part.

Portugal Pavilion

Álvaro Siza

Location: Lisbon, Portugal. **Date of completion**: 1997. **Client**: Expo '98. **Architects**: Alvaro Siza. **Scheme**: Pavilion for the celebration of Portuguese culture at Expo '98. **Photography**: Paco Asensio.

The Portugal Pavilion at Expo '98 is located next to the northwest corner of the Muelle de los Olivares. The border between the building and the adjacent area is covered by an awning supported on slender columns, forming an enormous, lateral covered walk along the eastern side of the building. This structure, made of reinforced concrete, has not had a specific use since the event: Expo '98 called for a great deal of flexibility and versatility in the use of space, but its representative function nevertheless required a clear and powerful image. The building, which was developed along a longitudinal north–south axis, consists of two units separated by a composite structural unit. The first of these is in fact a grand ceremonial square flanked to the north and south by two great porticoes, clad in glazed tiles of different colors, between which runs a very fine strip of concrete describing a curve, in the manner of a gigantic sail.

The second unit consists of a rectangular-based structure with a basement and two surface stories. These three levels are developed around a courtyard covering the ground as far as the lower story, to allow for the planting of trees. From one corner of the building a two-story annex projects, which is separated from the main building in the complex by a gallery.

Public service buildings

The focus of attention in this section will be on those small urban buildings which for practical purposes form part of the urban furniture of every large town and city. These might be small medical facilities, weather centres, water circulation control centres, or shipping navigation beacons and lighthouses, the proper use of which enhances the quality of life for the local population. They have been chosen for inclusion in this selection of contemporary architecture because of the innovation of their design; they have given added value to the landscape of each individual city.

Manliu mountain area

Enric Batlle and Joan Roig

Location: Manliu, Meranges, La Cerdaña, Spain. **Date of construction**: 1994. **Architects**: Enric Batlle, Joan Roig. **Associate**: David Closas. **Photography**: David Closas, Gregori Civera, Enric Batlle.

The project was developed around an already extant mountain refuge, in an area of the Catalan Pyrenees; it is at an altitude of 2000 m (6500 ft), next to a lake occupying the site of an ancient glacier, at the boundary between sub-alpine woodlands and alpine vegetation areas. The task was to construct an arrangement for the end of a mountain track leading to the refuge so as to provide information and channel visitors onwards. The biggest problem was to harmonize the existing uses, for open air stock rearing, with the increasing presence of the public enjoying the natural surroundings. The basic operations involved limiting vehicular traffic so as not to intrude on the surrounding meadowland, yet still provide minimum amenities for visitors, such as restrooms, litter collection points, drinking fountains, tables, and barbecue sites, which were nevertheless required to have a spontaneous, natural appearance.

Given the location and the project, there was only one material – stone – which could be used to construct virtually all the elements of the site without excessive handling and transport. Stone was, furthermore, the material used for the few buildings in the area and was also the most readily available. Consequently stone was used to construct the boundary walls, tables, barbecue sites, water fountains, traffic tracks, signage, and restrooms.

Signal box

Herzog & De Meuron

Location: Basle, Switzerland. **Date project begun**: 1989. **Date of completion**: 1995. **Architects**: Jaques Herzog, Pierre de Meuron, Harry Gugger. **Associates**: Hansueli Suter, Philippe Fürstenberger. **Photography**: Margherita Spiluttini.

Adjacent to the 18th- and 19th-century walls of the Wolf-Gottesacker cemetery is a substantial volume of copper: a railroad signal box and control center. It stands beside the railroad tracks, close to the new locomotive sheds. Distributed over its six floors are sophisticated control instruments and electronic equipment for managing switch points and coordinating the signals along the tracks. The concrete structure of the building is provided with external insulation, and is clad in copper panels approximately 20 cm (8 in) in thickness. These panels are open at a number of points to allow ingress of natural light. The orientation of the panels, opening out, casts lines of shadow on the façades, resembling the scales of a fish. This introduces a variation in the texture of the skin of the building, while at the same time emphasizing the dramatic character of its isolation. The building is, by definition, a striking point in the landscape which does not evoke any echoes of known forms or images, codified in terms of culture. It is a unique feature of its kind.

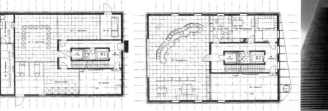

Grand Valley Women's Prison

Kuwabara Payne McKenna Blumberg Architects

Location: Kitchener, Ontario, Canada. **Date of construction**: 1996. **Design team**: Marianne McKenna, Bruce Kuwabara, Robert Sims, John Allen, Howard Sutcliffe, David Pontarini. **Scheme**: Dormitories, services, gymnasium, dispensary, chapel, school, storerooms, visiting rooms, reception, offices, and warehouse. **Photography**: Robert G. Hill.

roofs, and simple, unadorned materials. The natural lighting, good ventilation, and abundant use of color creates a healthy, friendly environment, aimed at encouraging a positive relationship between the inmates, the officers, and the visitors.

Located in a rural area of Ontario, this prison complex creates a balance between the private environment and communal areas. The project calls to mind the layout of a village located around a central park. In order to emphasize the residential nature of the complex, the different sectors of the project have been separated into independent buildings interconnected by a loggia. Likewise, arranged around the park are ten chalets, each for eight inmates, connected by footpaths and a perimeter trackway. KPMB has borrowed ideas from residential and agricultural architecture projects in the Kitchener-Waterloo community: generously dimensioned walkways, double pitched

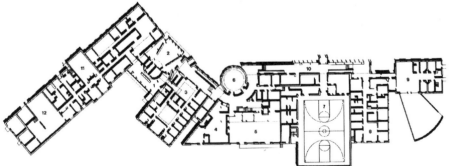

Samsung Medical Center

K.ITO Architects & Engineers Inc

Location: Seoul, Korea. **Date of completion**: June 1994. **Client**: Samsung Life Insurance Co. Ltd. **Architect**: K.ITO Architects & Engineers Inc. **Scheme**: Construction of a medical center: medical examination center, research institute, residential quarters for medical personnel and nursing staff, general medical modules. **Total surface area**: 113,805 m² (1.22 million ft²). **Photography**: Samsung Life Insurance Co.

The Samsung Medical Center, the largest general hospital in South Korea, is located in a new services area in the suburbs of Seoul, where major urban development has been under way. The Medical Center has a number of facilities, including a medical examinations center, a research institute, residential quarters for medical personnel and nursing staff, and the main buildings of the hospital, accommodating the specialist departments providing general medical services. The larger modules are located in the center of an area covering 200,000 m² (2.15 million ft²). This complex contains a nucleus which houses the elevators, while the hospital thoroughfares, broad and well lit, create a geometrical pattern with the patients' complex, the outpatient consultation clinic, and the examinations section. Each floor contains two ward units, a large, well-illuminated area surrounded by corridors and the patients' rooms, which are themselves designed to be as light and pleasant as possible.

Hospital del Mar, Barcelona

Manuel Brullet and Albert de Pineda

Location: Paseo Marítimo, Barcelona, Spain. **Date of completion**: 1994. **Client**: Municipality of Barcelona. **Architects**: Manuel Brullet, Albert de Pineda. **Associates**: Manuel Arguijo (structural analysis), Xavier Llambrich, Mateu Barba (works management), Jordi Barba (fixtures and fittings), Francesc Pernas (basic engineering), M. Hernandez, J. Alonso, A. Granell, J.M. Sanmartin (quantity surveyors), Alfonso de Luna (project associate), Cubiertas y MZOV (contractors). **Scheme**: Refurbishment of the Hospital del Mar: accommodation for patients, biomedical research facility, outpatient consultation buildings, offices for the Municipal Medical Research Institute, cafeteria-restaurant, services, offices for medical staff, and exterior landscaping. **Photography**: Ana Quesada.

This project involves refurbishment of the old Barcelona Hospital for Infectious Diseases (1925), with a double objective: firstly, the definition of a new organizational structure, both functional and physical, for the center which was used as the Olympic Hospital during the Barcelona Olympic Games in 1992; secondly, to adapt the Hospital to the changes in the city itself, and the urban development resulting from the construction of the Olympic Village in the area adjacent to the sea. The current project extends the surface area of the site intended for healthcare facilities, and at the same time addresses the redesigning of the Hospital proper. The new alignments of the façades of the Hospital were defined so as to adapt to the different layout imposed by the new Avenida del Litoral, and to the arrangement of the building complex, following the principle of personalizing the three central structures involved. As a final consideration, the architects sought to make best use of natural light as a unifying element for the open spaces of the Hospital complex.

Thames Tower

Brookes Stacey, Randall Fursdon

Location: Holland Park, London, UK. **Date of construction**: 1992–1994. **Client**: Thames Water Utilities. **Architects**: Brookes Stacey, Randall Fursdon. **Associates**: SMP Atelier One (basic engineering); J. Murphy and Sons (contractors); Charles Henshaws and Sind Ltd. (glazing and cladding contractors); Thermelek Engineering Services Ltd. (hydraulic engineering specialists); Atkinson Chemicals Ltd. (hydraulic systems); Hiltec Solar Ltd. (solar panels); Proctor Masts Ltd. **Scheme**: Water tower, as final point on a subterranean water pipe system. **Photography**: Peter Durant.

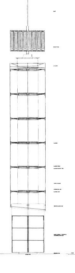

The tubular structure, 1.5 m (5 ft) in diameter and 15 m (50 ft) high, marks the final point of a spectacular project involving 80 km (50 miles) of subterranean water pipes. With sheet steel cladding, the tube is enveloped by a glass cylinder formed of curved 12 mm (½ in) glass sheets. Every 2 m (6.5 ft) the same element is inserted between the two skin structures: five cast steel arms, anchored in the tubular nucleus and deriving from the fastening mount for the glass panels, and providing support for the metal access gratings. An atomizing ring completes the unit. The pressure variations are converted by electronic barometric units and microprocessors into signals which activate the atomizing process inside the cylinder at the appropriate height. A curtain of blue tinted water then appears, flowing against the glass, and evoking memories of the ancient invention by Torricelli.

DRTE Arles

Jacques Filippi

Location: Quartier Fourchon 13200, Arles, France. **Date of completion**: 1995. **Client**: Bouches du Rhône Département. **Architect**: Jacques Filippi. **Associates**: Gay Puig (assignment supervisor), Marciano (structural engineers), Garcia (plumbing and air-conditioning), A.S. Ingenierie (electricity), Teste (landscaping). **Scheme**: Building for the Arles Directorate of Roadways, Transport, and Equipment. **Photography**: DRTE.

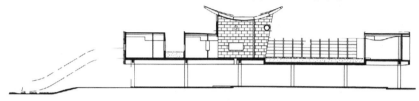

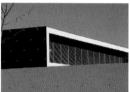

The DRTE (Directorate of Roadways, Transport, and Equipment) is not a part of either the city or the countryside, but serves the border in between, where appearances take on great importance, turning into issues of urgent and immediate consideration. Filippi understands that in certain landscapes it is not possible to take the architecture as a starting point for action, since the impressions created have nothing to do with the geometry or the topography, nor with an urban environment. The interior of this building is dominated by intense and vivid colors, with marked contrasts as a feature. As is the case throughout almost the whole region, the groundwater level is almost at the surface, and in this case is a mere 50 cm (20 in) below ground. This means that the site is virtually a marsh, and underpinning was carried out by driving piles down to depths of up to 15 m (50 ft) below surface level. The structure is a grid pattern of rounded columns, measuring 7 x 6 m (23 x 20 ft). The level of the floor slab was raised by a metre (3 ft) to avoid flooding, and the space created beneath the office block is used for parking. The lines of cars are interrupted by a number of elements painted in bright primary colors, accommodating the elevator, store rooms, and technical installations.

Punta Nariga Lighthouse

César Portela

Location: Costa da Morte, Galicia, Spain. **Date of completion**: 1994. **Client**: Autonomous State Port Authority and Spanish Port Authority. **Architect**: César Portela. **Associates**: F. Garrido, I.A. Suárez (technical systems), C. González (basic engineering), M. Cola (sculptural architecture), A. Oca, A. Carro (works supervision). **Scheme**: Construction of a maritime guidance and navigation marker lighthouse. **Photography**: Leopoldo Aloryo-Lamberti.

The lighthouse is located at Punta Nariga, on the cliffs of the Costa da Morte. It is a traditional design, not for the sake of creating a simple classic image, but rather to achieve permanence founded on construction techniques well suited to the conditions imposed by the location, as well as to complement the natural landscape and seascape in which it is set. The height of the focal plane is 50 m (120 ft), and it has a geographical range of 37 km (23 miles), a light beam range of 35 km (22 miles), and a beam intensity of 300,000 candlepower.

The structure is formed from three well-defined elements. The first of these is a platform which allows for public access. The triangular slab forming this platform also serves as the base for the lighthouse tower. One of its vertical elements merges with the natural rock; another rises above the level of the ground, like the arris profile of a medieval bastion; and the third emerges above the cliff, crowned by a bronze adornment resembling the figurehead of a ship. The second element, in the shape of a prism and likewise with a triangular base, reflected in the interior, accommodates the areas used for the technical installations and storage on the first level, with the second being used for the lighthouse keeper's accommodation. The whole is surmounted by a flat cover piece, which, being accessible, becomes an observation platform rising 7 m (23 ft) above the element beneath. It is the third element which forms the lighthouse shaft.

Offices

Dynamic action, flexibility, communications, and flow – all terms used to define the designs for the offices included in this section. Technology now comes to the aid of those working at tasks which were hitherto monotonous and solitary, and offices are no longer the exclusive domain of the bosses. Instead, the areas destined for office use have become the venue in which both ideas and products are created. The image created by the office is studied in minute detail, with the same care that goes into designing a logo or planning a publicity campaign. Taken all in all, the exterior and interior of an office reflect equally the true spirit of the company.

Riddell's

William P. Bruder

Location: Jackson Hole, Wyoming, USA. **Date of completion**: 1995. **Client**: Riddell's advertising and design agency. **Architect**: William P. Bruder. **Associates**: Ed Ewers, Dewayne Smyth, Maryann Bloomfield (design team). **Scheme**: Offices, meeting and conference rooms, library, and services. **Photography**: Bill Timmerman (also pp 632/633).

This is a three-floor office block, constructed for an advertising agency in Jackson Hole, located in the city's new commercial district, an area where the human imprint has not changed the attractive natural conditions of the surrounding landscape. It features an atrium to the full height of the three floors, a vertical space lit by a rising casement window, long and narrow, which, on reaching the roof, unfolds and is transformed into a light well. This open space is the nucleus of the whole structure, with the offices arranged around it. Riddell's advertising agency is located fronting onto a bend in the highway, and the façade reflects this shape. The remaining lines which delineate the building are determined by nonorthogonal geometry, a feature often encountered in Bruder's designs. The walls are placed in perspective, and jointed, which incurs a number of inevitable implications as far as spatial relationships are concerned: the space is rendered more dynamic, and its perception is distorted. Immediate comprehension is altered, and the space is expanded or reduced, depending on whether the walls are opening out or closing in; all these are changes which play with depth perception. The building echoes the architecture of the farms, ranches, and hay barns which proliferate in the region and are such a characteristic feature of the countryside. We can therefore speak of contextualization, in this case being understood as an imitation of a given situation, specific to the location in which the project has been created. But, in turn, this is also an image which is decontextualized, in that Riddell's is plainly not a hay barn, even though the façade overlooking the road takes its shape from that prototype.

Republic Plaza

Kisho Kurokawa architects & associates

Location: Singapore. **Date of completion**: 1995. **Architect**: Kisho Kurokawa. **Associates**: Tatsuaki Tanaka, Akira Yokohama, Hiroshi Kanematsu, Kazunori Uchida, Masahiro Kamei, Nobuo Abe, Yukio Yoshida, Ichiro Tanaka, Naotake Uekei, Iwao Miura. **Scheme**: 66 floors of offices and residential apartments. **Photography**: Musao Sudo.

As is the case with many other skyscrapers, the tower is matched by a lower body element, in this case a five-story podium. The podium is used for banking offices, and the tower for rented offices. On the eastern side, facing Raffles Place, is a cantilever canopy for vehicle reception. The columns of the building define an exterior portico corridor which provides access to the interior and the transitional area. The remainder of the first floor forms a reception area around the nucleus, accommodating the set of elevators. This nucleus element, which is repeated on all the floors, forms a central square rotated through 45°. The building podium is also connected to the reception area. On the northeast side is another canopy, and a number of escalators which convey pedestrians to the underground levels through a broad opening. The first basement floor offers a wide variety of shops and restaurants, and is linked to the subway terminus located beneath Raffles Place. The building, with a total of 66 floors, is surmounted by the residential accommodation of the owner, at the very peak of the structure.

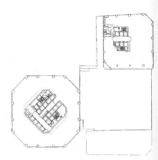

BBDO West

Beckson Design Associates

Location: Los Angeles, USA. **Date of completion**: 1995. **Client**: David Lubars (BBDO). **Architects**: Michael L. Beckson, Steven C. Heisler, Ed Gabor. **Associates**: LaSalle Construction (construction); The Sheridan Group (fixtures and fittings); Frederick Russell Brown & Associates (equipment); Nabih Youssef & Associates (structural engineers). **Photography**: Tom Bonner.

The old offices were completely demolished, and two stories created out of three. The strategy was to create a more concentrated working space, with a greater sense of action and dynamism. The architectural project was developed in parallel with a restructuring of the company: the old hierarchical organization, based on independent departments and closed offices, was replaced by open spaces and flexible teams of personnel, grouped on the basis of the clients being serviced. Even the President occupies a working area of the same dimensions as the rest of the staff. In the President's words: "...in our old offices, people wasted a lot of time at meetings. There was a lot of talk about what was going to be done, but there wasn't a whole lot of work actually being done. Beckson were asked whether they could come up with a solution which would bring people together as if they were in a meeting the whole time. As a result, communications happen by osmosis, due to the simple fact that you can see and hear the work other people are doing."

Lagertechnik office and parking lot

Baumschlager & Eberle

Location: Wolfurt, Austria. **Date project begun**: 1993. **Date of construction**: 1994. **Architects**: Carlo Baumschlager, Dietmar Eberle. **Associates**: Rainer Huchler, Ernst Mader (structural engineers). **Scheme**: Offices and parking lot. **Photography**: Eduard Hueber.

The shape of the structure was dictated by its location, the need for possible extensions, and the requirement for a private parking lot at a high level, a symbolic and promotional feature of Lagertechnik Wolfurt. The location is defined by a number of sharply differentiated features: densely populated urban areas to the south, the highway to the north, the elevated section of the freeway to the east, and farmland to the west. Against such a diverse background, each face of the building seeks to echo its immediate surroundings. The concrete structure is defined by a clear octagonal layout, the lighting of which allows for maximum flexibility of use.

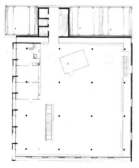

Cristal

Samyn and Partner

Location: Brussels, Belgium. Date of completion: 1998. **Client**: Immobiliere Bernheim-Outremer, s.a. **Architect**: Samyn and Partner. **Associates**: Setesco (structural engineers), SECO (general supervision), VENAC (acoustics). **Scheme**: Remodeling to create a new residential and office building. **Photography**: Ch. Bastin, J. Evrard.

The project included the restoration of three houses, the construction of a luxurious office block, and the landscaping of the surrounding public areas. The narrow nature of the site and the need to restore the three adjacent houses as part of the project allowed little freedom for the design. A context of

this type requires a clear expression of the function, with particular attention being paid to the scale of the building and the way it might be read, both from a distance as well as close at hand. Neighboring office buildings are higher, while the line of the façade is set back. In order to make the façade waterproof, it was converted into a roof surface, curved and asymmetric, in such a way as to reduce the dimensions of the building. This allows for a simpler transition between buildings of such different types, which characterize the two avenues. The

double curve of the roof also determines the scale of the building and adds interest to the diagonal view from the Avenue de la Joyeuse Entrée; this also reduces the shadowing caused by the façades of the neighboring buildings to a minimum. The outside of the structure is composed of horizontal lines of transparent and reflective glass panels. The project also involved the immediate surroundings, including a square for public use to close off the Avenue de Michel-Ange.

Central Plaza

T.R. Hamzah & Yeang

Location: Kuala Lumpur, Malaysia. **Date of completion**: 1996. **Architects**: T.R. Hamzah & Yeang. **Scheme**: Office building with swimming pool on the top floor. **Photography**: T.R. Hamzah & Yeang Sdn. Bhd.

The main interest in this project derives from a series of maneuvers conducted at the outset on the narrow prism structure. The building required bracing in the transverse direction to the prism due to structural problems involving resistance to the horizontal loads caused by the wind. This bracing arrangement was resolved by concentrating all the diagonal bracing elements required on the outside of the front faces, so guaranteeing the stability of the structure and contributing to its outer appearance. In order to avoid the excessive solar radiation encountered in this part of the world, the working areas of the offices were oriented to the north, introducing a degree of volumetric play into the plan of the façade in the area of the stairwell to the terrace roof.

A series of garden arrangements on each floor extends upwards across the façade, ultimately meeting the greenery surrounding the swimming pool on the top floor. The west side, which encountered problems due to excessive sunlight, is separated from the main body of the structure in order to provide shade on the enclosed area within, and to introduce an interplay of light and shade on this façade. The higher floors are provided with a system of sunshades, which are supported on a structure which rotates gently. The north façade, with a subtle curve entirely in glazing, provides a panoramic city view.

Remodeling an attic space in Vienna

Coop Himmelb(l)au

Location: Vienna, Austria. **Date of completion**: 1990. **Architects**: Coop Himmelb(l)au (Wolf D. Prix, Helmut Swiczinsky). Floor area: 4000 m² (43,000 ft²). **Photography**: Coop Himmelb(l)au.

of irregular terraced roof, suspended by a system of cables and braces. Glass is the key material in this structure, which forms an enclosure in which concrete and cement serve as the directing elements. To avoid excessive sunlight, the architects arranged blinds over the larger part of the glazed surfaces, while in the interior the predominant color on ceilings and walls is white. The floors present a myriad of materials, ranging from the warmth of parquet to the fragility of ceramics, in this case in a gentle grayish tone.

The principal element in the complex is the meeting room or conference hall located right in the middle of the corner area being remodeled. This opens to the outside via a number of large glazed spaces, and by a door with direct access to a surrounding terrace. The architects topped this central element with a type

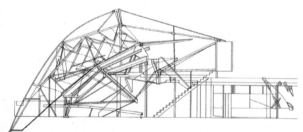

Banks

Money has not always been associated
with good taste, and the same is true of
architecture. Traditionally, the biggest
budgets have not always translated into
the best designs, still less into the greatest
innovations in the field of architecture. In
any event, it is certain that banks, deeply
involved in their mergers and acquisitions,
still need somewhere to carry out and
centralize their operations. Moving on
from the names traditionally associated
with bank buildings (Rocco Sen-Kee Yim,
Nikken Sekkei, Kohn, Pederson & Fox, for
example), there has been a succession of
new figures winning commissions for
constructing headquarters for some of the
big banks, such as Norman Foster with the
Commerzbank in Frankfurt, Kenzo Tange
and the OUB in Singapore, or I.M. Pei and
the Bank of China in Hong Kong.

Commerzbank

Norman Foster and Partners

Location: Frankfurt, Germany. **Date project begun**: 1992. **Date of completion**: 1997. **Client**: Commerzbank.
Architect: Sir Norman Foster and Partners. **Scheme**: Ecological office building.

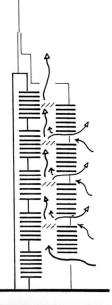

This project is the largest commissioned by the city of Frankfurt in recent decades, and represents a prime example of a skyscraper designed in line with ecological criteria. Each office is designed to provide natural ventilation through practically designed windows, which also serve to provide fine views of the city and of the landscaped courtyards in the form of cloisters located on every floor of the building. The relationship with the other buildings in the area is of great importance: the perimeter of the block has been rebuilt in the form of a low block which accommodates parking facilities and apartments, levelling up the height of the street and restoring the scale of the whole district. The tower itself, which is triangular in section, merges neatly with the existing buildings as well as with the new residential block, to smooth its passage into the urban context in such a way that it is only from the main access, on the north side, that we appreciate the tower in its full height from ground level. From Grosse Gallusstrasse, with its heavy flow of traffic, a grand stairway rises up, opening into a new public space dedicated to the city.

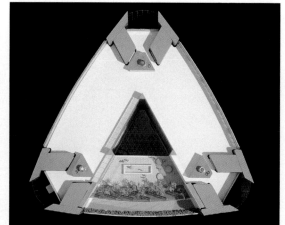

Citibank Plaza

Rocco Sen-Kee Yim

Location: Hong Kong. **Date of completion**: 1992. **Architect**: Rocco Sen-Kee Yim. **Scheme**: Building to accommodate the offices of Citibank in Hong Kong. **Photography**: Rocco Design Limited.

Known as plot 8888, the site chosen by Citibank Plaza to build its headquarters was the best and biggest in the Central district of Hong Kong. One of the aims of the new bank project was to avoid the indifference evoked by the agglomeration of tall buildings in the centres of major cities – buildings which totally ignore one another. Citibank wanted to demonstrate awareness of the massive presence of the nearby Bank of China, but at the same time sought to avoid direct confrontation; rather, it was looking for a play of contrasts with the existing building, using this juxtaposition as its main

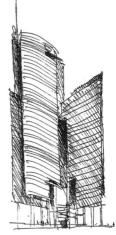

argument. To achieve this, it set the bulk of Citibank Plaza apart from its immediate surroundings, concentrating its mass on the farthest end of the site and leaving a south-facing plaza between the two structures. In addition to this, it was decided to split the building up in terms of volume, creating a division between two separate towers of 40 and 50 stories respectively. The architect opted for a "constructive synthesis," with a collage of unstable elements interacting to create a dynamic whole.

DG Bank Headquarters

Kohn, Pedersen & Fox

Location: Frankfurt, Germany. **Date of completion**: 1993. **Architects**: Kohn, Pedersen & Fox. **Scheme**: Offices of the DG Bank, with space for leased offices, a hotel, apartments, restaurants, and commercial areas. **Photography**: Dennis Gilbert.

In 1987 the DG Bank issued an invitation to tender for the construction of their headquarters in Frankfurt. What was required was a complex arrangement which would include, in addition to the offices belonging to the Bank itself, space for leased offices, a hotel, apartments, and commercial areas. It would be built in the central district near the train station, gracing the city's commercial artery, the Mainzer Landstrasse. The commission was placed with the American team of Kohn, Pederson & Fox, who developed an ambitious scheme: a floor area of 77,000 m² (830,000 ft²) and the tower housing the Bank's headquarters, at 208 m (680 ft), being the highest structure in the city. The complex location of the site provided the keys for implementing the scheme: it formed part of a new concentration of high rise blocks around the train station, in a quiet residential area. The great tower soars above all the buildings fronting onto the main road, while the other structures form a lower L shape surrounding the tower, accommodating the entrance linking to the immediately adjacent residential district. The scheme departs from the traditional skyscraper arrangement at the lower levels as well as in the tower, in order to respond to the heterogeneous nature of this largely concrete part of the city. This reaction to the urban context is provided not only on the basis of distribution within the block, but by creating in the interior a mixed complex of different uses, meeting the needs of this area of Frankfurt's central business district.

Long-term Credit Bank

Nikken Sekkei

Location: Chiyoda Ward, Tokyo, Japan. **Date of completion**: 1994. **Client**: Long-term Credit Bank of Japan. **Architect**: Nikken Sekkei. **Associates**: Takenaka Corporation (construction). **Photography**: Nácasa & Partners.

This 20-story building is located in the center of Tokyo, next to Hibiya Park. The T-shaped structure allows for the base of the tower to be much narrower than the rest of the building, which has made it possible for a small plaza to be created in front of the façade. Part of this plaza is occupied by two enormous glass boxes, 30 m (100 ft) high, which accommodate the access vestibules for the offices. The T shape represents a technical feat in itself (a computer was used to check the moment of rotation of the projecting elements), as well as being a demonstration of power. The result is that all the areas for public use are of a very special and spectacular character; the top floor is the most striking in this respect. The two ends of the building offer splendid panoramic views of the city of Tokyo, and accommodate a conference room and a reception hall 12 m high.

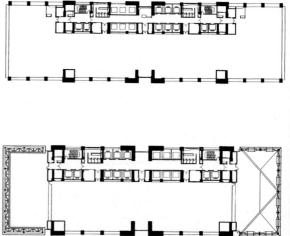

ING Bank

Erick van Egeraat

Location: Paulay Ede Utca 12, Budapest, Hungary. **Date of completion**: 1995. **Client**: Nationale Nederlanden Hungary Ltd., Budapest (J. Szamel); ING Bank, Budapest (Tibor E. Rejto); ING Real Estate, The Hague (P. Koch, Jan Everts). **Architect**: Erick van Egeraat. **Associates**: ABT Adviesburo voor Bouwtechniek b.v., Delft (structural engineers); Ketel Raadgevend ingenieurs b.v., Delft (mechanical and electrical services); Permasteelisa, Conegliano (glass construction); Henk Bouwer, Avi Lev, Delft (models). **Photography**: Christian Richters (also pp 650/651).

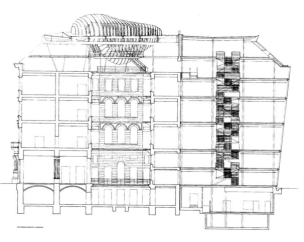

The building, located in the financial district of the Hungarian capital, dates from the end of the 19th century, and the façade contains elements of classicism and of Art Nouveau. The scheme involved the conversion of this residential building into the Budapest central offices of the Nationale Nederlanden Hungary and the ING Bank. The hall is an independent element, conceived as a separate spatial unit, which leads us through time from the *fin de siècle* to the present day. Emerging from the roof is the grand cupola in the shape of a "whale," which is invisible from the street. This whale-like volume, with its irregular curves, accommodates the conference room and, in a corner, the café. Its frame is formed by 26 laminated timber elements supported on a steel structure; a number of 400 mm (1 in) laminated glass beams, 3.5 m (11.5 ft) long, support a transparent glass curtain which creates the illusion of a great leviathan of the ocean deep.

Bank of China

Pei Cobb Freed & Partners

Location: Hong Kong, China. **Date of completion**: 1991. **Client**: Bank of China. **Architect**: Pei Cobb Freed & Partners. **Scheme**: 70-story building for the central offices of the Bank of China in Hong Kong. **Photography**: P. Warchol.

The Bank of China is an example of how the layering of uses in a building starts as a study in technical and functional planning to complement the intensity so characteristic of the urban environment, without reproducing the negative effects of its usual disorder. The creation of skyscrapers is intended to disassociate the resultant vertical arrangement of business centers from the idea of structural vacuity and monotonous, formal uniformity (void areas surrounding a nucleus). The fine façade of aluminum and glass is an external reflection of its complex structural system, spread among its 70 stories, while at the same time being a manifestation of a pure geometry based on asymmetry, an example of the fertile integration of

architecture and engineering.

The structural building rises on the site (with a total floor area of 132,895 m², 1.43 million ft²) from a base formed by four massive pillars, with anchor points in a cube 5.5 m (18 ft) in width, four stories high, which forms the geometrical base of the structure. Avenues and thoroughfares for pedestrians surround the building, urban gardens, rendered harmonious by greenery and cascades of water; these serve a double function, acting also as a barrier against the intense noise in the area.

OUB Center

Kenzo Tange Associates

Location: Singapore. **Date of completion**: 1986. **Client**: Overseas Union Bank. **Architect**: Kenzo Tenge Associates. **Scheme**: Headquarters of the OU Bank, offices, commercial center, apartments, and outside gardens. **Photography**: Osamu Murai.

The Overseas Union Bank fronts onto Raffles Place, and, at 280 m (920 ft), represents the tallest bank headquarters in Asia. The OUB Center is a slender building created from an interweaving of triangular prisms of differing heights and sizes. The largest is also the highest, and presents a tapering edge across the entire width of the structure, forming a visual extension of the axis of the road beneath. The smallest-dimensioned prism is the lowest, and is attached to the main prism element but without becoming entangled with it. As the base of the building, a low structure extends across the whole frontage of Raffles Place as far as the central train station, while a footbridge connects the atrium with a public parking lot for 3000 automobiles. The architect plays with the triangular shapes of the prisms in their double embodiment of flat planes and sharp edges, based on minimal manipulation of the elements' dimensions, emphasizing each of their formal qualities so as to adapt to differing urban contexts prevalent in this area of Singapore.

Corporate buildings

The corporate buildings described in this
section consist of offices and their ancillary
services, such as restaurants, conference
rooms, bars, and so on, as well as the
areas around them, in the form of parks or
squares. This type of architectural
combination provides accommodation for
companies, and, apart from fulfilling a
variety of different functions, these
buildings also serve as publicity generators
in their own right: in other words, they put
across a specific image which represents
the interests and the distinctive features of
the company. In this context, the work of
the architect is based on a clear
understanding with the client, and the
design will be the materialization of ideas
born of the dialog between them. There
are two clear objectives: first, to construct
a complex which will incorporate concepts
of functional performance and comfort,
and, second, to create an exclusive and
communicative symbol to elicit recognition
on the formal level.

Jean-Baptiste Berlier Industrial Hotel

Dominique Perrault

Location: Paris, France. **Date of planning**: 1986–1988. **Date of construction**: 1988–1990. **Client**: Société Anonyme de Gestion Immobilière. **Architect**: Dominique Perrault. **Scheme**: Industrial premises, restaurants, and parking lots. **Gross floor area**: 21,000 m² (226,000 ft²). **Photography**: Michael Denancé.

In 1986 the Paris City Council and the Société Anonyme de Gestion Immobilière issued an invitation to tender for a new building: an industrial hotel. Intended neither as an office block nor as an industrial building, it was to be simply a space, intelligently used and capable of accommodating a wide variety of activities. This not only involved providing a design for a new building, but the actual choice of site called for a specific solution in a difficult area between the ring road encircling Paris and the railroad tracks running from the Gare d'Austerlitz station. Given the apparent chaos of this situation, the clarity of Dominique Perrault's vision lends the area a whole new identity. The building provides 17,000 m² (183,000 ft²) of space for industrial operations of various sizes. What is provided is simply a space between wrought iron partitions, connected to the utilities. No other conditions are imposed other than the actual limitations of the block and the communications systems.

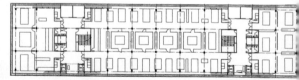

Centraal Beheer extension

Herman Hertzberger

Location: Apeldoorn, The Netherlands. **Date of completion**: 1995. **Client**: Centraal Beheer. **Architect**: Hermann Hertzberger. **Associates**: Dolf Floors, Dickens van der Werff, Jan van den Berg, Arienne Matser. **Scheme**: Reception area, visitors' area, function rooms, conference rooms, and services. **Photography**: Lock Images.

During the 1960s and 1970s, Hertzberger, through the medium of the journal *Forum* (edited jointly by Bakema and Van Eyck), studied the application to architecture of structuralist philosophy. He was seeking to create objective spatial structures which would respond to a previous and underlying arrangement of structures, before actually defining any specific elements. In other words, the first phase of the project, and the most important, consists of defining the fundamental structures of the architectural language, and establishing a syntax. Based on this, the building then develops in much the same way as a written text. Phrases are constructed on the site, based on the combination of the basic elements: windows, doors, furnishings, walls, rooms, stairways, office blocks, etc. The building which houses the headquarters of the Centraal Beheer in Apeldoorn is a clear example of structural architecture: its small, polyvalent units, subject to different interpretations

depending on the functional needs, are arranged on an orthogonal latticework, which makes the provision of subsequent extensions an easy task. The extension completed in 1995, however, represents a revision of all these theories. The structural techniques, the aesthetics, and, above all, the latent philosophy running through all these projects, spanning 25 years, is absolutely distinct.

Hertzberger's project involves the construction of a central building and an entrance area; being specifically areas which do not exist in structuralist architecture, they seem to grow like a woven fabric or a net.

One of the most arresting features is the design of the stairwells: they are all different, designed as unique, almost sculptural objects.

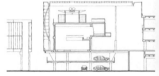

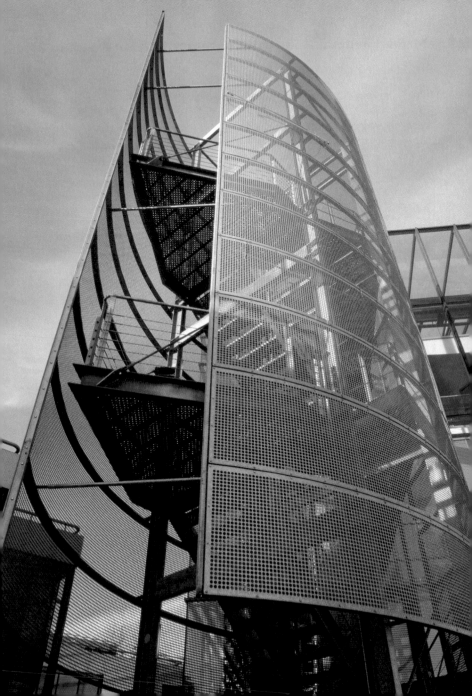

German Federal Railways Customer Service Building

Rhode Kellermann Wawrowsky

Location: Duisburg, Germany. **Date of construction**: 1998. **Consultants**: Arup GmbH (structural engineers), EGL (landscaping). **Design team**: Rhode Kellermann Wawrowsky. **Area**: 32,500 m² (350,000 ft²). **Scheme**: Offices and services. **Photography**: Holger Knauf.

Built on the site of a former locomotive repair workshop, this office building is arranged along a curved axis 220 m (720 ft) long. Opening off this central three-story corridor are 11 separate structures, creating a zig-zag line. This helps create a larger façade area, allowing all the offices to have windows and a view outside. This backbone structure also allows for the building to be extended at its ends. In addition, each of the peninsular buildings is organized around a central atrium. At the time of its construction, this building represented one of the most technologically advanced and best equipped centers of its kind, in operation 24 hours a day, providing important customer service.

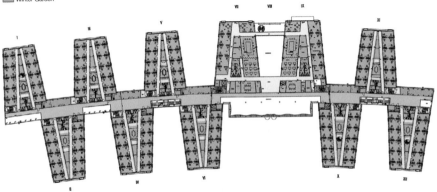

Office area

Plant + WC

Circulation area / Stairs / Lifts

Circulation area backbone

Training

Winter Garden

I   III   V   VII   VIII   IX   XI

II   IV   VI   X   XII

Oracle

Gensler

Location: Redwood Shores, California, USA. **Date of construction**: 1989–1998. **Client**: Oracle Corporation. **Architect**: Gensler. **Associates**: William Wilson & Ass. (contractors), Seccombe Design International (interiors). **Scheme**: Campus for the facilities of a leading software company: office buildings, conference and press center, gymnasium, parking lots, and exterior landscaping. **Photography**: Gensler.

In the mid-1980s a Canadian entrepreneur purchased this site in the popular tourist area of Redwood Shores, California. Gensler became involved with the project for reorganizing the area and converting it into the Centrum Business Park. Today, 11 years later, the final phase of the project is being brought to a conclusion. With six office buildings, covering a total area of 1.6 million m² (17.2 million ft²), a conference and press center, gymnasium, and four parking lots, the site has recently been converted into the headquarters of the Oracle Corporation, a leading software producer. The first building to be developed on the campus was the "access" structure, which now accommodates the Oracle executive offices. Architecturally speaking, the design is based on simple geometrical forms: a rectangular block supported by two cylinders, projecting an image which is both striking and strong. This building faces the lake, with which it interacts by way of its blue-green glass panels. With one single exception, the remaining office buildings are designed on the basis of a simple cylinder, 3.5 m (11.5 ft) in diameter, which intersects with a rectangular block, forming a 45° angle. This sole exception is an office block which retains the cylindrical element of its neighbors but has a completely different curved shape, giving contrast in the layout.

The Digital City

Studio Naço (Alain Renk, Marcelo Joulia)

Location: Villeneuve-d'Ascq, France. **Date of completion**: 1994. **Client**: 3 Suisses. **Architect**: Studio Naço (Alain Renk, Marcelo Joulia). **Associates**: Jean-François Pasqualini, Allard Kuyken, Beatrice Berián (architects), Muriel Quintanilla (designer), Olivier Dubos (graphics). **Gross floor area**: 8000 m² (86,000 ft²). **Photography**: Mario Pignata-Monti (also pp 668/669).

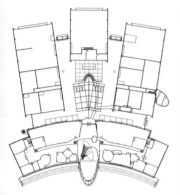

This building is dedicated to the creation and production of new images, whether printed on paper or distributed in multimedia and Internet formats. The offices are occupied by artistic directors, photographers, graphics designers, and all kinds of state-of-the-art technological equipment, virtual sets, and image banks. The type of relationships established between the people working there, the links with technology, and the transmission of information in ways other than the traditional, all have an unmistakable impact on the way in which the space is occupied. Given this context, Studio Naço have been obliged to recast their work as architects in order to face up to the challenge of this project. In this sense, their strategy has come closer to that of creators of images rather than constructors of buildings which are standardized, ordered, and typified. They seek to provoke an emotional response in the people using their architectural structures, and to create sensations by implementing unique spatial ideas and forms which are very unusual.

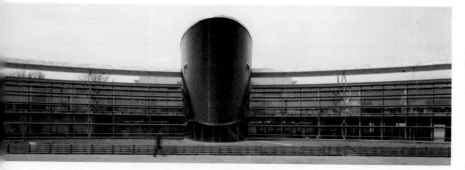

NTT Office Center

César Pelli & Partners, Fred W. Clarke

Location: Tokyo, Japan. **Date of construction**: 1990–1995. **Architects**: César Pelli & Partners, Fred W. Clarke. **Scheme**: Office for NTT, conference hall, telecommunications center, restaurant, and garden landscaping. **Photography**: Misuo Matsuoka, Kanedi Monma, César Pelli.

the conference hall, and, above these, the employees' restaurant. The building is divided into two clearly distinct parts: a strip section curving above the interior garden, intended for office use, and a triangular area with its façade facing outwards, grouping the services and communications nuclei.

On top of the initial rectangular shape, the architects set about enveloping the building to the greatest possible extent, pulling back from the borders of the site and with the edges rounded symmetrically on the side facing the highway. The scheme is divided into two buildings, presenting their exterior façades on this line. One tower is a slender entity merging with its plinth in the parking area, with a low body element in the rounded area of the elevated highway. A break in the construction of the perimeter allows a glimpse from the road of the interior; this interior is formed by an intermediate space providing a public garden that opens in a fan

shape from the entrance in the lower part of the façade, moving into the area delimited by the enveloping structure until the opposite face is reached, above the residential area. The lower body element is supported on the rounded façade, and accommodates a commercial center three stories in height, faced in Minnesota stone in a delicate warm pink color; this extends along the entire plinth of the building, seeking to provide continuity for the envelope. The tower rises 30 stories above ground level for use as offices, and six floors below ground to accommodate, at the deepest levels, the telecommunications center,

Leybold AG Headquarters

Günter Behnisch

Location: Werk in Alzernau. **Date of completion**: 1991. **Architect**: Günter Behnisch. **Scheme**: Headquarters of Leybold AG. **Photography**: Christian Kandzia.

Leybold AG manufactures innovative, high quality machinery, focusing in particular on the production of prototypes. The headquarters building consists of a circular entrance in the north, from which point the route proceeds via an escalator, above a light moquette floor occupying level +1. This gives access to all the functional areas: office levels +2 and +3, by means of regularly arranged vertical access elements; and the laboratory and production areas via communicating passages and stairways descending to level 0, which also accommodates the product reception and dispatch areas. In this way, the functions are separated into the different heights: clean production below, and the office areas above, independent and free of intersection. Thanks to this arrangement, it was possible to install one single, straightforward ventilation and dust filter system for the laboratory and production hall, in such a way as to allow the users to achieve clean-room conditions for their own equipment, easily and accurately. The office and production areas are linked visually by generous expanses of glass, with the marketing center (level +3) added in the form of a gallery, and the design facilities located below (level +2). The three office floors above are accessed by spiral stairways. The laboratory is designed to be self-sufficient and independent of the other sections. Finally, the outer bastion elements are of crucial importance, given their unifying role in enveloping the whole of the complex whatever its orientation or purpose.

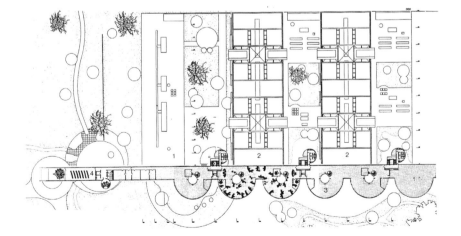

Apple offices, UK

Jamie Troughton & John McAslan

Location: Heathrow, London, UK. **Date of construction**: 1987–1989. **Client**: Stockley Park Consortium Ltd. and Apple Computers UK Ltd. **Architects**: Jamie Troughton & John McAslan. **Associates**: Nick Midgley, Aidan Potter, Jonathan Parr, Mark Wilson, Martin Campbell, Stephen Pimbley, Bobbye Desai, Birgit Klauk, Judy Slater. **Photography**: Peter Cook-Arcaid.

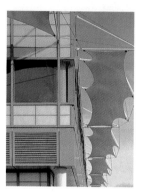

The complex consists of a large parallel piped block, divided into two surfaces. The interior is arranged around a central thoroughfare which acts as a separator and distributor of the space, dividing it longitudinally; the lighting blocked by its central arrangement is replaced by using a number of high skylights, which at the same time add structure to the roof. The façade has an outer design of great simplicity, born of the symmetrical and regular organization of the general layout. The main access, from the southern slope, gives onto a large reception area, from where connections are provided to the communal services. The two prism elements form an adjunct to the general structure of the

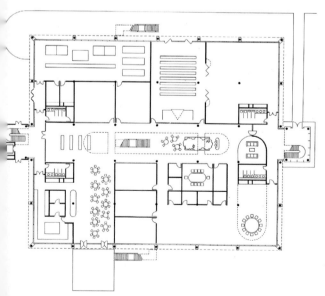

building on its eastern and western faces, and contain stairwells to provide communication between the floors, strengthened by the exteriors on the north and south elevations of the complex. The wing forms the link with the parking lot, completing the process of connection between the distinct elements of the building. On the top floor of the structure are the operational and administration areas, following a symmetrical arrangement which takes good advantage of the glazing of the general façade of the building.

IBM Solana

Peter Walker, William Johnson & Partners

Location: Dallas, Texas, USA. **Date of completion**: 1987. **Architects**: Peter Walker, William Johnson & Partners. **Client**: IBM Corporation and the Maguire Thomas Partnership. **Associates**: Ricardo Legorreta Architects, Mitchell/Giurgola Architects, Leason Pomeroy and Associates, Harwood K. Smith & Partners (planning); Carter and Burgess, Inc. (engineering). **Scheme**: Office center for IBM in California; exterior landscaping. **Photography**: Dixi Carrillo, Hargreaves Associates, Jim Heidrich, David Walker.

The general layout of the suburb of Solana has been in the form of sequential expansion of the three main functional sectors, starting from the access area from Federal Highway 114. These sectors are: the residential and recreational areas, the work of Ricardo Legorreta Architects; the commercial center, designed by the same company; and the administrative complex and regional headquarters of IBM, the creation of Mitchell/Giurgola Architects. The respect accorded to the essentially rural atmosphere of the locality has had a major effect on the project. The way in which the building structures are spread out, and the access routes around them, is characterized by taking the existing landscape into careful consideration. Entry to the residential area is gained from the highway ramp, across what has been dubbed Arrivals Garden, an area in which the spirit of the countryside predominates, although with a certain degree of styling mixed in: red stucco walls and the monolithic, vertical effect of the slender towers, in their vivid and varied colors. In the recreation and commercial areas, the idea of sequential perception has been carefully cultivated, together with the dramatic entrance experience. Components such as arcades, vertical towers, plazas, interior patios opening into the natural landscape, or sculpture gardens have been used. In the corporate complex, the radial arrangement of the modules favors integration with the surroundings. The presence of water, a constant feature throughout the whole of the development, plays a very important part in this sector in particular – which features a triangular pond, from where water flows into a magnificent lake of naturalistic design – as well as the vital practical role of providing the water supply.

TRW Central Office

Sasaki Associates

Location: Lyndhurst, Ohio, USA. **Date of construction**: 1989. **Architect**: Sasaki Ass. Inc. **Scheme**: Garden and landscaping design for a corporate center. **Photography**: Sasaki Associates.

Sasaki Associates were entrusted with landscaping the new TRW headquarters in a rural setting in Lyndhurst, Ohio. With an area of 49 ha (120 acres), the site was an old ranch with an extremely diverse topography. The design of the facilities has preserved and enhanced this landscape, integrating the roadways, buildings, services, and characteristics of the existing environment in a compatible and sensitive way, with minimal effect on the nearby residential areas. The greater part of the land consists of meadows surrounded by ancient woodlands. One striking natural feature is the Euclid river, which crosses the site; the seasonal floods have produced a range of gullies and ravines across the width of the area, creating a variety of natural landscapes. In order to preserve the existing qualities and character, Sasaki Associates and Urban Forest Management (Prairie View, Illinois) have established a register of more than 2500 trees on the site.

British Airways offices ("Waterside")

Niels A. Torp

Location: Heathrow, London, UK. **Date of construction**: 1992–1998. **Client**: British Airways. **Architect**: Niels A. Torp. **Associates**: Land USE Consultants (landscaping). **Area**: 105,000 m² (1.2 million ft²). **Scheme**: Office center for British Airways, restaurant, cafeteria, small commercial center, gymnasium, bank, and conference hall.

To obtain the most rational layout possible for its operations, British Airways decided to construct its office center, with capacity for 2800 employees, immediately adjacent to Heathrow Airport. Because the area is anything but "human" in terms of environment, it was felt that this large number of people would need to have confidence in themselves and in the environment surrounding them in order to work properly both inside and outside the complex. The only inhabited area anywhere around is the village of Harmondsworth, with an entertaining pub and a small church dating from the 13th century. The village itself needed to be protected from an "invasion" of 2800 new employees. The first decision was to convert one of the areas which had not been built on into a small park with a social center for use jointly by employees and the villagers. There was still the problem, however, of how to keep so many people motivated in such an inhospitable environment, surrounded by one of the biggest airports in the world. The architects decided to give the buildings the character of a "town," and to provide the large number of users with a sense of "community." The 55,000 m² (590,000 ft²) of the office complex was accordingly divided into six buildings set out in the shape of a U, inside which was sited a free-standing pavilion; this accommodates a school, linked to a leisure area, a restaurant, and the computer center. Between this pavilion and the office facilities an elegant park is provided for the use and enjoyment of staff from the six buildings.

Convention and exhibition centers

Convention and exhibition centers and trade
fair sites are characterized by the temporary
nature of the events to which they play host.
This means that there is a very intense flow
of visitors and exhibitors passing through in
specified periods of time, with the venue
being cleared again before the next event
begins. Added to this is the fact that, born of
the desire to provide an air of exclusivity, the
associated buildings seek to be aesthetically
striking, while not overlooking their
functional purpose. Trade fair complexes in
turn are national flag bearers: they are
structures which represent a country or a
region; they are buildings which are
intended for publicity, and their architecture
must be capable of reflecting the most
significant features of the geographical area
which they represent. Over the past few
years, exhibition pavilions have proved, for
architects, to be the perfect area for
experimentation, giving them the
opportunity to test out structural solutions
and new materials alike; in short, the chance
to speak their own architectural language.

New Leipzig Trade Fair Building

Von Gerkan, Marg & Partner

Location: Leipzig, Germany. **Date of competition**: 1992. **Date of construction**: 1993–1996. **Client**: Leipziger Messegesellschaft. **Architect**: Von Gerkan, Marg & Partner. **Associates**: PBI, Klaus Glass, Büro Wronn (consultants on façade); Ian Ritchie Architects, London (structural engineers); Wehnberg, Eppinger, Schmidtke (landscaping). **Scheme**: Exhibition areas, congress center, administration area, storage facilities, and parking lot. **Photography**: Ralph Richter, Friedrich Busam/architekturphoto.

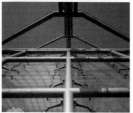

This enormous trade fair project for Leipzig continues the city's long tradition of fairs and exhibitions, and represents part of a new initiative by unified Germany to revitalize the former German Democratic Republic, East Germany, by making this fair one of the most important focal points for meetings and commercial interchange between Eastern and Western Europe.

The new fair facilities are located on the northern periphery of Leipzig, with good communications both to the main highways leading out of the city as well as to the airport. In addition to the traditional exhibition areas, the scheme also includes facilities for organizing congresses and gatherings in parallel with the fair. The central vaulted area accommodates the ticket sales counters, location boards, information points, and access to the upper area. More than 250 m (820 ft) long and 80 m (260 ft) wide, this great glazed hall is the biggest of its type ever constructed and is an impressive sight.

Tokyo International Forum

Rafael Viñoly

Location: 3-5-1 Marunouchi, Chiyoda-ku, Tokyo, Japan. **Date of competition**: November 1989. **Date of completion**: June 1997. **Client**: Metropolitan Government of Tokyo. **Architect**: Rafael Viñoly. **Associates**: Masao Shima Architects; Kunio Watanabe (Structural Design Group). **Scheme**: Four halls for theater, concerts, conferences (largest with capacity for 5000, smallest for 1500), fair site, exhibition halls, congress center, offices, commercial facilities, restaurants, and parking lot. **Total floor area**: 145,000 m² (1.56 million ft²). **Photography**: Nacasa & Partners, Tim Hursley.

In the central district of Marunouchi, in the business area and close to the commercial district of the Ginza, the site is strategically connected to the city's subway network, as well as to the railway stations of Tokyo and Yurakucho.

Right from the outset, the plan was to treat the most important sections of the scheme as separate entities. One element, on the western side, consists of the four large halls for concerts, exhibitions, and congresses, harmonizing with the surrounding urban landscape in size and linked by a common façade facing the city. The great hall, on the other side of the site next to the railroad tracks skirting the area, has an extended cylindrical shape that harmonizes perfectly with the plot perimeter. Running between the great hall and the other halls is a thoroughfare sufficiently wide to be turned into a plaza, providing a link not only between the different parts of the project but also with the rest of Tokyo, and creating a valuable space for public use in a city in which such facilities are a rare feature.

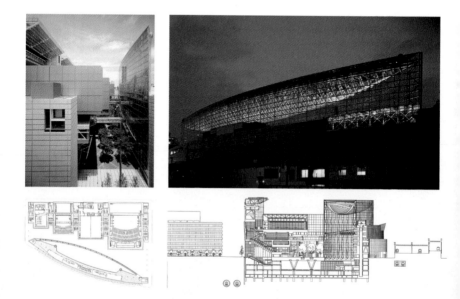

Kunibiki Trade Fair Building

Shin Takamatsu

Location: Matsue, Shimane Prefecture, Japan. **Date of construction**: 1993. **Architect**: Shin Takamatsu. **Associates**: Yamamoto-Toshibana A & E (structural engineers), Architectural Environmental Laboratory (fittings). **Floor area**: 8733 m² (94,000 ft²). **Scheme**: Exhibition hall, conference and meeting rooms, offices, and services. **Photography**: Nacasa & Partners.

This building is used for major fairs and congresses, for the everyday commercial needs of the Shimane prefectural authorities, as well as for small-scale congress events. The name Kunibiki literally means "meeting of lands," and refers to the legend of the gods of Izumo who brought the Japanese islands together to create the country. The basic thinking behind the project was to separate the different elements of the scheme and to transform them into independent structures. Accordingly, in front of the great exhibition hall there is a linear office block, at the front of which are positioned the cylindrical bodies of the conference rooms. The most outstanding feature of the trade fair building, however, is a lobby 24 m (80 ft) high, located at the front, featuring geometrical shapes suspended in the air (three cones, a sphere, a glass cube, and a cylinder), which contain the lighting elements and a tearoom providing refreshments for visitors to the building.

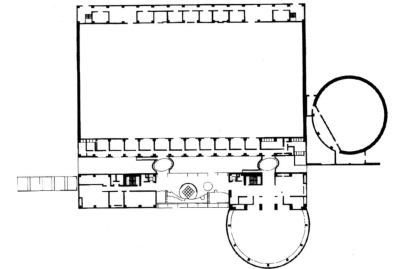

Kunibiki Trade Fair Building 701

Lille Congress Center

Rem Koolhaas

Location: Lille, France. **Date of construction**: 1994. **Architect**: Rem Koolhaas. **Scheme**: Congress halls, concert hall, and exhibition area. **Photography**: Ralph Richter/architekturphoto.

The Grand Palais congress center was essentially an OMA development. In principle it consists of a large bridge structure which links the two earlier areas, but it has evolved in such a way that it presents an ovoid form incorporating three functions: Zenith (concert hall), Congrès (congress hall) and Expo (exhibition area). The building can be adapted to different uses, with the structure becoming virtually invisible in the concert hall, yet with the exhibition area displaying a forest of columns in different sections. The roof becomes a technological landscape, which accommodates equipment, the façade itself changes depending on the internal requirements, combining metal (opaque) for the service and loading areas, plastic (semitransparent) in the section which looks out onto the city, and concrete (fire resistant).

EXPO Lisboa´98

Location: Lisbon, Portugal. **Date of construction**: 1995–1998. **Scheme**: Complex for the Universal Exhibition at Lisbon, EXPO '98. International and multitheme pavilions and commercial areas, with recreation and leisure facilities, parking lot. **Photography**: Paco Asensio.

Lisbon regarded Expo '98 as its starting point for the launch into the next millennium, and the project was planned to provide the definitive metropolitan take-off point for this Atlantic capital. Concentrated on 50 of the 300 ha (125 of the 740 acres) assigned for urban development, the Portuguese Expo involved the construction of one or two dozen self-contained units, of differing dimensions and for different uses, of which only some were demolished at the end of the event. It was then that

the site took on a second lease of life, with the new infrastructure and access created for the original event being adopted to support continued use of part of the site for the functions already assigned to it: residential use, tertiary educational purposes, or recreational facilities. Most of the theme pavilions which had been intended as permanent structures were planned with an eye to the future, which has meant that excellent results have been achieved in bringing them back to life. Portugal is the only country with its

own individual location; the other countries taking part erected their pavilions beneath the undulating covering of the new Lisbon fair site. The Expo includes, among others, the Portugal Pavilion by Alvaro Siza, the Knowledge of the Sea Pavilion by Joao Luis Carrilho da Graça, and the Oceanarium designed by Peter Chermayeff.

Cartuja 93

Corporativo

Location: Seville, Spain. **Date of construction**: 1993. **Client**: Cartuja 93. **Architects**: Corporativo. **Scheme**: Leisure and cultural area. **Photography**: Expo 92 Photographic Archive and Cartuja 93, David Cardelús.

In the case of Seville, the urban development project which provided the physical support for Expo 92 was extended into the Cartuja 93 project, with the aim of optimizing the "assets" created during the event. There were two basic objectives on which the project was focused: development of the center by way of scientific and technological innovation, and development in the metropolitan area in terms of cultural and leisure resources. The first of these involved the provision of facilities such as the science and technology park, the university campus, and the tertiary educational resource center, while the second allowed for the creation of the cultural area, linked to the monumental La Cartuja complex, a theme park, the Alamillo urban park, and other leisure and sports facilities. The construction of the island provided a miniature encapsulation of all these aims, inasmuch as it involved civil engineering works, the release of land for urban growth, and provided enrichment for the urban landscape, while at the same time keeping the natural surroundings.

Millennium Experience

Richard Rogers Partnership

Location: Greenwich, London, UK. **Date of construction**: 1996–1999. **Client**: The New Millennium Experience Company Limited. **Architect**: Richard Rogers Partnership. **Associates**: Ove Arup & Partners (supervision), Buro Happold (structural engineers and services), Fedra (fire resistance engineering), McAlpine (building contractors), Bird Air (roof), Bernard Ede (landscaping). **Scheme**: Design and construction of the site, the structure of the complex itself, and the outside installations: catering, reception area, parks, pier, exhibition areas, services. **Photography**: Grant Smith.

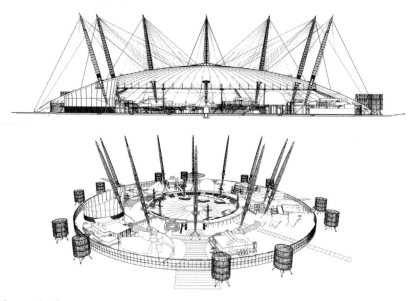

This complex for celebrating the entry into the Millennium will be inaugurated on 31 December 1999, and will play host to exhibitions and festivities marking the start of the new century. The "Millennium Dome" measures 1 km (0.6 mile) in circumference, with a diameter of 365 m (1200 ft), and maximum height of 50 m (165 ft). Its roof is suspended on a series of steel masts, 106 m (348 ft) high, and is secured by more than 70 km (42 miles) of cable. The roof is made of Teflon fibreglass, with an open space in the interior well suited for the various celebratory events. Work began in June 1997, with the construction of the main body of the complex, next to the "Millennium Pier," an artificial island, a leisure area designed in an undulating shape, with lighting and music to aid relaxation, and, finally, the Greenwich Dome, which will incorporate exhibition areas and a cafeteria. The pier (costing £2 million) is the longest of a series of state-sponsored construction projects of this type, aimed at improving river traffic through London. The artificial island (the "Living Island") has been landscaped with a number of native plant species, and is scheduled for completion in the summer of 1999, before the dome itself.

Brussels Exhibition Center. Pedestrian Route

Samyn et Associés

Location: Chaussée Romaine, Brussels, Belgium. **Date of construction**: 1995–2000. **Client**: Parc des Expositions de Bruxelles. **Architect**: Samyn et Associés. **Associates**: Setesco (stabilization), Atenco (basic engineering), Gh. André, Y. Avoiron, F. Berleur, B. de Man, J.P. Dequenne, A. d'Udekem, F. el Sayed, Th. Henrard, L. Kaisin, D. Mèlotte, N. Milo, J.Y. Naimi, N. Neuckermans, T. Provoost, J.P. Rodriguez, O. Steyaert, Ph. Samyn, B. Thimister, G. van Breedan, M. Vandeput, S. Verhulst. **Area**: 14 ha (35 acres). **Scheme**: Exhibition center, pedestrian route providing a link between halls, parking lot, business center, post office, press center, garden landscaping, crèche. **Photography**: Ch. Bastin, J. Evrard, Andrés Fernández, Bauters Sprl.

To give an idea of the enormous numbers of visitors who arrive at the complex through the North Gate (Porte Nord), the parking lot, for example, provides 12,000 spaces; more than 70% of the visitors gain access to the area through this entrance, which means one million people a year, not counting delivery trucks and vans, to visit an exhibition area of 14 ha (35 acres). Obviously, this means there is an urgent need for a large area to be created to provide reception facilities, capable of handling the massive number of people arriving through the North Gate. Those using public transport continue to enter through the gentle landscaping of the south access route.

The entrance hall of the Brussels Exhibition Center consists mainly of an enormous parabola roof in wood and glass, a structure covering a total area of approximately 26,000 m² (280,000 ft²)in latticework measuring 15 x 16.2 m (49 x 53 ft).

A thoroughfare 10 m (32 ft) wide and 90 m (292 ft) long, constructed in three sections, provides a direct link between parking lot C and the reception area. Located beneath the glazed canopy of the roof and 6 m (20 ft) above ground level is the covered area for commercial vehicles accessing the halls. Functioning literally as an axis, this also provides the way into a network of aisles between the existing halls, allowing the public independent access to the different facilities.

Valencia Congress Center

Norman Foster

Location: Valencia, Spain. **Date of construction**: 1996–1997. **Architect**: Norman Foster. **Scheme**: Congress halls, auditorium, landscaped garden area, lobby, facilities for equipment, offices, cafeteria, restaurant, press centers, and exhibition areas. **Photography**: Paco Asensio.

This new congress center provides the focal point of an area of heavy urban development on the outskirts of Valencia. The building has a gentle convex shape, with two curved façades of different lengths. The scheme includes three auditoria of various sizes and capacities, each of them equipped with simultaneous interpreting cabins and the smallest able to be divided into two areas. The large glass façades are protected by external slatted blinds, based on movable sheets of translucent glass, which help save energy and provide a very pleasant light. In front of these vertical blind elements are a number of curved pools, which help reflect the natural light into the interior. The roof, which covers the whole of the structure, is of zinc-coated aluminum, and, thanks to the subtlety of its design, appears to float above the body of the building while in fact being supported on a number of large concrete porticoes. The whole complex resembles the prow of a great ship in the open sea.

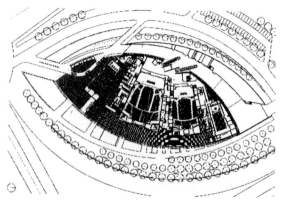

Brisbane Convention and Exhibition Center

Philip Cox

Location: Southbank, Brisbane, Australia. **Date of completion**: June 1995. **Client**: Government of Queensland. **Architect**: Philip Cox. **Associates**: Cox Rayney, Ove Arup (structures and engineering). **Scheme**: Convention and exhibition center; five exhibition halls, a further hall, and 20 meeting rooms. **Photography**: Cox Group Brisbane.

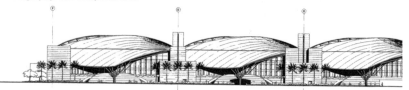

The Center contains five exhibition halls, one of which contains a mechanical system for raising or lowering the seats to allow for gatherings with more than 4000 participants. Other facilities include a hall with capacity for 2000 people and 20 meeting halls varying from 15 to 1000 m² (160 to 10,750 ft²). The halls are contiguous along the building, and can be extended to provide an exhibition area of more than 25,000 m² (270,000 ft²) in total area.

The Center is designed to create the impression of waves when viewed from the gardens, using a series of shell-shaped forms based on the geometry of the parabola. The main idea behind the design was to develop a structure which descends as far as possible down the façades so as to endow it with a human scale.

The Brisbane Convention and Exhibition Center has won five national architectural awards, as well as the Royal Institute of British Architects Engineering Award for the year 1996.

Torhaus

O.M. Ungers

Location: Frankfurt, Germany. **Date of construction**: 1991. **Client**: Frankfurt Fair. **Architect**: O.M. Ungers. **Scheme**: Gallery and high rise building for the fair's administrative offices. **Photography**: Francesc Tur.

The Torhaus is located in the center of Frankfurt, next to the freeway access road. There are also two railroad tracks crossing the site on overpasses, resulting in a triangular open space which was causing some problems in the fair's activities. The solution was this glass and stone building, which made communications possible between both parts of the site. Its name ("Tor" means "gate" in German) is a reference to this converted complex providing a symbolic gateway to the city. The structure consists of a horizontal strip element and a tower set on an irregular base. The service facilities are located in the first element, and are spread over four floors: nursery school, hairdressers, food shopping outlets, offices for consultants and interpreters, press offices, and a business center are located in this module, the southeast face of which accommodates the heating and air-conditioning systems. A pedestrian throughway passes onto the third floor in the form of a moving pavement, and around this element the towers rise up, providing an additional 24 floors to house the administrative offices of the Fair. The main body consists of two integrated elements: the interior element in glass, and the outer element in stone, protecting the interior element and forming a backdrop for it. The structure totals 29 floors, and reaches a height of 117 m (385 ft). The fact that the building still inspires admiration today is the best tribute that can be paid to this spectacular skyscraper.

Research Centers

The specific nature of some architectural categories means that additional strengths are required; this is the case with buildings intended for research, which call for a specialized process of design. Architects must be prepared to confront the technical challenges which the researchers pose for them. Accordingly, the structures in this section are the result of teamwork, providing an answer to all the problems which arise in the course of development of the project. The main challenge is to support the technical research work by creating properly functional areas which at the same time will provide a pleasant working environment, i.e. paying particular attention to the use to which the building is to be put, but likewise to the people who are going to work in it.

Seibersdorf Research Center and Offices

University of Cincinnati Research Center

OCAS

M & G Research

Design Cube

Institute of Neurology

IMPIVA

Skirball Institute of Biomolecular Medicine

Wexner Visual Arts Center

Social Science Studies Center

Heureka

Pacific Design Center

Hysolar Institute

Lucille Halsell Botanical Garden

Graz Botanical Garden

ESTEC

Seibersdorf Research Center and Offices

Coop Himmelb(l)au

Location: Seibersdorf, Austria. **Date of construction**: 1995. **Client**: Austrian Research Center. **Architects**: Coop Himmelb(l)au (Wolf D. Prix, Helmut Swiczinsky). **Associates**: Sam, Hopfner, Hornung, Mündl, Pillhofer, Spiess, Péan, Postl (design team). **Scheme**: Offices and laboratories. **Photography**: Gerald Zugmann, Hélène Bisnet (also pp 720/721).

The task was to refurbish and extend an existing warehouse on the Seibersdorf Research Center site. The building was to be modified and enlarged in such a way that it could accommodate the Center's offices. The research group had the peculiarity of involving professions from a variety of disciplines, and the planning required that the

building should reflect this style of work. The presence of different systems at the same time was to be represented not only in the method of working, but also in the structure itself. Sections of the building which were broadly differentiated were overlapped, with different structural systems existing side by side, the old and the new manifested simultaneously on the same level. This can be seen in the dimensions of the building, the structure, and the surfaces; there is no façade as such.

The element added to the original warehouse takes the form of a two-story beam structure, supported on a series of inclined pillars, some of them arranged in the shape of a cross, depending on the structural requirements. This is in effect a framework from which are suspended the slabs of concrete which form the floors. The direction of this framework structure does not follow that of the previous building, but is situated perpendicular to it, and, at one end, passes above the roadway. This accordingly creates a bridge effect, which then in turn launches out into a number of different directions.

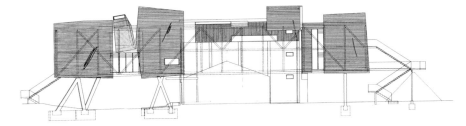

University of Cincinnati Research Center

Michael Graves

Location: Cincinnati, Ohio, USA. **Date of construction**: May 1995. **Client**: University of Cincinnatti. **Cost**: $32 million. **Architect**: Michael Graves. **Associates**: KZF Inc. (associate architects), Smith, Hinchman & Grylls Assocs. (design), Hargreaves Associates (landscaping), Monarch Construction (building contractors). **Scheme**: Research institute. **Photography**: Timothy Hursley.

Since embarking on his architectural career in 1964, Michael Graves has developed from the neo-avant-garde abstraction of his origins to the language of the postmodern, which characterizes his most recent work. It was in the realization of a number of extension and enlargement projects that he was brought into direct contact with history, so classical and vernacular allusions began to appear in his work, together with abstract forms in a linguistic combination which defines his architectural style. Color, defeating one of the prejudices of modern architecture, and the use of the façade as a pictorial and scenic element have acquired great importance. Likewise, the system of axes used to create the layout and the free combination of elements hark back inevitably to the classical tradition.

In May 1995 work was completed on the Engineering Research Center for the University of Cincinnati, Ohio. In terms of structure, the building can be seen as a mixture of a grand longitudinal pavilion design, and four other transverse elements, with the entrance extending from between them. Despite the variety of materials (ochre and terracotta masonry), or the shape of the windows (round or square), the façades present a sense of ordered uniformity. Similarly, in the copper-clad roof, the suggestion of industrial shapes appears beneath a large longitudinal vault.

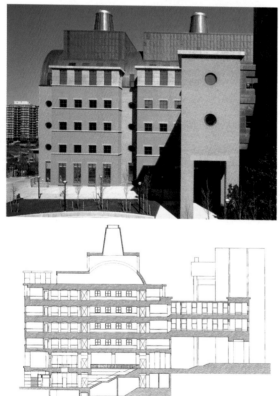

OCAS

Samyn and Partners

Location: Ghent, Belgium. **Date of construction**: 1991. **Architects**: W. Azou, M. Bouzahzah, K. Delafonteyne, H. Dossin, T. Hac, C. Hein, T. Khayati, A. Mestiri, Ph. Samyn, B. Selfslagh, D. Spantouris, J. van Rompaey, L. van Rhijn. **Consultants**: Samyn and Partner, NV Sidmar (structure), Heacon (hydraulics). **Scheme**: Offices, laboratories, test workshops, and parking lot. **Area**: 9000 m² (97,000 ft²). **Photography**: Ch. Bastin & J. Evrard, G. Coolen nv.

The Research Center for the Applications of Steel (OCAS) is located at the intersection of a freeway and a highway, bordering the facilities of the steel company Sidmar. OCAS consists of office buildings, laboratories, and experimental workshops. The greatest possible degree of spatial flexibility was specified, in order to be able to incorporate new machinery and technical resources without interfering in day-to-day Center operations.

The project was designed in a circular bank structure 180 m (590 ft) in diameter. Access to all the sections

of OCAS is provided through a gate, located in its geometrical center. The different functions are arranged along two orthogonal axes. The laboratories are located on the first floor, in a bridge structure 162 m (530 ft) in length and 19.5 m (64 ft) wide. The two major experimental workshops are perpendicular, with a parabolic roof allowing light to enter over a length of 42 m (138 ft), and rise to a height of 16.5 m (54 ft). Direct access to the workshops is provided by means of an interior throughway, for moving heavy loads.

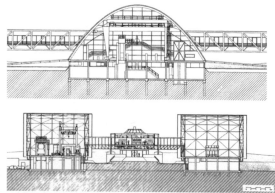

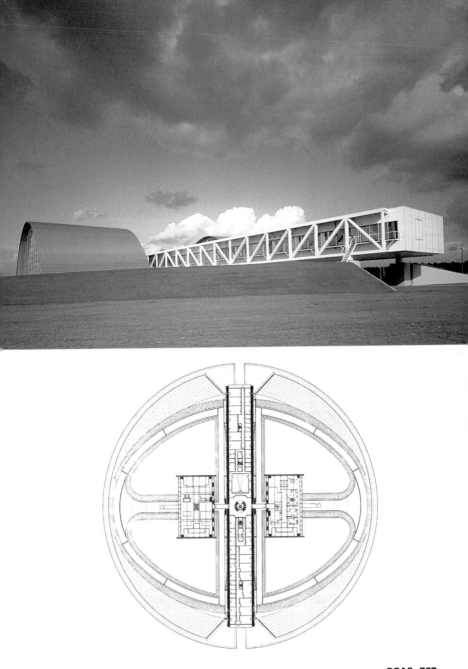

M & G Research

Samyn and Partners

Location: Venafro, Italy. **Date of construction**: 1992. **Architects**: Ph. Samyn, A. Cermelli, A. Charon, M.D. Ramos, M. Van Raemdonck, B. Vleurick, Studio H. **Consultants**: SETESCO (structure), CANOBBIO (roof structure). **Area**: 2700 m² (8900 ft²). **Photography**: Matteo Piazza.

These chemical laboratories are in Venafro, a township in the south of Italy located in a long valley surrounded by hills, fields of crops, and traditional buildings. Right from the initial sketches, the idea was to create a roof which would form a single volume, of an awning type, oval in shape, with dimensions of about 85 x 32 m (280 x 105 ft) and a height of 15 m (49 ft), supported by transverse arches and longitudinal cables. The whole structure is located in the center of a pool, likewise oval in shape, which not only has a landscaping function but also provides a means of regulating the heat of the laboratory facilities.

The interior space is lit by the inherent transparency of the membrane, and by a series of perimeter arches, adapted to serve as windows. The membrane is made of PVC-coated polyester. Inside, research programs are carried out which call simultaneously for heavy machinery and delicate experimentation. Located beneath the awning are the equipment and a second two-story structure which accommodates offices and services, these being accessed by a system of linking passageways.

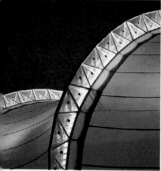

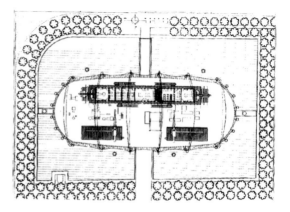

Design Cube

Ortner & Ortner

Location: Klagenfurt, Austria. **Date of construction**: 1992–1995. **Client**: EDD-Designentwicklungs. **Architects**: Ortner & Ortner. **Associates**: Sabien Krischan; Reinhold Svetina (structure). **Photography**: Ralph Richter/Architecturphoto, Lang & Lang.

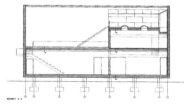

Ortner & Ortner have certainly made their presence felt. A gigantic box shape (18 x 26 m, 59 x 85 ft, in plan and 12 m, 39 ft, in height), indigo blue in colour, raised above a white gravel surface on 18 concrete pylons, secured at the four cardinal points as a reference to a higher order of things: a pure structure. Visitors use the metal access ramp, ascending from ground level and emerging in the interior of the box. Once inside, natural light filtering through an awning canopy illuminates a patio of façades in red and a gray floor, the same rough gray as the concrete blocks which compose the outer casing. The façades are clad in panels of vitrified plywood. Opposite the entrance, above the longitudinal axis, is the façade of the exhibition and conference hall, of a height and width such as to occupy the northern half of the structure; on the left, following the transverse axis, the façade extends over three stories of the administration section, then at half height above the terrace which extends over the hall. On the right, a stairway leads to the balcony, the only element to reach beyond the limits of the box shape, and providing a view of the outside world.

This structure is separated from the box by a narrow perimeter strip, defined by the passageway above the entrance, the inclined ramp from the balcony to the terrace, the admission of light into the hall, and the new light source and stairway on the way from the entrance to the elements of the building.

Institute of Neurology

Burton Associates, Tod Williams, Billie Tsien

Location: La Jolla, California, USA. **Date of completion**: 1996. **Architects**: Burton Associates, Tod Williams, Billie Tsien. **Scheme**: Multidisciplinary center for neurological research. **Photography**: Pablo Mason.

The project was to create a multidisciplinary center for neurological research, with an environment which would favour both practical experimentation as well as theoretical research, in a major complex which would attract specialists from all over the world. The site is surrounded by land used by the Scrippscampus , with a view of the eastern hills of the Pacific Ocean. Located on a hilltop, the center, occupying some 5000 m² (54,000 ft²), consists of three main buildings arranged across a plaza. This semicloistered arrangement allows for the unfolding of an interior landscape, where the discovery of the different spaces seems to be of more importance than the actual shape of the buildings. The three structures involved are: a three-story center for theoretical work; a U-shaped laboratory wing surrounding the plaza; and an auditorium. A series of passages and stairways extends around the perimeter, passing between the different levels of the complex and providing a range of different views over the plaza and the hills of the surrounding countryside. The truly outstanding feature of this project was the very close cooperation between the teams of architects and of landscaping specialists. Far from imposing themselves on one another, these professionals worked together in the same direction, constantly adding new details which enrich the final result.

IMPIVA

Ferrater, Bento and Sanahuja

Location: Castellón, Spain. **Date of construction**: 1996. **Architects**: Carles Ferrater, Carlos Bento, Jaime Sanahuja.
Associates: Carlos Martín, Carlos Escura. **Scheme**: Offices and services. **Photography**: Paco Asensio.

The Institute of Small and Medium-sized Businesses (IMPIVA) on the outskirts of Castellón is among the last of the town's buildings before one enters the orange groves which proliferate throughout this part of the Mediterranean, and is located in a technology park. This is a somewhat chaotic area in architectural terms, in which various styles compete. In the midst of this, the architects of IMPIVA opted for a building based on a rigorous geometrical composition, in the manner of the abstract artists of the avant-garde. The focus of the project is to provide leased offices and facilities for companies in their first few years of existence, at a time when they need the greatest possible flexibility.

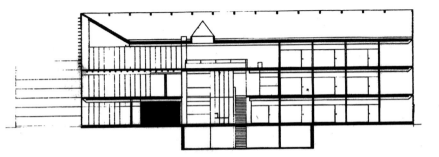

Skirball Institute of Biomolecular Medicine

James Stewart Polshek and Partners Architects

Location: New York, USA. **Date of construction**: 1992. **Architects**: James Stewart Polshek and Partners, Architects. **Scheme**: Annex to Tisch Hospital, for biomolecular research. **Area**: 51,000 m² (549,000 ft²). **Photography**: Paco Asensio.

The layout of this project aimed to meet a variety of needs simultaneously: a main entrance, a connecting nucleus, and an internal garden acting as a structural delimitation.

The principal lobby area measures 1560 m² (16,800 ft²), and is covered by an aerodynamically shaped aluminum and glass canopy. Its double height makes the entrance to the hospital and medical school a comfortable space of generous dimensions. In formal terms, the linking element with the north wing is the most freed up: a curved glazed structure and an anthropomorphic appearance provide a welcoming atmosphere for the admissions and waiting room section of the hospital. The use of different materials on the fasade provides a hint of the different functions inside: the laboratory floors are clad in granite, the wards in brick.

Movement between the laboratories is facilitated by a double passageway. Each module is divided into a working area, with tables mounted on the outside wall, and a rest and recreation area facing the passage, creating a circular corridor around the nucleus. The height of the floors intended for the laboratories has been restricted so as to allow maximum sunlight to enter. This principle is also applied to the medical areas; there are four suites arranged on each floor, with the greatest possible number of windows.

Wexner Visual Arts Center

Peter Eisenman

Location: Minneapolis, Minnesota, USA. **Date of completion**: 1991. **Architect**: Peter Eisenman. **Scheme**: Lecture theaters, laboratories, library, workshops, exterior public plaza, teaching staff accommodation, and exhibition hall. **Photography**: Leff Golberg/Esto Photographics.

From the outside, this appears a compact building divided into two parts: a solid structure as the plinth, with large rectangular openings on one side and arcades on the other; and a much lighter timber and glass upper element. A secondary structure supports an awning which provides protection from the sun and serves as the horizontal termination of the building. The apse element is a solid body with very narrow, high vertical openings accommodating the windows in a Romanesque apsidal structure.

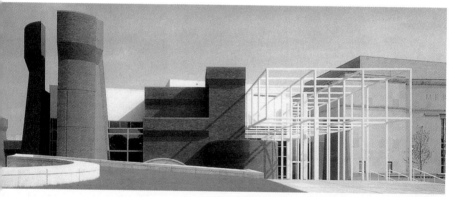

Social Science Studies Center

James Stirling, Michael James Wilford

Location: Berlin, Germany. **Date of completion**: 1990. **Client**: Social Science Studies Center of Germany. **Architects**: James Stirling, Michael James Wilford. **Scheme**: Building to accommodate a science and study center. **Photography**: Richard Bryant-Arcaid.

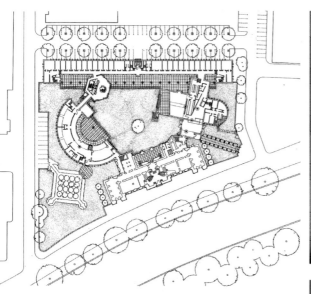

The arrangement of the different structures around the large central patio, and the colorful, bright finish, are the key features of this academic center in Berlin. The new facility incorporates a majestic façade which miraculously survived the war; that of the old School of Fine Arts. The variety of the elements, in their design, form, and shape, was one of the basic criteria for the project. Its location with respect to the original building meant that a highly involved technique had to be adopted using the composition of fragments method: each specific function is introduced in an individual architectural module, the location of which accords with the development of the project as a whole.

Heureka

Mikko Heikkinen and Markku Komonen

Location: Tikkurila, Vantaa, Helsinki, Finland. **Date of construction**: 1987–1988. **Client**: The Science Center Foundation. **Architects**: Mikko Heikkinen and Markku Komonen. **Associates**: Juva Oy, Matti Alho (project management), Kimmo Friman (associate architect), Paloheimo & Ollila Engineers, Matti Alho (basic engineering), Ernst Palmen, Finnish State, Municipality of Vantaa, and a number of private companies. **Scheme**: Central hall, exhibition hall, theater, auditorium, access bridge, cafeteria, offices, and services. **Photography**: Jussi Tiainen.

Designed for the demonstration of the scientific foundations of the universe, this center's appearance has the characteristics of an exhibition facility, a complex which is homogeneous in terms of structure, but compact in its expressive content. The Heureka center is located

on a site bounded by the intersection of a railroad line and the course of the river Keravanjoki. The structure was designed as a series of pure geometrical shapes and planes: a cylindrical central hall, a curved hall, a spherical theater, and an auditorium in the shape of a fan, all leading from a basic prism element. The structure also comprises a bridge which marks the presence of the river. Its access area features a metal fascia and a system of highly stylized tensioning elements, while another characteristic space is provided before entering the building proper, the stone garden, which dominates the way in. This accommodates a geological map of Finland, the aim of which is to impress the visitor, right from the outset, with the message of the building. The exterior and the supplementary structures harmonize with these informational elements, in a mixture of content and form or style.

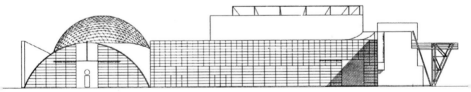

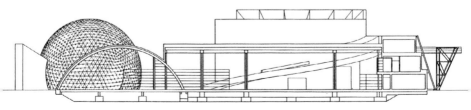

Pacific Design Center

Cesar Pelli & Associates

Location: Los Angeles, California, USA. **Date of completion**: 1998. **Client**: Municipality of Los Angeles. **Architect**: Cesar Pelli & Associates. **Scheme**: Exhibition center for furniture and design (furniture, carpets, drapes, decorative items, and accessories): exhibition halls; parking lot; terrace; patio and public plaza, with ampitheater and exhibition gallery (Murray Feldman Gallery). **Photography**: Marvin Rand.

The project is an extension of the original Pacific Design Center site, the Blue Whale, with six levels, to which in 1988 Cesar Pelli made an addition of 76,000 m² (818,000 ft²), approximately double what was there originally. The reason for this expansion was the increased demand for exhibition space, which was what then prompted the construction of two additional buildings. To provide a sense of continuity for the new structures, some elements of the earlier buildings are included in the new ones: the base includes a plinth clad in the same blue tinted glass that is in the original structure's base. It was decided to implement the construction of the new modules in two phases: first, a steel structure, with panels of green glass in the base; and the second, a structure likewise of steel, but clad with panels of red glass. The green section is a structure of 40,000 m² (430,000 ft²), with eight floors, crowned by a cupola or lightwell, again of glass, in the form of a hexagonal pyramid, following the form adopted by the floor plan of the container element. The Pacific Design Center has become a distinctive symbol of the area, thanks to the colors, which are such a striking contrast to the harmonized shades of the surrounding buildings.

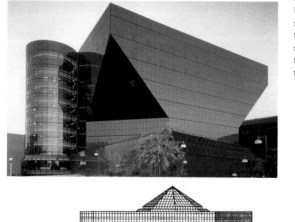

Hysolar Institute

Behnisch & Partner

Location: Stuttgart, Germany. **Date of completion**: 1987. **Client**: IPE, DFLUR. **Architects**: Behnisch & Partner. **Scheme**: Accommodation for offices, laboratories, storage facility, and ancillary areas. **Photography**: Behnisch and Partner.

There are two institutions housed in the Hysolar Institute: the Institute of Physical Electrotechnology, and the German Research Center for Aerospace Navigation. The first of these carries out basic research into semiconductor electrodes which make use of the energy provided by light; the second is engaged in exploring ways of optimizing the yield from this energy.

This commission was essentially straightforward: accommodation for offices, a certain amount of laboratory space, a storage facility, and ancillary areas. This offered sufficient margin for some stylistic experimentation but there was limited time for the design and construction, which prevented Behnisch from pursuing the project in its usual manner.

As a result, at first sight it seems surprising that this project comes from the studios of Behnisch and Partner. The materials, the coloring, the unrestricted layout, and what in the firm's other works would appear discordant, on closer observation becomes recognizable, however. It is precisely this quality which is one of the decisive characteristics of the Hysolar Institute in the city of Stuttgart.

Lucille Halsell Botanical Garden

Emilio Ambasz

Location: San Antonio, Texas, USA. **Date of completion**: 1987. **Architect**: Emilio Ambasz. **Scheme**: Botanical garden consisting of a complex of greenhouses.

The San Antonio Botanical Garden is a complex of different greenhouses on a large area of land with an irregular surface. Though, in other zones with cooler climates or fewer hours of sun, glass greenhouses are usually employed to make better use of the sun's rays, in this area of Texas, where the weather is very hot, this practice would be counterproductive.

The complex consists of a number of circular buildings, partially visible – all of them in whitish concrete to achieve a greater identification with the dry landscape – on which rest the spectacular glass structures, which remind one vaguely of old architectural forms: pyramids and truncated cones. A kind of sunken street, the main axis, joins the different parts of this greenhouse complex. One reaches it via a semicircular set of steps built into a wall that takes us into the bowels of the earth. From here, a narrow gallery leads to a more open space presided over by a solitary palm tree. Carrying on, one arrives at another, larger area flooded by a strange light from the roof, which projects pyramidal and hemispherical shapes. This filtered light has allowed a varied flora to grow. From here, some revolving doors lead to a porch and a patio, a central space where there are other buildings (square on the right and long and circular on the left).

This is without doubt a project in which intelligent action has been used to synthesize different growing environments.

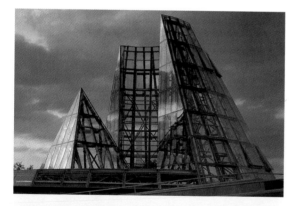

Botanical garden in Graz

Volker Giencke

Location: Graz, Austria. **Dates of construction**: 1989–1990, 1993–1994. **Client**: University of Graz. **Architect**: Volker Giencke. **Associates**: Ove Arup & Partners, Szyskowitz & Graber (engineering). **Photography**: Ralph Richter/architekturphoto, Peter Eder, Atelier Gienoke, Hans-Georg Tropper.

In each of the three cylinders a different climate has been created: subtropical, arid, and temperate. Under a flat and inclined roof, which rises out of the ground, there is the cultivation zone. Designed by computer, the main structure takes the shape of the cylinder sections using parabolic ribs, while the secondary one follows generatrix lines. The sections are made of an aluminum alloy for lightness, and are as small as possible, allowing 98% of natural light to enter the building. The water heating system uses pipes with a parabolic structure that give a constant temperature throughout the inside. Cooling is done by a new propulsion system that mixes water and air to generate steam, instantly dropping the temperature to 5°C (41° F).

The exterior enclosure is formed by a double layer of transparent acrylic elements that cover the structure like a skin. The growing area is ventilated by units in the roof that open hydraulically.

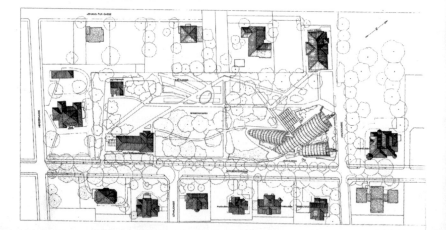

ESTEC

Aldo van Eyck, Hannie van Eyck

Location: Noordwijk, Netherlands. **Date of completion**: 1989. **Client**: ESTEC. **Architects**: Aldo van Eyck, Hannie van Eyck. **Scheme**: Building to house the European Center for Space Research and Technology: conference and audiovisual rooms, restaurant, conservatory, stores, offices, kitchen, and services. **Photography**: Alexander van Berge.

The plan for the new complex is dominated by a classical scheme that subdivides the building into a tripartite octagon. In essence the project has been described as an atrium inscribed in a large square.

The atrium was given a circular treatment, while the sides of the square are like arches. The building would need to be highly flexible, so the architects employed hendecagonal columns to form a sinuous and flowing arrangement, combining both curved and straight lines. This method is very successful in yielding simple and natural juxtapositions, matching polygons that can freely assume the curved line. Thanks to this system, the building could be divided up into various geometric shapes of great purity, but with fluid and undulating forms, in accordance with the topographical characteristics of the ground. The complex has been endowed with a range of color tones that runs the whole range of the spectrum, in order to define the different functional areas. In the same way, the slope of the roof allows the whole space to be reorganized, playing the game of volumes and vacuums, presences and absences, that contribute to the visual morphology of the complex.

ESTEC 753

Factories

Industrial activity has become an indicator
of the extent of a country's development.
The idea that people are a further factor in
production has evolved thanks to a greater
social conscience, so a new concept of
"factory" has developed, according to
which it has become quite a challenge to
ensure that the worker feels like a human
being within its walls. The architectural
projects included in this chapter reveal a
range of idiosyncratic industrial activities
related to the products being made, which
might be described as unusual.
In spite of their obvious diversity, there are
several constants that all of these buildings
must adhere to, in order to be able to
achieve optimum functionality. These
include: setting the plant up properly for
the production process, elimination of
superfluous elements that will increase
costs, and installing the right equipment to
ensure that the workers are operating
under the most favorable conditions.

Ricola warehouse

Herzog & de Meuron

Location: Mulhouse, France. **Date of design**: 1992. **Date of completion**: 1993. **Clients**: H.P. Richterich, Ricola AG, Laufen/CH. **Architect**: Herzog & de Meuron. **Associates**: André Maeder (project leader), Dieter Kienast (landscape architect), Marc Weidmann (polycarbonate panels). **Scheme**: Storage and production facility. **Floor area**: 2760 m² (29,000 ft²). **Photography**: Margherita Spiluttini

The new warehouse for the company Ricola-Europe S.A. is located to the south of the city of Mulhouse, in an industrial zone in the middle of the forests of Alsace. The plot, which was quite large, is almost flat, and the new warehouse was to be for both storage and production. Herzog and de Meuron proposed a rectangular building on one level, totally transparent inside.
The longer sides are dominated by two large canopies, which give protection from both sun and rain. These are two large sets of translucent polycarbonate panels on which plant outlines are screen printed. These reflect the landscaping outside and the luminous atmosphere inside.

The Box

Eric Owen Moss

Location: Culver City, California, USA. **Date of construction**: 1994. **Client**: Frederick Norton Smith. **Architect**: Eric Owen Moss. **Associates**: Lucas Ríos. Scott Nakao, Scott Hunter, Eric Stultz, Todd Conversano, Sheng-yuan Hwang, Paul Groh, Thomas Ahn (design team), Joe Kurily (structure), John Snyder (electrics), Peter Brown-Samitaur (construction). **Scheme**: Reception and meeting room. **Photography**: Tom Bonner (also pp 612/613).

The Box is not an item of new plant, but rather an annex to an old industrial building which is in tune with this type of space. The plan is rectangular and the structure is of wooden struts with a central pillar and a longitudinal lantern. The Box is a very small structure, about the size of a family house, not counting the surface area of the existing building. Its functions are minimal: it houses a reception on the ground floor and a meeting/conference room upstairs. Conceptually, it is a box (hence its name) but a box where things start to happen (and that is Moss's ingenious game).

In spite of their spectacular appearance, Eric Owen Moss's buildings are hard to understand without visiting them and, despite their extravagant look, they are made with very few materials and with a uniform finish. Their strength comes from their plasticity, from the flow of forms, and from the implicit movement. They are full of games, puzzles, and spatial riddles. Moss does not build spaces, he presents sensations and experiments with sequences of images that have to be re-elaborated in the mind of the observer. The forms of his architecture are improbable because they are geometrical wagers and great adventures.

Toto

Naoyuki Shirakawa Atelier

Location: Kitakyushu City, Japan. **Date of construction**: 1994. **Client**: Sun-Aqua Toto Ltd. **Architect**: Naoyuki Shirakewa Atelier. **Associates**: Sankyu Inc. (construction). **Photography**: Nobuaki Nakagawa.

By night one can see TOTOTOTOTO written on a black background. The letters consist of points of light floating in the air. By day, one can read the same on a blue plane. This sign is designed to be seen in motion, at the speed that the automobiles travel on the highway.
Shirakawa's architecture derives in general from clear geometrical principles and simple spaces. This is an architecture that employs geometry as a major source and tool of the project. Its apparent complexity derives from the play instituted throughout development, in terms of its own properties and the specific requirements of each case.
Shirakawa's buildings normally feature patios, which are a fragment of privatized nature, and which provide light. The TOTO project, however, is not a building of explicitly opened up interiors. Its structure is based on an axis which runs parallel to the axis of entry. The structure and function of the factory are dependent on this passage, which is open at both ends. The rest of the building consists of spaces attached to this.

Holz Altenried warehouse and showroom

Carlo Baumschlager, Dietmar Eberle

Location: Hergatz, Germany. **Date of construction**: 1995. **Client**: Bernd Altenried. **Architects**: Carlo Baumschlager, Dietmar Eberle. **Associates**: Michael Ohneberg (design), Oliver Baldauf (supervisor), Büro Plankel (structure). **Scheme**: Warehouse, showroom, and offices. **Photography**: Ed Hueber.

The project consisted of creating a storage area and a showroom, with a small space for offices and administration area.
It is divided between an unlit warehouse on the first floor, a light upper floor housing a well-illuminated area for samples, and a complex of offices and auxiliary services, located at the west end of the building. The façades that compose the greater part of the structure, as well as the roof, are slightly bowed outward, as if the building were swollen. The skin has been molded over wooden battens to the shape determined by the changing profile of a succession of wooden laminated and glued ribs that is, in fact, the structure of this box of curved walls. These ribs are prefabricated spruce arches; each has a different profile. The larch covering is homogeneous: there is no difference between the surface of the façades and that of the roof.
The project, through its geometry and its method of construction, suggests the work of artisans, as though it were a handmade object. It is quite clear that the objective of the construction of this building is an advertisement for the Holz-Altenried company and its work with wood.

SCHNITT A—A

Technical Center for Books, Marne la Vallée

Dominique Perrault

Location: Bussy-Saint-Georges, France. **Date of design**: 1992. **Date of construction**: 1995. **Architect**: Dominique Perrault. **Associates**: Maxime Gasperini, Jérôme Besse (assistants), Daniel Allaire (engineer), Pieffet-Corbin (economist). **Scheme**: Book store, workshops, offices, meeting rooms, and services. **Photography**: Georges Fessy (also pp 756/757).

The basic functions of the technical center are, firstly, the storage in good condition of individual books or collections that are rarely consulted, with special emphasis on temperature and relative humidity. Secondly, in order to ensure efficient functioning and the ability to respond to the demands of users, it must be possible to transmit or transport documents flexibly, rapidly, and easily, within 24 hours of an order having been placed.

A technical image, homogeneous surfaces bearing simple, clearly conceptual symbols: this is an extremely organized, pure, and beautiful structure, thanks to the clear absence of anything superfluous. A silent building, certainly, despite the fact that it houses an infinite number of texts.

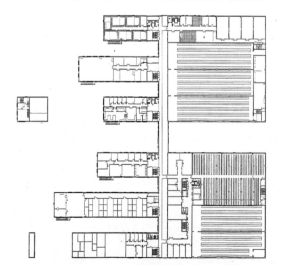

Grain treatment plant

Samyn and Partners

Location: Marche-en-Famenne, Belgium. **Date of construction**: 1995. **Architects**: Gh. André, J.L. Chapron, A. Charon, R. Delaunoit, Ch. Fontaine, D. Mélotte, S Peeters, Ph. Samyn, D. Singh, B. Vleurick; Bouny Construction sprl (construction), Menuiserie Fréson sc (structure and carpentry). **Scheme**: Workshop, store, offices, laboratories, and services. **Floor area**: 1400 m² (15,000 ft²). **Photography**: Ch. Bastin & J Evrard.

Located in the forest of Ardennes, this building consists basically of a grain treatment workshop, cold storage, and a number of offices and laboratories. The plot is an irregular space surrounded by splendid oaks; which prompted Philippe Samyn to design the building with a simple and striking shape. This is an oval glass dome formed by a structure of wooden arches. In fact, this is one of the simplest of structures in architecture, which relates this building to the Mongolian yurt and the Zulu hut. Philippe Samyn takes advantage of the research done into these types of structure by Mutschler and Otto in Mannheim (1975), Kikutake in Nara (1987), and the experimental buildings erected in Dorset, UK, in 1982 by Edmund Happold and the architects Ahrends, Burton & Koralec. Inside the dome two auxiliary buildings have been put up alongside the central workshop to house the cold rooms and offices.

Phosphate plant

Gustav Peichl

Location: Nordgraben, Berlin-Tegel, Germany. **Date of construction**: 1985–1987. **Architect**: Gustav Peichl.
Scheme: Installation of a purifier, outdoor landscaping. **Photography**: Uwe Rau.

This purifier installation, made between 1985 and 1987, forms part of a residential area plan for the neighborhood of Nordgraben, in Berlin-Tegel (Germany), a traditionally industrial zone. The proposal was to construct a space that would constitute a major advance, in the form of a qualitative improvement in all senses (technological, aesthetic, environmental, and in urban planning).

One of the motifs repeated almost constantly in the design is the creation of as much open space as possible, with the proliferation of lawn-covered slopes complemented by trees, alongside adjacent avenues or inside the plant. The northern part of this complex must be open to the general public as an urban park, while the western sector remains as part of an area including the adjacent residential housing zone.

The individual functional units are shared radials in the center of the plant, tracing the form of a star that is formed by the mixing tower and the central block, the three waste removal tanks with their respective filtering systems. The three tanks are covered by a layer of earth, in such a way that a triangular green-colored embankment can be created by the slopes of the lawn. For the roof, metal sheets have been used incorporating channels to prevent the accumulation of water.

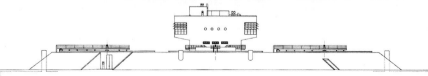

Herman Miller furniture factory

Frank O. Gehry.

Location: Rocklin, California, USA. **Date of construction**: 1989. **Client**: Herman Miller Furniture Manufacture and Distribution. **Architecture**: Frank O Gehry. **Associates**: Stanley Tigerman. **Scheme**: Construction of the production and distribution units of a furniture factory. **Photography**: Hedrich-Blessing.

The building is located on an inhospitable plot on the edge of a lightly undulating piece of land. Natural vegetation is scarce and the climate is very dry. The plan adopted to counteract the sterility of the environment was the architectural creation of a species of plaza, crowded and warm, as if it were a small town of about 300 people. Frank O. Gehry also used planting as an important element conferring spatial order. The most dramatic feature of this ambitious project is the curious hemispherical dome in the oriental manner, designed by Stanley Tigerman, which is located on a small neoclassical-style building housing a conference and meeting room.

Vitra Conference Pavilion

Tadao Ando

Location: Weil am Rhein, Germany. **Date of construction**: 1993. **Client**: Vitra GmbH. **Architect**: Tadao Ando. **Scheme**: Conference pavilion for design production company Vitra: lobby, conference room, personnel training rooms, offices, library, outside gardens with patio and services. **Photography**: Friedrich Busam/ architekturphoto.

The firm Vitra produces high-quality designs for furniture, whether in the classical style or by contemporary designers such as Bellini or Philippe Starck, among others. This conference pavilion is situated close to the company's factory in southern Germany and various activities take place there, from training of personnel to conferences on all kinds of matters. Tadao Ando decided, because of the extraordinarily flat site, not to give the building any height, so as not to disturb the tranquillity of the area. The building has been sunk into the ground: parts of it are buried underground and part of the plot is taken up with a patio. The building is made up of three elements: a rectangular block parallel to the walls that delimit the sunken patio, another rectangular block that penetrates into this patio at an angle of 60° and a cylindrical block that creates a space cutting the two rectangular ones. The pavilion building has two levels, conference rooms, a library, private offices, and a lobby. All these spaces open onto the sunken patio, which functions as a device to attract and retain those elements of nature, light and wind, between the spaces of the building. This patio reinforces the austere silence of the architecture around it.

Funder Werk 3 factory

Coop Himmelb(l)au

Location: St. Veit/Glan, Carinthia, Austria. **Date of construction**: 1988–1989. **Architect**: Coop Himmelb(l)au.
Associates: Wolf D. Prix, Helmut Swiczinsky. **Scheme**: Woodworking factory: power plant, production
workshop, and bridge connecting two workshops. **Photography**: Gerald Zugmann

The project was to build a woodworking factory which was to be emblematic of a new industrial architecture. The primary concept is that of dismembering the workshop, dividing it into a number of autonomous elements, like the different pieces of a Cubist still life. The building consists of two parts, the power plant and the production workshop, which is much larger. These two areas are connected by a covered bridge between them. In the production warehouse the roof has been constructed of steel and concrete, with three small gables and a large slab measuring 650 m² (7000 ft²). The walls consist of prefabricated sections of concrete and steel at the bottom, on which are placed brass fillets. The southeast façade is divided by an inverted corner, made of steel and glass, in which one can see a framework of beams and crosspieces placed on the diagonal.

Financial Times

Nicholas Grimshaw & Partners

Location: London, UK. **Date of completion**: 1988. **Architect**: Nicholas Grimshaw & Partners. **Floor area**: 14,000 m² (150,000 ft²). **Photography**: Jo Reid.

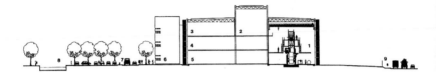

The main task was to design new premises for two printing presses. The structure is noted for its simplicity and symmetry. With a rectangular plan, it has two lateral sections of 18 m (59 ft), with a backbone or axis of 12 m (39 ft). These sections face north (where the presses are) and south (where the administration and auxiliary services are). One of the most outstanding aspects of the complex is the transparent glass roof of the printing press area, so the presses can be seen from outside.

This roof is an enormous window measuring 96 x 16 m (315 x 52 ft), and consisting of square panes screwed into each corner and sealed with silicone. Six columns positioned in the centers hold two semicircular steel sections of differing diameters, linked by flat plates. Each face of the column has steel projections for protection purposes. The façades of the long sides are also made of glass; in contrast, the dispatch end of the building and the stairwells in the entrance are solid.

The entrance façade, which is located on the south side, is guarded by separate, curved stairwells lined with aluminum.

West 8 MTR Terminal

Koen van Velsen

Location: Stonecutters Island, Kwai Chung, Hong Kong. **Date of completion**: November 1996. **Architect**:
Koen van Velsen. **Client**: Modern Terminals Ltd. **Scheme**: Offices, ticket offices, and technical workshop.

This 15,000 m² (160,000 ft²) complex consists of a six-story building for administrative offices, entry and exit ticket offices, and a technical workshop which provides operational support for the fleet. The buildings are located on a piece of reclaimed land next to Stonecutters Island, with views towards the jetty to the south and the cargo terminal to the north. Within the context of the

cargo terminal, with its heavy, aggressive landscape of cranes and steel containers, it was essential to create an architecture style that was not suppressed by its surroundings. It was also imperative that the buildings should be appropriate to the utilitarian nature of their functions and be constructed of materials that are simple and efficient. The administration building

responds to this premise by having basic functional elements, such as the staircase and high towers, that appear like sculptured objects separated from the framework, which is covered with ceramic tiles like the office installations. This separation is emphasized by the use of brightly colored ceramic tiles in the elevator and on the elliptical staircase, later covered by a block of glass with a light inside to project the client's logo.

The ticket offices, used to check the state of the containers when they enter or leave the terminal, are long steel structures, 45 m (150 ft) across, to give maximum flexibility to the operations at ground level. The metal floor between the ticket offices and the workshop equipment also accentuates the architectural response to the context. The total cost of the project was approximately 150 million Hong Kong dollars.

Skyscrapers

Skyscrapers are undoubtedly a celebration
of technological progress, a grand gesture
to man's capacity to construct ever higher
in his attempts to reach the heavens. But
they are also a product of territoriality, of
the property market, of speculation. The
basic questions to be answered by today's
architects are the same as those faced by
those who designed the first skyscrapers
in Chicago at the end of the 19th century.
How to relate the skyscraper to an
environment alien to its scale? How to get
to and from the ground? How to build the
structure? How to dress the skeleton?
Those erecting skyscrapers now are at
least aware of urban problems and try to
confront them by responding to the
environment in which their giant projects
are situated.

Petronas Towers

Cesar Pelli & Associates

Location: Kuala Lumpur, Malaysia. **Date of construction**: 1997. **Client**: Kuala Lumpur City Center. **Architect**: Cesar Pelli & Associates. **Associates**: Adamson Associates (associate architect), KLCC Berhad Architectural Division (surveying), Thornton-Tomasetti Engineers, Ranhilt Bersekutu (structural engineers), Flack + Kurtz, KTA Tenaga (mechanical engineering), Lehrer McGovern (management), STUDIOS (interior), Balmori Associates (landscaping). **Photography**: J Apicella, P Follet/C.P. & A

The most important design decision in this project was to make the towers symmetrical: this characteristic carries all the figurative and symbolic charge. Between them lies the key element of this structure's composition: empty space, an essential concept in all Asiatic cultures.

Although each tower has its own vertical axis, the axis of the whole complex is between them, in the empty space. The force of the void is empowered by the pedestrian bridge that connects the two towers (of 88 stories) at levels 41 and 42, where there are public observation platforms looking over the sprawling city.

The bridge, with its support structure, creates a door to the sky, a door 170 m (560 ft) high, a door to the infinite. The towers diminish six times in plan section as they get higher and, in the last setbacks, the façades lean slightly inwards, completing the form and reinforcing the vertical axis of the towers, which is emphasized by the needles on the summits of these towers. Every attempt has been made to reduce the effects of excess sunlight on the interior of Petronas Towers. For this reason the continuous strips of window are of reduced height and are protected by sunshades that, together with the multiple setbacks in the façade plane, create a constant set of shadows that together form a three-dimensional façade. The cladding material is stainless steel, which amplifies the multiple reflections of Malaysia's light conditions.

Osaka World Trade Center

Nikken Sekkei

Location: Osaka, Japan. **Date of completion**: 1995. **Architect**: Nikken Sekkei. **Scheme**: Building containing offices and spaces for public use: shops, restaurants, cafeterias, and auditorium. **Photography**: Kouji Okamoto.

The World Trade Center Osaka (WTCO) is the identifying landmark of the district of Nenko, on the artificial island of Sakishima. With its height of 256 m (840 ft) distributed over 55 stories and a total floor area of more than 150,000 m² (1.6 million ft²), the highest building in the west of Japan has quickly become a visual reference for the whole bay and the Kansai region. Its distinctiveness, impossible in the center of a city, is achieved not only through its sheer size, but also through the various public spaces inside, which make it accessible to the general public not necessarily visiting any of its office suites. A large atrium, 3000 m² (32,000 ft²) and 21 m (70 ft) high, known as the Fespa, forms a lively yet relaxing public area. It serves as access to both the tower's main nucleus of vertical communications, and to the different public facilities, such as shops, restaurants, cafeterias, and an auditorium for 380 people, in a global design thought of as a large indoor park. This large atrium not only serves the building but integrates the complex into its urban environment, both in function and in scale, serving as the main access route to Cosmo Square.

Suntec City

Tsao & McKown

Location: Singapore. **Date of completion**: 1997. **Architect**: Tsao & McKown. **Scheme**: Building containing offices, convention center, shops, cafeteria, restaurants, and various leisure areas. **Photography**: Richard Bryant/Arcaid.

The scale of recent development in Singapore is matched only by the speed at which it has been carried out. In this context the Suntec City operation is remarkable. The team of Tsao & McKown has made a real effort to create a civic space, where there is still room for the pedestrian in a high-rise environment. Located at the confluence of the city's main traffic arteries, there have been a number of modifications to the road system at the site in order to provide better communications with the historic part of the city. Between this and Suntec City, a public pathway is being constructed along a green strip of land running parallel to the water, with which it will later be joined. An operation of this magnitude, which at present is the largest private complex in the country, addresses itself to the urban context of the towers, but also pays special attention to pedestrians, bringing its vastness down to a more human scale.

Puerta de Europa Towers

Burgee & Johnson, Dominguez and Martin

Location: Madrid, Spain. **Date of completion**: 1996. **Architects**: Burgee & Johnson, Dominguez and Martin. **Scheme**: Office building, underground parking lot, first floor, mezzanine, 24 stories of offices, and heliport. **Photography**: Robert Royal.

Why are there two glass towers bowing to each other at the entrance to Madrid? What is the reason for constructing two buildings that seem to contradict traditional structures, which generally demand vertical transmission of loads? There are no immediate answers. These have to be sought in the origin of the project and the preconditions imposed on it, as well as in the wish of its developers to construct something original. This area of expansion to the north of Madrid has been the object of numerous remodeling projects lately. The two blocks had to be separated by a sufficiently wide strip of land to avoid three existing subway stations, the corresponding walkways below for pedestrians, and the rights of access to and from an unbuilt-up street. Later there was a need to build a road under the plaza to relieve traffic congestion. Starting with these requirements the New York architect John Burgee proposed the construction of two towers leaning at 15°, meeting at a common point on the axis of the Paseo de la Castellana.

This scheme filled the role that the municipal planners had assigned to the towers as part of an array of tall buildings aligned along the street. It also managed to emphasize the image of these two unusual structures, in addition to resolving the excessive separation between the two that lessened their impact on the city's skyline.

Umeda Sky Building

Hiroshi Hara

Location: Osaka, Japan. **Date of completion**: 1993. **Architect**: Hiroshi Hara. **Scheme**: Office building: two towers of 40 stories joined by a platform, and gardens. **Photography**: Tomio Ohashi.

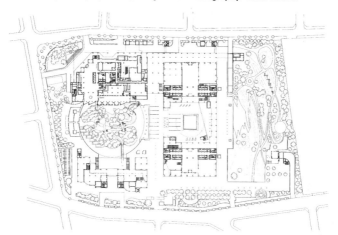

Located to the south of Tokyo, Osaka is one of the Japanese cities where Asian economic activity has been concentrated in an attempt to decentralize the country's business. Until a few years ago, the area where this project is located, Umeda City, was a vacant plot in the north of the city, very close to the Kanjo railroad track, which connects Osaka peripherally. As in any other project of this type, the developers needed a symbol capable of representing the newly created area: in the modern city this translates unfailingly into an imposing skyscraper. Skyscrapers have been erected as symbols not only of the modern city, but also of technological progress. According to the board of Japanese architects, it was not a case of building the highest skyscraper, but of conceiving a new type, in the form of two towers connected at their summits. For Hiroshi Hera this was a structure that could be the image of the city of the future.

Melbourne Central

Kisho Kurokawa

Location: Melbourne, Australia. **Date of completion**: 1991. **Architect**: Kisho Kurokawa. **Scheme**: Offices, commercial and leisure spaces, underground access to a subway station. **Photography**: Tomio Ohashi (also pp 784/785).

This complicated structure by the Japanese architect Kisho Kurokawa is located in the financial district of Melbourne. In its more than 26,067 m² (280.582 ft²) there are offices, spaces for shops and leisure pursuits, together with underground access to a subway station. By the juxtaposition of various activities in a single building complex it is hoped to revitalize a part of the city that had lost all its urban dynamism. The 2.6 hectare (6.4 acre) plot does not take up the whole area of the block where it is located, and coexistence with the adjacent buildings was a clear objective of the project. The lower part of the building, over which the glass tower juts out, in contact with the immediate urban environment, attempts by the composition of its space to testify to the complexity of the city. Under the huge glass cone a large central space opens out like a giant atrium, and this is the heart of the shopping center. A number of balconies on different levels look out over the space, and vertical movements are made architecturally to communicate between them. The building is presented, there is no doubt, as an attempt to combine all the convolutions of a city into a heterogeneous mix of uses, materials, and forms.

750 Seventh Avenue

Kevin Roche, John Dinkeloo and Associates

Location: 750 Seventh Avenue, New York, USA. **Date of completion**: 1991. **Architect**: Kevin Roche, John Dinkeloo and Associates. **Associates**: Weiskopf & Pickworth (structural engineering). **Scheme**: Skyscraper for company use. **Photography**: Paco Asensio

This surreal sight, on the edge of the theater district next to Times Square, is a steel tower with a short, thick antenna on top, which makes it appear like an enormous mobile telephone. It is customary in this area to present a progressively stepped envelope, and so Roche decided on a spiral shape in order to achieve a more dynamic design than the traditional set of boxes piled one on top of another. The final result has been harshly criticized by some of the most important architects of the AIA (American Institute of Architects). What does provoke a certain amount of admiration and surprise is the cladding based on satined glass. This is a kind of glass wickerwork with a horizontal line of ceramic and a vertical line of dark gray reflective glass. These two components give the building a really strange and dramatic texture.

Carnegie Hall Tower

Cesar Pelli & Associates

Location: W. 57th Street, New York, USA. **Date of completion**: 1999. **Client**: Rockrose Development Corporation. **Architect**: Cesar Pelli & Associates. **Associates**: R. Rosenwasser Associates (engineering). **Floor area**: 49,000 m² (527,000 ft²). **Photography**: Paco Asensio.

On W. 57th Street, between Sixth and Seventh Avenues, there is a curious quartet of buildings. Carnegie Hall Tower, light and golden, is practically stuck onto the edge of the brilliant, dark Metropolitan Tower, often referred to as the "Darth Vader Building," a symbol of the 1980s' shiny confidence.

The second highest building in New York, Carnegie Hall Tower is a commercial development that utilizes the space of the adjacent Carnegie Hall. Pelli has managed to relate his new building to the iconic concert hall. The tower, which has 60 floors, extends its illustrious neighbor's range of shades and shapes, reinterpreting the size, color, and ornamentation of the concert hall. Pelli compares his position as architect working inside the framework of the city to that of the assistant to a great painter like Raphael. The Tower comprises two interlinked soffits, of different sizes. It is raised 10 m (33 ft) above the level of the street in order to complement the five-story Russian Tea Room.

Shanghai World Financial Center

Kohn, Pedersen & Fox

Location: Pudong, Shanghai, China. **Date of construction**: 1997–2001. **Architect**: Kohn, Pederson & Fox. **Scheme**: Tower and base: hotel, observatory, commercial area, and underground parking lot. **Photography**: Edge Media NYC.

Located in the financial and commercial center of Lujiazui, the building is being erected as a distinctive landmark of the Pudong district. Within Shanghai's economic resurgence, Pudong is the most favored area of expansion, and the large majority of the skyscrapers planned for the 21st century are to be built there. The Shanghai World Financial Center was started in 1997 and is due to be completed in 2001. The plan for this 460 m (1510 ft) high, 95-story skyscraper, which will have 300,000 m² (3.2.million ft²) gross floor area, includes a hotel, a viewing zone, commercial premises, and underground parking, within the two elements of the project, the tower and the base. The tower will contain the hotel and, on the top floors, the viewing zone, while the remainder will be distributed in the base. Its aerodynamic shape, the enormous hole in the top, the sharp edges, a smooth skin that will reflect the changes of light throughout the day, are the tools being used to make this building the reference point for the urban landscape of Shanghai.

SITE PLAN

Jin Mao Building

Adrian D. Smith (SOM)

Location: Shanghai, China. **Date of completion**: 1998. **Architect**: Adrian D. Smith (SOM). **Scheme**: Building containing offices, hotel, shopping center, cinema, convention center, landscaped exterior public space, and underground parking lot. **Photography**: Steinkamp/Ballog Chicago

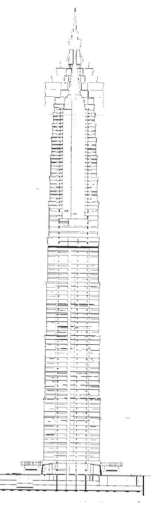

Recently completed, this 88-story building, with its stepped sections at the highest levels and, above all, the style of its pinnacle, is reminiscent of the shape of Chinese pagodas. Integration into the urban environment, which is one of the project's objectives, has been entrusted to an image already well absorbed into the country's collective consciousness. The first 50 stories of the tower are to be used for offices, while the rest will contain a luxury hotel with outstanding views of the city. An accompanying building is designed to house a shopping center, cinema, convention center, and services for the hotel. There are independent entrances to the skyscraper on each of the four sides of this building, which is surrounded by a landscaped public area which acts as an intermediate zone between this structure and the surrounding streets, reinforcing a symmetry that we also find in the layout of the elevator wells. Three underground levels for parking cars and bicycles complete the project's design.

Millennium Tower

Foster and Partners

Location: London, UK. **Date of completion**: At planning stage. **Architect**: Foster and Partners. **Scheme**: Tower for commercial and residential use. **Photography**: Richard Davies.

London's Millennium Tower, designed by Norman Foster, has been the object of debate for a long time. The feasibility and necessity for a building with these specifications in this particular area, plus financing problems, have caused protracted disputes between the architects and the local city planners, leading to constant delays in proceeding with construction: the tower has still not been built.

The building consists of a tower 385 m (1260 ft) in height, to which has been added a mast measuring another 60 m (197 ft) Within its 91 stories, the tower will house a communications zone at the top and, below this, 12 stories of apartments. The rest of the complex will consist of offices (60 stories), three restaurants, a viewing area, a shopping center in reception, and various levels for parking and storage. With its clearly futuristic design, the tower is intended to become an emblem of the new millennium in London.

Homes

Residential architecture is of fundamental significance inasmuch as it refers to the evolution of our way of life. This field has the privilege to examine at close quarters today's domestic dreams, to investigate new lifestyles, and to speculate on changes in the family, social, and even work environments. In fact, the house is the concrete manifestation of the interests, wishes, and whims of both purchaser and architect. This section includes a selection of homes built just before the year 2000. The choice has not been based on economic, aesthetic, or fashion criteria; we wanted to go beyond these dictates and include homes that mark a schism, that are today's innovations and tomorrow's classics. Nor are they intended to be prototypes, or examples to be followed. They are included because they are characteristic of their time, their location, and their owners. These projects have been grouped into different chapters, although all have features in common.

First, respect for the environment, not specifically at an ecological level but in the way in which the buildings relate to the landscape. Second, respect between client and architect, so that the wishes of the former are an inspiration for the latter. Third, proper choice of materials used in the construction as, apart from determining tonality, light reflection, and surface textures, the materials complete the final image of the house, influencing this on many levels. Finally, the exclusivity that is implicit in this type of project, since they are usually born out of very personalized commissions. The tastes and resources of each owner vary, so each project is unique. Moreover, the architects have the opportunity to immerse themselves in their creative work, suggest fresh ideas, and try out new functional or structural concepts.

Multifamily urban homes

Although throughout the Modern Movement era the design of multifamily housing was the central question and exemplified the architectural situation of the moment, at the present day it would be questionable to view the status of multifamily homes in the same terms. The reason is not that architects have lost interest in such an important subject, but that it is difficult to offer concrete and realistic solutions to a problem that includes ever more parameters. City planning, regulation, and economic speculation are responsible for many of the horrors produced in this field. Those responsible for the examples included here have been able to avoid these pitfalls, however, by investigating this area in depth. These are not mere exercises in how to prettify façades, but projects that contribute to a social, urban planning, and architectural debate.

Homes in Haarlemmerbuurt

Claus en Kaan Architekten

Location: Binnenwieringerstraat 8, Amsterdam, Netherlands. **Date of completion**: April 1995. **Promoter**: Lievan de Key. **Architects**: Felix Claus, Kees Kaan. **Associates**: Floor Arons, Roland Rens, Michael van Pelt (design), Stracke (construction) **Scheme**: Apartments. **Photography**: Ger van der Vlugt

The Haarlemmerbuurt area is between the port of Amsterdam and the canals. This is a very lively area; its atmosphere is a mixture of the bourgeois environment of the canals and the landscape along the banks of the river Ij. The history of this part of Amsterdam is reflected in the façades of the houses: like a film set, the streets are a string of architectural styles from all periods, tied one to another at random. In the case of Binnenwieringerstraat 8, the work was to an existing building: it was very small, only 3.5 m (11.5 ft) wide by 8 m (26 ft) deep. For that reason, the architects decided to use an adjacent space to locate all the services and installations needed so that the old structure could house comfortable apartments. Indeed, after the remodeling, the old house contains only three rooms. The project allowed the old building to be preserved, including its typical constructional details done by artisans (which would be impossible to reproduce today), without having to cause any damage when installing staircases, pipework and so on. Everything necessary to comply with current regulations and requirements is built into the annex. The old house, instead of becoming a museum to 19th-century living, has been turned into an open space measuring 7 x 3 m (23 x 10 ft), a well-appointed example of social housing.

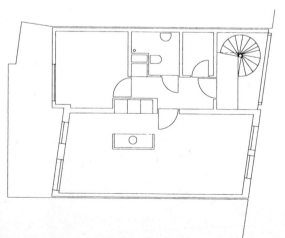

Homes in the Calle del Carme and the Calle d'En Roig

Josep Llinàs Carmona

Location: Barcelona, Spain. **Date of design**: 1992–1993. **Date of construction**: 1994–1995. **Architect**: Josep Llinàs Carmona. **Client**: Procivesa. **Associates**: Eva Monte, Joan Vera, Jaume Martí. **Scheme**: 28 homes, commercial premises, and garage. **Photography**: David Cardelús

In the historical center of Barcelona, the district known as the Barrio del Raval is undergoing a series of renovations and clean-up operations, which are being performed on a dense fabric of very run-down houses. The plot involved in this project, which became available following the demolition of several houses, faces a narrow, dark lane, the Calle d'En Roig, and a lively shopping street, the Calle del Carme. The ground floor of the apartments funnels into the Calle del Carme, allowing pedestrians to come and go. On the next floor up, there are three turrets that allow the section to widen out and let light into the dark Calle d'En Roig. It is the first floor that is best suited to the existing perimeter thanks to the shape of the turrets and the screen between them, which protects the privacy of the terraces of the first-floor apartments from the neighboring façade. The three almost free-standing turrets are located on a new line of façade rising out of a discontinuous footing at the base of the new structure.

Homes in the Calle del Carme and the Calle d'En Roig 817

Apartment building in Basle

Jacques Herzog, Pierre de Meuron

Location: Schützenmattstrasse, Basle, Switzerland. **Date of design**: 1991. **Date of construction**: 1992–1993. **Client**: Pensionkasse des Basler Staatspersonals (BS). **Project supervisor**: André Maeder. **Architects**: Jacques Herzog, Pierre de Meuron. **Associates**: Dieter Jüngling, Rina Plangger. **Photography**: Margherita Spiluttini

apartments there is a view of the trees next door.
The ground floor consists of an extra high hallway, which allows access to a museum at the back of the plot. The first two floors are used for commercial premises.
The front of the apartments, in the façade that looks out onto the street, is enclosed by cast-iron slats that run the full width and height of each floor. The choice of this unusual material is related to elements of the street furniture, such as the

gratings over the drains; the building adopts this urban image as a reflection of the city outside.

This is a small building on a very long and narrow plot of land in the medieval part of Basle: it is 6.3 m (21 ft) wide and 23 m (75) deep.
The distribution of the floors is based on a large courtyard garden in one of the neighboring plots, which looks out onto the south side. The new building is organized around this garden, so that from the

Homes for postal workers

Philippe Gazeau

Location: 46, rue de l'Ourcq, Paris, France. **Date of construction**: 1993. **Client**: SA HLM Toit et Joie. **Architect**: Philippe Gazeau. **Associates**: Agnès Cantin, Jacques Forte; Fougerolle Construction (construction). **Scheme**: 26 homes for postal workers. **Photography**: Jean-Marie Monthiers.

The plot where these 26 homes are located is extremely long and narrow. It is in an architecturally very heterogeneous neighborhood, notable for regular urban-style façades onto the street and lower, more irregularly shaped buildings to the rear. The first problems to solve on this project were organizing the space so that light and ventilation reached the middle of the plot, and designing the new structures to harmonize with the existing buildings all around. On the side of the rue de l'Ourcq, two tall blocks were designed, eight floors, supported by the two shared side walls, and set back a considerable distance from the street.

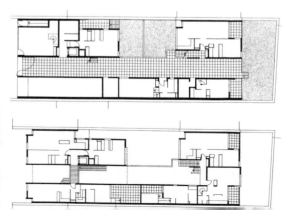

Apartment building in La Croix Rousse

Jourda & Perraudin Architectes

Location: Rue Grataloup, Lyon, France. **Date of design**: 1990. **Date of construction**: 1995. **Client**: OPAC, Lyon. **Architects**: Jourda & Perraudin Architectes. **Associates**: Gavin Arnold, EZCA, Claude Brenier, Catherine Vardanégo. **Photography**: Georges Fessy (also pp 812/813).

This apartment block is located in the La Croix Rousse district in Lyon. This is a neighborhood which has long been inhabited by craftsmen, so most of the houses here have craft workshops, with a large amount of work space, and are served by a few local businesses providing essential services. This new structure aims to have some continuity with the existing building types.

The key decision consisted of concentrating all the available space into the apartments themselves, by making the stairs a completely separate element, attached to the rear of the property. This structure consists of the stairs to the different floors, but it is much more substantial than would be required just for that function. This feature is used for going up and down, getting to the elevators, or moving between apartments, so it is a real communal space for the whole block.

The six floors of the building contain two small single apartments on the first and second floors, and two duplex apartments on the four upper floors. The mansards house small studio/workshops.

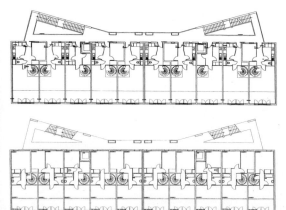

Apartment building in Oporto

Eduardo Souto de Moura

Location: Rua do Teatro, Oporto, Portugal. **Date of design**: 1992. **Date of construction**: 1995. **Architect**: Eduardo Souto de Moura. **Client**: Eng. Miguel Cerquinho. **Associates**: Graça Correia, Pedro Mendes, Silvia Alves, Francisco Cunha, Manuela Lara; Soares da Costa/San José (construction). **Photography**: Luis Ferreira Alves.

The Rua do Teatro is in an area of Oporto outside the medieval walls. This new apartment building is located on a plot that is much wider than the others around it. Given that the neighboring houses are quite small, Souto de Moura designed this project to effect continuity with them. The two neighboring houses are on a different alignment: the one on the left is taller and not set back very far; and that on the right is smaller and set back much further. Consequently Souto de Moura's design strictly respects the different alignments of the neighboring houses: his own building compromises between the two.

Kop van Zuid residential complex

Frits van Dongen

Location: Landtong, Rotterdam, Netherlands. **Date of construction**: 1998. **Architect**: Frits van Dongen. **Associates**: A.J. Mout, R. Puljiz, A.J. de Haas, M. Heesterbeek, F. Veerman, J. van Hettema, J. Molenaar. **Scheme**: 625 homes in a cooperative, sports club, six tennis courts, children's play area, 1000 m² (10.100 ft²) of commercial premises, 200-place parking lot. **Photography**: Daria Scagliola and Stijn Brakkee.

This complex, which alone contains 625 homes, is located on an ex-docklands plot with three sides facing the river: the two longer ones on both flanks, and the third at the end. Located on the lengthened wharves, the complex consists of a system of linear blocks that form three semi-enclosed courtyards. The blocks running across, with high density housing, are higher, while the land parallel to the wharves is closed in by smaller blocks, separated by the ends of the others; these are single family homes set out in rows. There are five large, equidistant blocks, although they are all different from each other. In addition to the three courtyards, there is a large open space in the middle of the complex, on top of the parking block: this is to be developed as a public garden area.

The initial design more or less guarantees that the complex will avoid seeming too regular. In each stepped block, the access corridors, located on its spine, are joined two by two, forming a double space, so that the entrance to the higher apartments is via a raised passageway. In addition to this, halfway along the block there is a large glazed courtyard that allows maximum light to enter the common areas of this interior spine, where there are restrooms, kitchens, and, in many cases, cupboards and storerooms. The single family homes, which face the wharves on the side, are of particular interest: here regularity is firmly restored in the minute details of each dwelling unit.

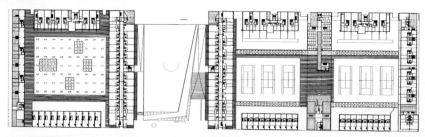

Apartments in Tilburg

Wiel Arets S.L.

Location: Timmermanspad Street and the corner with Kuiper Street, Tilburg, The Netherlands. **Date of construction**: 1993–1995. **Architect**: Viel Arets S.L. **Client**: Stichting Verenigde Woningcorporaties SVW. **Associates**: Michel Melenhorts (coordinator), Tina Brandt, Reina Bos, Andrea Wallrath; DVHV Amersfoort (budget). **Scheme**: 67 three-room apartments divided into three blocks of 37, 14, and 16 units. **Photography**: Kim Zwarts.

An old industrial zone in the center of Tilburg is being transformed. It has been decided, for example, to house the De Pond Museum, which has an important collection of contemporary art, in one of the old factories in the once run-down area. The apartments that Arets designed are distributed between three blocks on Timmermanspad Street, where the museum is to be. Two blocks are located in a U shape at one end of the museum, making room for an interior garden alongside one of the façades; the third, a long block, with views over the De Pond Museum garden, is just inside the plot, opposite its main entrance. Each apartment has 77 m² (830 ft²) of floor area;

access to each is via a common corridor, some 3 m (10 ft) wide. The external treatment of the blocks' façades differs according to whether the block is a main one, facing the street, or a rear one, protecting the corridor from which there is access to each unit. The first type is of rough stucco, called "putz," with interior balconies from which one can watch movement in the street. The second type, which looks over the garden areas, is made of open brickwork containing relatively large windows, which light the access corridor of the building.

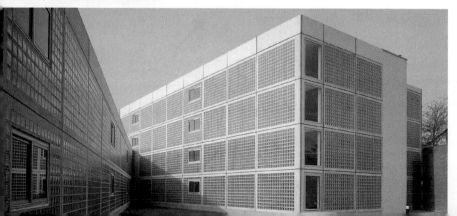

Résidence Les Chartrons

François Marzelle, Isabelle Manescau, Edouard Steeg

Location: Rue Poyenne, Bordeaux, France. **Date of design**: 1991. **Date of construction**: 1994. **Client**: Sonacotra. **Architect**: François Marzelle, Isabelle Manescau, Edouard Steeg. **Project supervisor**: Edouard Steeg. **Scheme**: 102-room residential complex. **Photography**: Vicent Monthiers Schlomoff.

Résidence Les Chartrons, in the center of Bordeaux, is an experimental attempt to find quantitative, functional, and aesthetic parameters that will ensure an acceptable quality of life in this type of residential complex. A starting point is the fact that all the rooms have their own bathroom, consisting of a basic module repeated and varied throughout the complex. This module, repeated five times, forms part of a larger unit comprising five bedrooms, which share a common living room and kitchen. The layout of this unit is

very simple: organized as a duplex, there are two bedrooms and the communal areas on the lower floor, while the three remaining bedrooms are upstairs. Although an interior staircase joins the two floors, making the unit rather like a conventional house, there are independent entrances to the five bedrooms, making the system of staircases for the whole complex relatively complicated and significant in style.

The layout consists of two blocks of four floors in parallel, with a fairly small interior courtyard. The use made of the courtyard, which contains some communal services, is determined by the fact that all the staircases and passages leading to the various rooms leave from this point.

113, rue Oberkampf

Frédéric Borel

Location: 113, rue Oberkampf, Paris, France. **Date of completion**: November 1993. **Clients**: Ministry of Telecommunications and Post. **Architect**: Frédéric Borel. **Associates**: Joel Gallouedec, Carola Brammen, Massimo Mattiussi; SCGPM (contractor); G.I.I. (engineering). **Scheme**: 80 apartments, building for a post office, and a small shopping center. **Floor Area**: 7000 m2 (75.000 ft²). **Photography**: F. Borel.

The site for this project is a narrow urban plot, measuring 20 m (66 ft) on the street and 87 m (285 ft) long. One added difficulty on the plot was the presence of shared walls, to a height of 23 m (75 ft). Contained within natural limits, similar to the walls of a fortification, the project became a microterritory, an urban microcosm. The particular requirements of the scheme, a post office, small shopping center, and a building of small apartments (studios and floors with two rooms) for young people, became the active parameters of the overall project.

The post office, the stores, and the entrance to the apartments are organized around transparent elements through which one can see a small fraction of the infinite: "presence and absence of distance." A small bit of landscaping, in the form of a garden visible from the street, is laid out in the central area. The apartments are spaced around the periphery and have views of the garden: the fragment of ground that breathes, the last façade, looking to the sky.

The final block, deep into the plot, has three levels of apartments, each with a terrace, facing south. The floor layout, designed to attract young couples, suggests somewhere that can be adapted for a family: the service room situated in the middle of the domestic space can become a nursery, a bedroom for the parents, a library/studio or even the living room.

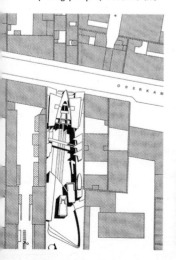

Apartments in the historic center of Maastricht

Mecanoo

Location: Herdenkingsplein "Memorial Plaza", Maastricht, The Netherlands. **Date of design**: 1990–1992. **Date of construction**: 1994. **Client**: Municipality of Maastricht (plaza), Stichting Pensioenfonds Rabobank (apartments). **Architect**: Mecanoo. **Associates**: Technical consultants ABT, Delft. **Scheme**: 52 apartments. **Photography**: Christian Richter.

The apartments are located behind a screen of varnished cedar that hides the living rooms. The balconies and galleries, by which one reaches each of the apartments from the stairwell, are in line with the outer portico, which is paved in marble. This connects the two blocks containing the apartments, creating the illusion of a single façade when in reality they are independent buildings. The interior distribution of the block that faces the plaza is reminiscent of traditional Dutch houses, with each apartment occupying the whole of the corridor. The block that is set further back is occupied by a duplex, also stretching from façade to façade, and apartments in the corner, facing the plaza. The side wall is painted white, to differentiate it from the living room window side.

In the indoor courtyards there are gardens for the ground floor apartments and some small storage cubicles made of a special local stone, rescued from a nearby demolition site. The same stone is used to line the stairwells and in the reconstruction of the wall around the plot.

Grand Union Walk

Nicholas Grimshaw & Partners Ltd

Location: Grand Union Walk, Camden, London, UK. **Date of completion**: 1986–1989. **Client**: J. Sainsbury plc. **Architect**: Nicholas Grimshaw & Partners Ltd. **Associates**: Neven Sidor, Mark Fisher, Hin Tan, Ingrid Bille, Sally Draper, James Finestone, Thomas Fink, Rowena Fuller, Andrew Hall, Christine Humphrey, Gunther Schnell, Ulrike Seifritz, Simon Templeton. **Scheme**: Commercial and residential complex: major store, workshops, and attached apartments. **Photography**: John Peck.

The principal objective of this commercial and residential complex was to try to reconcile the potential of high-tech architecture with the needs of municipal planners. It was decided to construct a complex comprising a major store, a series of workshops, and a group of attached apartments on a triangular plot. The shape of the land made viable a functional separation into modules, due to the different directions of the sides of the plot, one of which faces the Grand Union Canal. The commercial and workshop schemes were allocated two modules, while the northerly side, on the canal, was reserved for the nucleus of the apartments, thus offering an interactive combination of architecture and nature. The important role given to the physical presence of the water in its relation to the building means that consideration also had to be given to the security of future inhabitants and the environmental protection of the canal. Use of the unusual bowed structures reduces the problems of an oblique frontage, reinforces the private nature of each of the balconies, and gives a better view over the water. The architects based their plans on some essential points: the almost industrial process for installing the structures; the alternation of surfaces straight and curved, transparent and opaque; and, lastly, an effective ratio of external and internal space.

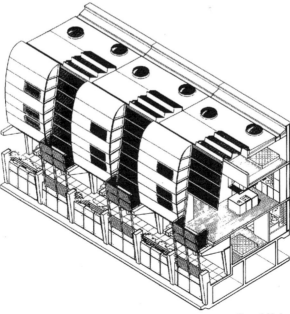

Multifamily suburban homes

The demographic and migratory
explosion has called for the urgent
construction of residential complexes in
the suburbs. These blocks, only planned
in economic terms, have temporarily
solved the problem of housing provision
for a considerable increase in the urban
population. These box-like buildings have
involved no advances either socially or
structurally. Currently the suburbs, where
the city gradually turns to country, are
colonized by multifamily residential
architecture more attentive to durability
and comfort. There are, however, projects
that seek a balance between functionality
and aesthetics: on the one hand,
investigating the nature of residential
architecture, assimilating new concepts of
the family; and, on the other, adapting to
an ambiguous environment which is
being defined at the rate that buildings
are erected on the land, establishing its
character and appearance.

Homes in Fukuoka

Steven Holl

Location: Fukuoka, Japan. **Date of construction**: 1989–1991. **Architect**: Steven Holl. **Project supervisor**: Hideaki Arrizumi. **Associates**: Peter Lynch, Thomas Jenkinson, Pier Copat; Shimizu Corporation (structural engineering); Schwartz-Smith-Meyer/Martha Schwartz (landscaping). **Photography**: Richard Barnes.

surface and the pavement of the porticoes. These are the fundamental elements of a system of public spaces and walks that articulates the whole block.

This is a complex of 28 apartments located in a suburban area of Fukuoka, comprising what is basically a single block, although there are two concepts involved: "articulated space" and "empty space," a container of silence.

The block encloses four large south-facing courtyards, that on the lowest level featuring a pond. These are designed as spaces for meditation, away from the everyday life of the home. These four spaces, which are higher than street level, are articulated with the rest of the complex by being connected to a number of porticoed areas which face inwards towards the block: these double-height spaces are linked to the stores, the café terraces, and the children's play area. The silent spaces facing south and the activity-packed porticoes facing north are separated by only one story. In addition, a single flight of stairs connects one type of space to the other, bridging the difference between the pond's flat

Homes in Makuhari

Steven Holl

Location: Makuhari New Town, Chiba, Japan. **Date of construction**: 1996. **Client**: Mitsui Fudosan Group. **Architect**: Steven Holl. **Project supervisor**: Tomoaki Tanaka. **Gross floor area**: 8415 m² (90,500 ft²). **Scheme**: 190 apartments and small stores. **Photography**: Paul Warchol (also pp 840/841).

The objective of the project was to design a complete block of the city of Makuhari, on the Bay of Tokyo. The main operations involved:
1) Opening the original ring of buildings at the four corners, by what Holl calls "gates," each one related to a cardinal point: north, south, east, and west gates.
2) Turning and changing the spaces in the blocks as appropriate to favor the best sunlight.
3) Locating a central block to divide the original courtyard into two parts, thus generating two smaller courtyards, called the north courtyard and the south courtyard. These basic areas form what Holl defines as weighty and silent space that witnesses the ordinary and most prosaic events of life.

Some unusual work is included in the scheme, for the most part in the form of single family homes, of which there are six, one for each of the gates and the two courtyards.

The houses that correspond to the four gates are usually suspended or half-suspended over the large gaps between the blocks which form the gates themselves, while those related to the courtyards, which incorporate ponds, tend to be built in a seemingly unstable situation, tipped towards the surface of the water.

M-30

Francisco Javier Sáenz de Oíza

Location: Polígono 38, La Paz, Madrid, Spain. **Date of completion**: 1991. **Client**: Land, Environment, and Housing Council, Community of Madrid. **Architect**: Francisco Javier Sáenz de Oíza. **Scheme**: Construction of 400 homes over 8 floors. **Photography**: Francesc Tur.

A review of the architectural scene over the last few decades shows that the restructuring by planners of suburban areas tends to involve the construction of social housing, a structured element in the often sprawling periphery. The building was planned as one continuous block, in a spiral shape, that runs along the contour as far as the road junction, where it turns back inside, to form an open ring. Sáenz de Oíza decided to adjust the route of this side road, so that, on the northeastern slope of the land, the building is facing inwards, to give better definition to the complex's access zone and the underground parking lots serving the building.

The sinuosity of the structure is another of the keys to the project, since from it are derived two architectural realities: the building itself and the space it encloses, the lung to help it breathe and the communal facilities on view. The selection of solid brick 15 cm (6 in) thick as the principal building material contributes to the homes' insulation from the annoyance of traffic noise.

Nemausus I

Jean Nouvel and Jean-Marc Ibos

Location: Nîmes, France. **Date of completion**: 1987. **Architect**: Jean Nouvel and Jean-Marc Ibos. **Scheme**: 114 homes, 146 parking places, garden area. **Photography**: Pierre Berenger.

The architects have tried to distance themselves from the typical compact, solid image of social housing, and have opted for an apartment complex where the accent is on those features underlining the sensation of mobility and dynamism. The design of these homes has been inspired directly by cultural and aesthetic references to the "loft." The need to keep to a budget, as well as maintain the industrial nature of the area, have meant basing the project on the use of industrial materials and raw

materials, achieving a curious combination that re-creates in a personal space the kind of decoration more often found in a manufacturing space. With this experimental project a number of objectives have been achieved: creating homes that are larger than usual; gaining the extra space within the budget for

smaller homes; and, finally, using part of the terrace area to extend the living area, thereby taking advantage of the site's superb climatic conditions to the full.

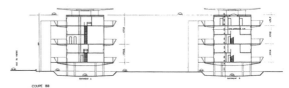

Wozocos

MVRDV

Location: Woonzorgcomplex Joh. De Deo, Reimerswaalstraat, Amsterdam-Osdorp, The Netherlands. **Date of construction**: 1994–1997. **Client**: Woningbouwvereniging Het Oosten, Amsterdam. **Architect**: MVRDV. **Associates**: Willem Timmar, Arjan Mulder, Frans de Witte; Bureau Bouwkunde; Pieters Bouw Techniek, Haarlem (structural engineering). **Scheme**: 100 homes for elderly people in the west of Amsterdam. **Photography**: Hans Werlemann.

MVRDV was contracted to design a block of 100 apartments for elderly people in an area to the west of the center of Amsterdam. After analyzing the town planning regulations drawn up by Van Eesteren for this area, they reached the conclusion that only 87 of the 100 homes planned could be built without blocking the sunlight to the neighboring buildings. Where could the other 13 be located? They decided to hang them from the northern façade, literally suspending them in the air. In the building there is a corridor along the north façade that is reached by the only stair and elevator well, and in which are situated the entrances to each of the homes, including those that

overhang; and a south façade, onto which the apartments give directly. The homes consist of three smaller rooms opening from a peripheral room that contains the kitchen and a sitting room/dining room/bedroom with a balcony. The size of the balconies varies, as does the color of their covering material, and, like the windows, their placement seems to be independent of the internal layout, some of them coinciding with the dividing wall between each of the homes.

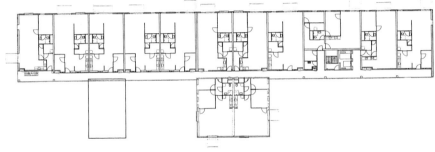

La Venerie residential complex

Dubosc & Landowski

Location: Montargis, Loiret, France. **Date of construction**: 1994. **Client**: OPAC du Loiret. **Architect**: Dubosc & Landowski. **Associates**: Andrea Mueller, Monica Alexandrescu. **Scheme**: 48 homes. **Photography**: J.M. Monthiers.

In this complex of homes two symmetrical blocks face each other to create a more controlled inner space, protected and integrated into the urban framework of Montargis. In this case maximum use is made of the useful surface that this construction can offer. This is achieved by placing the staircases outside the building, thus reducing the communal areas, which are usually dead space. The homes are placed transversally to the blocks, which allows them to have a double orientation. On the ground floor, where the layout is vertical, there are duplex homes for four or five people with their own access and garden. The second level is formed by units for one or two people; these are laid out longitudinally and are reached via a staircase and corridor outside. The top two levels are occupied by homes for two or three people and have recently been reorganized as duplex apartments.

The materials used are of industrial origin, which allows greater ease of installation and a minimum of maintenance in subsequent years.

The La Venerie residential complex has a new architectural plan which tries to make the social dimension of collective housing compatible with the autonomy of individual living in the 20th century in France.

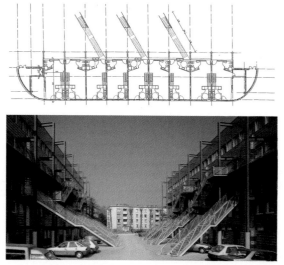

Social housing in Alcobendas

Manuel de las Casas

Location: Alcobendas, Madrid, Spain. **Date of design**: 1993. **Date of construction**: 1996. **Client**: Ivima. **Architect**: Manuel de las Casas. **Associates**: José Luis Cano, Indagsa (structural engineering), Ortiz & Cia (construction, fittings), Felicidad Rodríguez (model), Iciar de las Casas (gardens and landscaping). **Scheme**: 198 social housing units and garages: 183 three-bedroom homes (70 m², 750 ft²), 15 two-bedroom homes (60 m², 650 ft²), 84 parking spaces. **Photography**: Ángel Luis Baltanás, Eduardo Sanchez.

The complex consists of a series of blocks perpendicular to the road, and others parallel to the edge of the plot, which visually shut in the complex. The layout of the blocks is determined by the curve of the street, creating a façade and closing off the noise and sight of the traffic. The complex is treated as one single residential unit, in other words, the plot is enclosed in such a way that the spaces between the blocks are for private pedestrian use. The blocks are five floors high and are of high density – four apartments per floor. Inside, the homes are planned as linear units with the service rooms and storage spaces grouped around a central nucleus, the majority of them having two façades for better ventilation. The structure and the outer enclosure are dealt with by means of a system based on large, 12 cm (4.5 in) thick panels of reinforced concrete, which act as load bearing walls. These panels are used both for the façades and for the inside walls, which gives great strength to the building.

Residential block in Graz

Riegler & Riewe

Location: Bahnhofstrasse, Graz, Austria. **Date of design**: 1991. **Date of construction**: 1994. **Architect**: Riegler & Riewe. **Associates**: Margarethe Müller, Brigitte Theissl. **Scheme**: 27 homes. **Photography**: Margherita Spiluttini, Paul Ott.

There are two different types of home in this block: some of 50 m² (540 ft²) with two and a half rooms, and others of 78 m² (840 ft²) with four and a half. The whole building, which is three floors high and 75 m (250 ft) long, is designed, so that, with its outer skin, it looks less bulky. A number of sliding doors run the whole length of the façades. The façade which gives access to the homes is broken by the stairwells. Sections of metal grating have been used to cover this façade, fixed on the stairs and movable on the apartments; on the side that gives onto the garden, however, nylon has been used. The continuous movement of these panels, which provide both privacy and protection from the sun, gives an ever-changing appearance to the home. The façade closest to the street looks out onto the pavement of the access approach to the entrances, up stepped ramps. On the other side, a garden provides more direct contact with the exterior, on the side of the building where each home has a longer façade and where there are two rooms.

Apartments in Graz

Ernst Giselbrecht

Location: Graz, Austria. **Date of construction**: 1998. **Architect**: Ernst Giselbrecht. **Photography**: Paul Ott.

The building is aligned north to south and has four floors, with duplex homes grouped two and two. Those upstairs have balconies and views of the surroundings, while those on the ground floor have direct access to the garden. The entrances, stairs, and balconies are not placed symmetrically and, while forming part of the building, appear like independent elements that vary in form according to their use or function. The dividing walls of the apartments stretch across the whole width of the building and constitute the dominant rhythm of the interior structure. Each pair of homes is joined by a linking gallery.

This layout of walls and apertures allows the apartments to be subdivided freely, thus providing a structural system governed by the spirit of classic modernism.

Thanks to the generous amount of glass, the whole building can be seen from the entrance.

The staircase looks like one continuous element that runs up through the building as far as the roof. The transparency of the tops of the internal divisions allows the different rooms to be imagined as independent bodies in a common space. The place is perceived to be larger, there is an overall view of the apartment, and the walls are dissolved in the home's large, multifunctional interior space.

Hotels and residences

The projects included in this section differ from the other residential categories in just one specific respect: they are temporary residences. The buildings that house them must provide hospitable spaces that can tolerate considerable turnover of users. So, apart from addressing the particular functional requirements of each project, the design will need to make flexible use of space to meet the needs of many different clients.This chapter includes, among others, hotels in different parts of the world, student residences, and guest houses for visitors. Although they vary regarding location and use, all the examples have something in common: they succeed in creating pleasant surroundings in robust buildings, despite the wear and tear they might undergo.

Visitors' center in Yusuhara

Kengo Kuma

Location: Takaoka, Kochi Prefecture, Japan. **Date of completion**: March 1994. **Architects**: Kengo Kuma & Associates, Todahiro Odani & Associates, Plaza Design Consultant. **Associates**: K. Nakata & Assoc. (structural engineers). **Scheme**: Restaurant and hotel (eight Western-style and eight Oriental-style bedrooms). **Photography**: Fujitsuka Mitsumasa

Yusuhara-cho is at the source of the Shimanto, a river whose waters are maybe the clearest in Japan. The place is extraordinarily beautiful: the river, the valley, the cedar-covered slopes, the terraced banks where rice is grown... all this makes the park a special place which is sought out by many visitors.

Kengo Kuma is aware that the place is the reason for building the center.

In fact, this building is for housing visitors and, therefore, its occupants are there precisely to appreciate the beauty of the environment. For that reason, the architecture must be in keeping with the landscape and must open a dialogue with the natural world.

The building has two floors and a markedly linear shape running north to south. The gross floor area is approximately 1300 m² (14,000 ft²). It is clearly divided into three modules with different functions: in the first are the restaurant, kitchen and services; in the second, the bedrooms (Oriental-style downstairs and Western-style upstairs); and, finally, there is a building for machinery and equipment.

The restaurant module is the most interesting and complex. It is based on an opposition between two planes: that of the roof and that of an artificial pool. These two planes define an interior space with no precise limits, which varies continuously with the light.

Hotel Kempinski

Helmut Jahn

Location: Munich, Germany. **Date of construction**: 1996. **Architect**: Helmut Jahn. **Associates**: Peter Walker (landscaping). **Floor Area**: 38,300 m² (412,000 ft²). **Photography**: Helmut Jahn.

The Hotel Kempinski is the first building of the neutral zone at Munich airport, dedicated to commercial and business activities, and promoted as a city within the airport itself. In this spirit, it is modular in style, forming part of a series of buildings being planned.

The organization of the hotel corresponds to the airport's system of different levels. The rooms, a total of 400, surround a central covered garden.

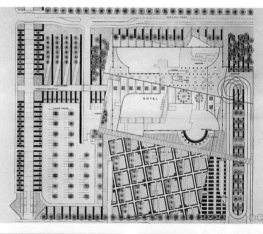

Hotel Martinspark

Dietmar Eberle & Karl Baumschlager

Location: Dornbirn Vorarlberg, Austria. **Date of completion**: 1995. **Architects**: Dietmar Eberle & Karl Baumschlager. **Scheme**: Design and construction of a hotel, and its restaurant as an annex. **Photography**: Eduard Hueber

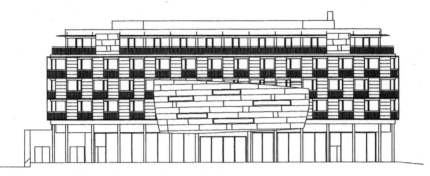

The rooms of this small, rectangular shaped hotel are distributed around a central patio. The appearance of the hotel is characterized by the façade, based on sliding blinds made of blue panels. The blue panels slide over glass windows, on all of the floors, creating a moving mosaic.

On the western façade of this sober building, there is a large structure of oxidized copper: this is the restaurant. It is supported on very fine metal pillars and its windows are long narrow slits opened at different heights, which coincide with the longitudinal lines of the joints of the copper sheet. The inside of the restaurant is simplicity itself. There are no decorative elements, so that diners can appreciate the singular form of the space without any kind of distortion.

Hotel Paramount

Philippe Starck

Location: New York, USA. **Date of completion**: 1990. **Client**: Ian Schrager, Philil Pilevsky, Arthur Cohen, Morgans Hotel Group. **Architect**: Philippe Starck. **Associates**: Anda Andrei (associate architect), Michael Overington (works director). **Photography**: Peter Mauss/ESTO Photographics.

The plan for the hotel included 610 rooms, two restaurants, an elegant club, a gymnasium, a crèche space, areas for shops and exhibitions, and even a small cinema. The hotel aspires to offer functional comfort in the context of almost poetic design. The emblematic façade of the building has made respectful use of its original structure. The first floor is defined by a series of 12 pointed arches over a glass surface with no visible frame or joins. The central interior courtyard is a rectangular space of double height. The whole area becomes a stage set, an idea that is reinforced by the checkerboard carpet reminiscent of the game of life itself.

The intermediate floor, occupied by one of the hotel restaurants, is in the form of a gallery that is open to the interior courtyard. A glass screen reveals the ambiguous function of these balconies, which act both as viewing points and display cabinets at the same time.

The architectural forms used in the hotel are based on chromatic and structural neutrality. Their severity and rigidity are transferred outside by the use of the color gray on stucco or plaster ornaments, roofs, and paving. The hotel's interior color scheme looks energetic and sensual, lending vitality to the activities taking place. The color motifs are repeated in the bathrooms. The polished surfaces and the mirrors multiply the visual perspectives and the sensation of size. The recurring rose red theme evokes lyrical references. The interior of the rooms has been designed personally by Starck himself with the very clear intention of creating a comfortable atmosphere that is like a second home.

Sea Hawk Hotel

César Pelli & Associates

Location: Fukuoka, Japan. **Date of completion**: 1995. **Architect**: César Pelli & Associates. **Scheme**: Hotel/resort, exterior gardening. **Photography**: Taizo Furukowa, Osamu Murai, César Pelli, Yukio Yoshimura.

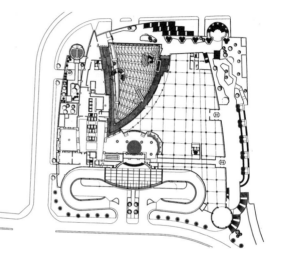

Built on the edge of the sea, visible from the city and constructed like a lighthouse, the hotel's design creates a collection of sculptural forms on the bay. The curves of the roof and walls relate to the elements: water and wind. The complex consists of buildings of different sizes. On the 34 floors of the high tower (in the shape of a boat) there are 1052 rooms, all with a view of the sea. The composition of fragmented curves echoes the profiles of a baseball stadium's monumental roofs. This tall tower contrasts with the round shapes of the lower building's glass cupolas. The walls are finished in ceramic tiles that form a rich texture of different colors and designs. The foyer is an elegant and quiet entrance for hotel guests, as opposed to the high, luminous and lively space of the glass atrium. In the form of a glass horn and open to the sea, the atrium is designed as an urban plaza with fountains and trees that invite both private conversations and public performances.

Cooper Union Residence

Prentice & Chan, Olhausen

Location: New York, USA. **Date of completion**: 1992. **Architect**: Prentice & Chan, Olhausen. **Scheme**: Student residence: dormitories, meeting room, communal service area, campus. **Photography**: Paco Asensio.

The design for this project managed a synthesis of both 19th- and 20th-century styles, in accordance with existing codes for the area, and the inclusion of a campus. One of the most significant elements is the sequence of grilles superimposed on the façade, that emphasize the square and rectangular shapes of the building. There are three separate structures and the proportions of the complex are very rational. The expression of the old and the new is achieved by the different widths of the layers of the façade: the narrow bands conserve the character of the neighborhood, while the wide outer wall of the tower has a more contemporary look. Inside there is a campus with private spaces. The design offers two bedroom apartments reminiscent of the "loft" concept, together with meeting rooms and communal areas. Large windows create a light and well-ventilated interior.

Ponsada Santa Maria do Bouro Hotel

Eduardo Souto de Moura, Humberto Vieira

Location: Braga, Portugal. **Date of design**: 1989. **Date of construction**: 1997. **Client**: Enatur. **Architects**: Eduardo Souto de Moura, Humberto Vieira. **Associates**: Manuela Lara, Antonio Loussa, Marie Clement, Ana Fortuna, Pedro Valente. **Photography**: Luis Ferreira Alves.

The purpose of this project was to make use of the stones available from a ruin to construct a new building, which involves various different aspects and functions (some already decided, others still pending). The scheme does not involve reconstruction of the building in its original form or plan.

In this case, the ruins are more important than the "convent," since it is the ruins that are open and manipulable, just as the building was in its time. The layout does not claim to express or represent any particular house by reproducing some original plan, but it does rely on a type of architecture that has remained more or less unchanged over the years. During the design process, we looked for clarity between the form and the scheme as a whole. Faced with two possible courses, we rejected pure and simple consolidation of the ruins to aid contemplation, choosing to introduce new materials, uses, forms, and functions "between things," as Le Corbusier said. "Picturesque" is a question of destiny, not part of a project or program.

Hotel Il Palazzo

Aldo Rossi

Location: Fukuoka, Japan. **Date of design**: 1986. **Client**: Mitsuhiro Kuzawa. **Architect**: Aldo Rossi.
Associates: Shigeru Uchida (artistic direction). **Photography**: Nacása & Partners Inc.

The project began at the end of 1986, when Mitsuhiro Kuzawa, owner of the hotel, commissioned the architectural design from the Italian Aldo Rossi and the artistic direction from Shigeru Uchide. He also requested the assistance of an excellent group of creative people to develop particular aspects of the scheme. The objective was to change the perception of the hotel, to have it thought of as socially, culturally, and intellectually functional rather than merely providing accommodation. The structure was to influence the urban landscape of the city (Fukuoka, Japan) by its visual significance, so that the hotel could make an impact on an already varied landscape. Those in charge of the project, Aldo Rossi and Shigeru Uchida, have been leading names in architecture and interior design for many years.

Sapporo Beer

Toyo Ito

Location: Sapporo, Japan. **Date of construction**: 1989. **Floor Area**: 300,000 m² (3.2 million ft²). **Architect**: Toyo Ito. **Photography**: Nacása & Partners.

The Sapporo Beer Company is one of the many industries located between Chitosa airport and the city of Sapporo. The project was a collaboration between the client, the Sapporo brewery, Y. Uede (of Uede Cultural Projects), S. Fukukawe (landscaper), and Y. Kanno (composer).

The Guest House, which is designed to accommodate visitors to the brewery, was built in a garden which occupies a third of the plot and comprises the Odin Pool, the Hill of Elms, the Forest of Fairies, the Plaza of the Fire and the Marshland, in representation of a Scandinavian landscape. The Guest House was designed to blend into the existing topography, so it is entirely buried, except for the façade, which looks out onto the garden. This made the whole complex more an earth-moving job than an architectural construction. The bar, the restaurant, and a rest area are located in polygonal spaces lit by skylights and decorated with painted ceilings and textiles. The ventilation towers, the skylights, and the awnings at the entrance appear above ground level; they are designed to simulate the wings of an aircraft, thus reflecting the nearby airport.

The project is a welcome resting place for visitors to the factory. They arrive at the Guest House, and descend into the earth, where they find a warm and bright atmosphere.

House of Water and Glass

Kengo Kuma

Location: Shizuoka, Japan. **Date of completion**: 1996. **Architect**: Kenzo Kuma. **Scheme**: House for guests of a Japanese company. **Floor Area**: 1125 m² (12,100 ft²). **Photography**: Futjitsuka Mitsumasa,

The House of Water and Glass is located on the edge of a cliff, on the coast of Ataml, looking out over the Pacific Ocean. The materials used are all light, such as glass, steel, or wood; these, according to Kengo Kuma, are materials of the present. The floor of the top level is covered by a sheet of water 15 cm (6 in) deep. Three glass structures, two square and one oval, have been placed over this and are reflected on the water. These are covered by a roof of metal sheets. Access is from the parking lot through an open door in a granite wall, which leads directly to a bridge of concrete and steel. On the floor below there is a bedroom in the Japanese style, a room for administration, a meeting room, and a gymnasium. On the access level floor is the dining room, to the right the kitchen and the sushi bar, and to the left visitors' rooms. On the top floor, the two rectangular structures contain guest rooms, and in the oval one there is a dining room.

The central idea of the House of Water and Glass is the study of different ways of seeing, in this case, nature: all in a general atmosphere of calm and equilibrium and with a rational use of materials.

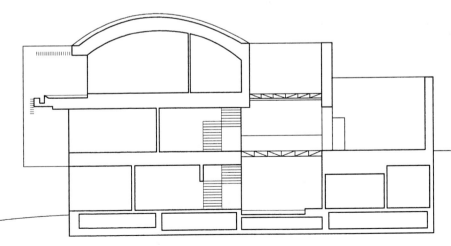

Timanfaya National Park Visitors' Center

Alfonso Cano Pintos

Location: Lanzarote, Canary Islands, Spain. **Date of construction**: 1993. **Client**: National Institute for the Conservation of Nature. **Architect**: Alfonso Cano Pintos. **Scheme**: Visitors' center for Timanfaya National Park, with staff accommodation. **Photography**: Alfonso Cano Pintos, Steve Chasen.

Alfonso Cano Pintos thought it right that the building should have a certain presence: he rejected the idea that the architecture could visually "contaminate" such an extreme landscape.

The scheme for the building had various functions. Firstly, the principal task of the complex is that of collecting and disseminating information on what the visitor is going to see in the National Park. For this there has to be a space for an explanatory exhibition and a projection room, as well as a small shop for selling books and objects related to the park, a multipurpose room, a library, administrative offices for the center, and other complementary facilities. In addition, another building meets the requirements of the park's personnel: two homes for the 'rangers', changing rooms, first aid station, stores, and parking lot for all-terrain vehicles.

The quality of the materials used, the white of the lime-wash on the outside, the scrubbed concrete and the steel plate emphasize the contrasts between artificial, man-made creation and the natural world.

Hotel Arts

SOM (Skidmore, Owings & Merrill), Bruce J. Graham

Location: Barcelona, Spain. **Date of completion**: 1992. **Client**: Hotel Arts. **Architects**: SOM (Skidmore, Owings & Merrill), Bruce J. Graham. **Scheme**: Building for the Hotel Arts: restaurants, convention rooms, and shopping center. **Photography**: David Cardelús.

As a kind of gateway to the waves, the towers, which are visible from all over the city, have become a symbol of the new efforts to open Barcelona to the sea, an issue which has been ignored for too long. The hotel makes a striking impression: a metal structure that can be seen all down the length of its 43 floors. It is the skeleton itself that provides the overall image of the project from any viewpoint. Behind this structure, an aluminum curtain wall encloses the building within, and gives depth to the façade, providing a rich pattern of light and shadow across it.

At the foot of the tower, to smooth the transition to ground level, there are 16,000 m² (172,000 ft²) of shops, restaurants, cafés, and a major store, built around a large pool open to the sea. Over this, as if floating on the water, is positioned an enormous fish covered in anodized aluminum. Frank O. Gehry collaborated in the project to install this, which, in addition to giving shade to the courtyard/pool, is a distinctive symbol for the shopping area and the whole stretch of beach.

Vantaa Home for the Elderly

Heikkinen & Komonen

Location: Vantaa, Finland. **Date of completion**: 1993. **Client**: Foibe Foundation. **Architect**: Heikkinen & Komonen. **Associate**: Janne Kentala. **Scheme**: Home for the elderly: residential blocks and communal service block. **Photography**: Jussi Tiainen (also pp 861/862).

This residence for the elderly is a new example of an architectural style that in the last few years has again caught the eye of international critics. Although all the buildings belong to the same

complex, the plan was to keep the different sections away from each other and to separate the buildings, to ensure that the residents do not feel as if they are in a hospital, but in their own home. The architect has divided the residents' apartments into a number of blocks and concentrated the communal areas in an independent building. The service block divides the plot longitudinally, following the topological line of the terrain. On one side is the hospital and the

old buildings of the Villa Rekola, on the other the apartments. The central building contains a restaurant, a library, rooms for residents' activities, a gymnasium, a swimming pool, a sauna, the specific facilities for residents with senile dementia, and various other services such as the hairdresser's and chiropodist's premises.

Group of homes for the Cheesecake Consortium

Fernau & Hartman

Location: Mendocino, San Francisco, USA. **Date of completion**: 1994. **Architect**: Fernau & Hartman. **Associates**: T. Gray, K. Moses, E. Stussi. **Gross floor area**: 8000 m² (86,000 ft²). **Scheme**: Complex of single family homes, verandahs, pergolas, platform for visitors' tents, laundry, library, and workshop. **Photography**: Richard Barnes.

The project consists of the construction of a complex of homes in a forest area in Mendocino County, to the north of San Francisco, for a group of friends. The scheme was finally built in three groups, each with various components: a building of two floors with communal services on the first floor and an apartment on the second floor, a residential wing with five apartments, a laundry and a library, and finally a workshop for repairing cars, developing photos, making furniture, or playing ping pong.

In total, there is a floor area of 5000 m² (54,000 ft²) of construction and 3000 m² (32,000 ft²) of covered areas: verandahs, pergolas, platforms for occasional visitors' tents, and terraces that connect the different buildings and encourage life in the open air.

At the same time, it has been ensured that all the rooms are easily accessible to elderly people, with ramps and elevators suitable for wheelchairs.

Semidetached and row houses

Homes with shared walls presuppose an obligation for neighboring buildings to have respect for each other. There are two strategies for approaching this situation: the first is based on a study of the surroundings, adapting to the parameters of proportion and style, and making use of existing architectural features. The other strategy is to start with a real building and use its originality to highlight its qualities and those of the neighboring buildings. Both approaches result in contemporary homes that have regard for the place they occupy, whether in cities or in small towns and villages. All the projects presented here pay special attention to how to make the best use of space, which is smaller than in the case of free-standing buildings. The architects' efforts are concentrated on their wish to create environments that give the impression of size.

Home/studio in Islington

Caruso St. John

Location: London, UK. **Date of completion**: 1994. **Architects**: Adam Caruso, Peter St. John. **Associates**: Alan Baxter and Associates (structural engineers). **Scheme**: Home and studio. **Photography**: Hélène Bisnet.

Adam Caruso and Peter St. John were involved in the conversion of an old store on two floors in Islington, North London, into a home and studio. The store, rectangular in shape and measuring 4.7 m (15 ft) wide by 9.8 m (32 ft) deep, provided a useful area of approximately 45 m² (484 ft²) per story. The floors were completely open, with no walls or even a pillar intruding on them. Caruso and St. John decided to replace the old façade with a glass wall. This consists of double glazed Climalit glass (8+24+6) with both insulation and acoustic properties. The panes are translucent but, although they let light through, they visually insulate the inside from the outside. They act like a silk screen or China paper. During the day the façade is hermetically sealed, as if it were made of a metal sheet. At night it becomes a light that illuminates the street.

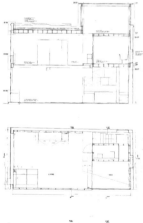

Price/O'Reilly House

Tina Engelen, Ian Moore

Location: Redfern, Sydney, Australia. **Date of construction**: 1996. **Architects**: Tina Engelen, Ian Moore. **Photography**: Ross Honeysett.

This two-story house is built on a piece of land that was formerly occupied by two traditional flat-roofed houses. The local authorities insisted that the new house should look like a traditional house and not like a store.

The main façade is divided into two vertical sections; both the horizontal elements and the proportions of the sections are designed to be in keeping with the neighbouring houses. In contrast, the rear façade consists of one opening 6 m x 6 m (20 x 20 ft). The layout inside has been adjusted accordingly. Behind the main façade are the small rooms of the home, divided into two levels: garage, storage area, and services (first floor); bedrooms and bathroom (second floor). Meanwhile, next to the garden, a single, double-height space has been constructed, which functions as sitting room, dining room, kitchen, and, eventually, photographic studio facilities.

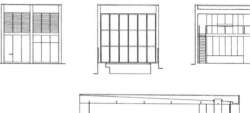

Home/studio (for an Ikebana artist)

Hiroshi Nakao

Location: Tokorawa, Japan. **Date of completion** 1996. **Architect**: Hiroshi Nakao. **Associates**: Hiroko Serizawa. **Scheme**: Workshop and home with three bedrooms. **Photography**: Nacása & Partners.

The house is a tomb. It is an exterior injected into the world, converted into an interior, and closed. This is definitely an inverted tomb. The outer walls are clad with a steel which changes dramatically from black to red as it rusts. And later, it subtly and bit by bit changes back to black. The house is submerged in the occurrence and recurrence of black. The inside is painted black. Like a flat image sliding over the world, the black temporarily takes over and silences all substance. And it requires one only to feel and wait. Wait for whatever manages to recover its deep memory and make it talk: light. An interminable cycle of reflections that appear and spread to illuminate the contours of the material (or the flesh) or to mute them, in a continuous process of renovation. The house organizes the dynamics of memory and forgetfulness. Space, its center, is in turn compressed and stretched. Depth is unfolded horizontally and vertically. In this space, our bodies, unstable and withdrawn, acquire a new rhythm and another gravity. The house organizes the movement, we throw ourselves down and we stand up. Memory and forgetfulness, standing and lying down. The house is definitely a tomb. A tomb that claims thought, life. A black box that tries to create life.

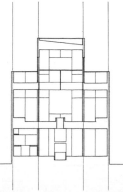

Offices and home of architect Stanley Saitowitz

Stanley Saitowitz

Location: Redfern, Sydney, Australia. **Date of construction**: 1993. **Architect**: Stanley Saitowitz. **Photography**: Richard Barnes (also pp 894/895).

The location, to the south of Market Street, consists of a typical 7.5 x 24.5 m (25 x 80 ft) urban plot. The fact that the client and architect were one and the same person, added to the prototypical characteristics of the plot, meant that the project would be a research exercise.

The aluminum sheet façade and full-width windows contrast with neighboring Victorian buildings, revealing interiors of a different scale and architectural design. The building is split into three units, each with ample double height space. The top section is occupied by Stanley Saitowitz's office, lit by a large central skylight. The middle section is the architect's home, and the first floor has the garage.

The framework consists of two rows of pillars located 1.5 m (5 ft) from the neighboring properties. These two projections contain all the building's services and stairs. In this way the central bay is left completely clear.

The construction system itself and the fittings create the architectural image. The strategy was to select materials, like chromium plating or wood veneer, which did not need to be finished: they could be covered eventually but could safely remain.

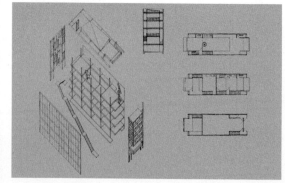

Zorn Residence

Krueck & Sexton

Location: Chicago, USA. **Date of completion**: 1995. **Architect**: Krueck & Sexton. **Photography**: Korale Hedrich Blessing.

The Zorn house is located in a residential area of north Chicago. It is positioned on its plot in such a way that it breaks the symmetry of the adjacent façades and enjoys views to the south. The house was designed as a simple brick and glass building, the interior of which revolves around a double height communal area. The south facing wall is the most transparent and is designed to receive the maximum light.

A long, narrow, vertical window opens to the west, projecting slightly from the plane of the façade, and offers views of the street at the same time as it extends along the roof in order to provide overhead diffused lighting for the central area of the second floor.

The starting point of Krueck & Sexton's architecture is the concept of a rectangle. Initially designed as a pure rectangle, the house has been transformed, slightly broken up, moved around a bit, and had parts added. Some of the additions were in height and some in width. In this way the various areas have been given expression and the building finally becomes a unified composition with all its features.

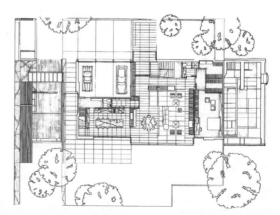

Duffy House

Bercedo + Mestre

Location: Sitges, Barcelona, Spain. **Date of completion**: 1998. **Architect**: Bercedo + Mestre. **Associates**: D. Schleipen (design), J.M. Ambros (technical architect). J. Marín (construction), R. Mayne (carpentry), Islathermic (aluminum) **Scheme**: Single family home. **Photography**: Jordi Miralles, Dominik Schleipen

The project consisted of the refurbishment and extension of an old, self-built house which was very run-down and damp, on a single floor, with a central corridor and small rooms on both sides. The house stands on an urban plot nearly 7 m (23 ft) wide between a four-floor and a three-floor building. What was created is an intimate setting, a private space which brings together different scenes and atmospheres. Shapes are therefore simple and stark. Part of the framework of the existing house has been demolished in order to insert an inner courtyard just beyond the entrance. In contrast to the reticence of the façade which overlooks the street, walking through the entrance the visitor encounters something quite unexpected. From this initial paradox, interior and exterior spaces constantly overlap, providing unaccustomed visual relationships and complex situations. This is a house which one constantly exits and enters. The architects have managed to develop a

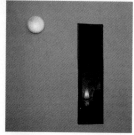

private exterior space in which the owners can live life in the open air.

Single family homes in Montagnola

Mario Campi, Franco Pessina.

Location: Lugano, Switzerland. **Date of construction**: 1988. **Client**: Mr. Corecco. **Architects**: Mario Campi, Franco Pessina. **Associates**: Benedikt Graf, Gianmarco Ciocca, Enzo Vanetta. **Scheme**: Three single family homes. **Photography**: Eduard Huelver.

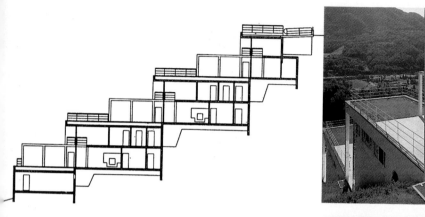

The project consists of three single family homes. The architects present these in a single block which blends naturally with the topographical relief, sloping down from west to east. In the southern area, chosen to accommodate the access staircase backing onto the various dwellings, the style of the façade looks more closed and compact, with six stepped floors which translate the concepts of duplex and double height, and provide alternative access doors. The opposite elevation is more open. On this northern face, the basic geometry of the building is organized into the three dwellings.

Inside, Campo and Pessina make space and light the focal point of their work, arranging the various rooms according to the panoramic views. The three units have been treated in the same way, although the highest one is smaller. All in all, the complex presents seven horizontal planes which, over the living room, develop more vertically due to a gap in the floor separation framework which causes the double height. One of the most effective strategies of the complex is the use of space: the roof of each unit functions as a terrace.

Homes with panoramic views over Lake Gooi

Neutelings & Riedijk

Location: Fourth quadrant of the shore of Lake Gooi, Huizen, The Netherlands. **Date of construction**: 1994–1996. **Client**: Bouwfonds Woningbouw SL Haarlem. **Architect**: Neutelings & Riedijk. **Associates**: Willem Bruijn, Gerrit Schilder; Juurlink & Geluk, Rotterdam (landscaping). **Scheme**: 32 single family homes with integral garages. **Photography**: Stijn Brakkee.

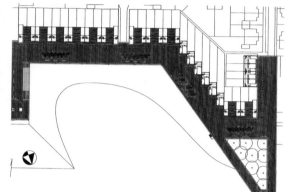

The project forms part of a larger plan consisting of 152 homes, the first phase of which comprises these 32 homes with panoramic views. Their internal layout is designed to make the most of their special position: water on one side, a great deal of light on the opposite side.

There are two types of home in this new project by Neutelings & Riedijk; both are designed within a 6 m (20 ft) bay and both exploit the visual perspectives of the lake to the maximum. Those which face the lake directly are built in pairs with the living room of one resting on the living room of the other, occupying the full width of both homes, 12 m (39 ft). Those which

are at an angle to the lake are built back to back, with one set back from the other, producing an indented façade for the development. All the houses have gardens, their own integral garage, and either a generous roof terrace (homes facing the lake) or a terrace suspended over the back garden (homes at an angle to the lake).

The promenade between the edge of the lake and the homes has been designed to blend with them.

Double house

Thomas Herzog and Michael Volz

Location: Pullach, Munich, Germany. **Date of completion**: 1989. **Architects**: Thomas Herzog and Michael Volz. **Associates**: Michael Streib, Julius Natterre, Bois Consult, Lausana (statics), Rainer Wittenborn (color design). **Scheme**: Single family home, exterior landscaping. **Photography**: Dieter Leistner.

This home is configured as a combination of traditional materials and techniques together with other more innovative materials and techniques for additional quality. The outcome is a house which synthesizes aesthetic simplicity with more intelligent pragmatism and becomes a kind of prototype or model which can be used with a moderate degree of naturalness in different kinds of environment. The initial theme of the project was to build a residential building, with two apartments, on a flat, vacant plot in Pullach, on the outskirts of Munich, an area of traditional styles of rural architecture.

The requirements of the client, who wanted a wooden building, with particular attention paid to the problems of energy saving, and yet with a fairly limited budget, had to be addressed. This whole set of factors had a decisive influence on the design of the future home, finally dictated by the technical aspects of solar energy, on which subject Herzog's team (with Michael Volz and Michael Streib) were constantly advised by the Freiburg Solar Energy Institute.

Patio Villa

Rem Koolhaas (OMA)

Location: Rotterdam, Netherlands. **Date of construction**: 1984–1988. **Architect**: Rem Koolhaas (OMA). **Associates**: George Heintz, Götz Keller, Jeraen Thomas, Thÿs de Haan, Jo Schippers, Petra Blaisse, Yves Brunier (landscaping). **Scheme**: Single family home on two floors, garden, and garage. **Photography**: Peter Aaron/ESTO.

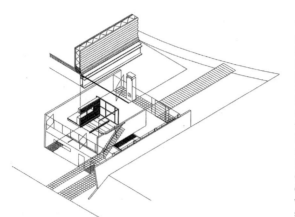

The two floors have different floor areas due to the slope. The glazed patio is the central organizational feature. With its off-center layout, four different areas become apparent: to the north, the dining room; to the south, the garden and living room; the Oriental metal wall of the prism houses the kitchen; on the other side, between the cube and the unobstructed wall, lies the rectangular stairwell flanked by its sinuous protective structure.

This villa is a virtually philosophical reflection on the architectural possibilities of designing a home today.

The whole of the interior has been laid out around a prism of light which not only acts as a central area but also affects the question of transparency and clarity. There is an almost total absence of physical barriers between rooms in the home.

On the outside the building has been designed with a desire to parody the traditional style of local villas, with the use of chromatics and glass borders as expressive motifs. The simplicity of all the details and components, the lightness of the dividing walls, and the lack of furniture give the lifestyle of its inhabitants a feeling of sober yet elegant luxury.

Silver House

Thom Mayne and Michael Rotondi, Morphosis

Location: Los Angeles, USA. **Date of completion**: 1987. **Architect**: Thom Mayne and Michael Rotondi, Morphosis. **Scheme**: Family home on the outskirts of Los Angeles. **Photography**: Morphosis.

This home, consisting of three floors built in a most unusual way on a completely irregular plot, has the living area on the top floor and the bedrooms and bathrooms on the lower floors. In this way, the inhabitants can see the Pacific Ocean, which would otherwise have been concealed by the row of houses on the other side of the coastal highway. The plans also clearly show the intersection of two separate units: a central block which contains the bathrooms, kitchen, and elevator, and a second diagonal unit which contains the remaining rooms. Special attention has been given to the circular entrance located on one side of the building's central unit. This leads to a lobby which provides access to a courtyard to the left and a guest area to the right, opposite the bathroom and sauna. The top floor contains the study and living room, located between the kitchen and dining room. Finally there is also a basement, which is used as a garage and storeroom with its own service area.

Single family suburban homes

The suburbs have in the past often been
associated with entropy, ambiguity, and
even indifference. Their appearance may
be uncared for as a result of precarious
and speculative property deals. The last
few decades of the 20th century, however,
have seen an upsurge of interest in
renovating these areas. Firstly, at a town
planning level, there have been efforts to
improve the infrastructure and give
districts on the periphery the advantages
of both city and country. Secondly, on an
architectural level, in-depth studies have
been carried out on the type of houses
required in suburban areas, and their
functional requirements. Over recent
years suburban homes have become
highly sought after. The examples shown
here demonstrate the special nature of the
location and the ideas of clients and
designers for them.

Burnette House

Wendell Burnette

Location: Sunnyslope. Arizona. USA. **Date of construction**: 1995. **Scheme**: Single family home, garden, and garage. **Photography**: Bill Timmerman.

The Burnette House is in the Sonora desert in the city of Sunnyslope. It is located at the end of an old abandoned route which led into the desert, cutting its way across the territory. In its center, the house is cut in two by an interior courtyard, which is the access from both the garden and garage. It is an ambiguous place where all levels of the house meet and where light penetrates at irregular angles, producing a strong contrast between light and shade. A staircase, consisting of squares of steel plate of different sizes, apparently suspended in the air, terminates at a small pool which reflects the staircase and makes the floor seem to disappear.

The side walls of the Burnette House have even, vertical slits every 2.5 m (8 ft) on the south wall and every 1.25 m (4 ft) on the north wall, which act like a sundial. Depending on the time of day and the season of the year, the shafts of light passing through the slits trace a specifically slanted line on the floor.

Wilbrink Villa

Ben van Berkel

Location: Amersfoort, The Netherlands. **Date of project**: 1994. **Architect**: Ben van Berkel. **Associates**: A. Krom, P. van der Evre, B. Medic BV, ABM **Description**: Single family home, courtyard, and garden. **Photography**: Hélène Bisnet, Kim Zwarts.

From the street, the house looks like a single slope covered with gravel: the main façade appears to have sunk below ground level. The slope is divided by a ramp running down to the garage and a pedestrian walkway leading to the central courtyard. So the house does not have a specific, recognizable entrance but a gradual one.

The shape of the central courtyard is irregular. It is open to the west but is reached from the pedestrian walkway. The garage cuts it off from the road, which enables it to become the living heart of the house. It receives sun from the south and all rooms open onto it via large glass doors.
The interior of the house is L-shaped, with the living

room right in the corner. The short wing houses the services (kitchen, pantry, laundry) and the long wing the bedrooms. The bathroom is an extra building added to the house, with wood clad external walls. It juts out from the main structure and helps to close off the courtyard area.

Rotterdam house/studio

Mecanoo Architekten

Location: Rotterdam, Netherlands. **Date of construction**: 1989–91. **Client**: Erick van Egeraat and Francine Houben. **Architect**: Mecanoo Architekten b.v. **Associates**: Erick van Egeraat, Francine Houben (design), Theo Kupers, Bjarne Mastenbroek, Cock Peterse, Inma Fernandez, Birgit Jurgenhake, Marjolin Adriaansche, Van Omme & De Grooth (contractor). **Scheme**: Single family home with studio, garden, swimming pool, and garage. **Photography**: Scagliola, Brakee, Francine Houben.

The building is located at the end of a row of houses built in the 19th century and surrounded by single family homes and apartment blocks built by some of the Netherlands' current top architects. The first floor houses the lobby, garage, and the architects'/owners' studio. The studio leads through glass doors to a Japanese garden. The pool is separated from the house by a wooden platform. The living room is on the second floor, with excellent views over the river. This is a large floor which, in addition to the living room, accommodates the kitchen and dining room. There is a terrace adjoining the south wall, with views over the canal. The north façade, made of glass, continues to the top floor, where a library serves as an anteroom to the three bedrooms situated here.

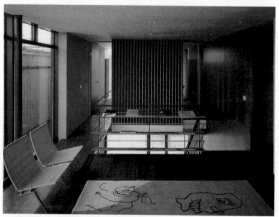

Lawson-Western House

Eric Owen Moss

Location: Los Angeles, USA. **Date of completion**: 1994. **Architect**: Eric Owen Moss. **Photography**: Tom Bonner.

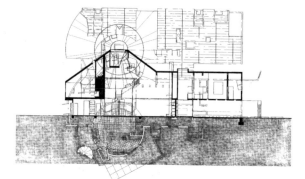

The functional, spatial, and formal ideas of the clients were garnered and interpreted by the architect and became the true starting points of the project's design.

The house is in one of the most prosperous parts of the city of Los Angeles. Its position, along the northern boundary of the plot, meant that a garden could be located in front of the south façade. Automobile and pedestrian access is from one end of the building, creating a sequential interior pathway which leads to the kitchen, the true functional and spatial nucleus of the home. The first floor accommodates the interconnected communal areas; the kitchen has a perimeter ring, for service and storage areas and from where the main staircase of the house starts. The large living room is a very high, vaulted room containing a metal fireplace; adjacent to both of these is the dining room, a room of more domestic proportions. The floor is completed by a playroom adjoining the kitchen on the west side, plus the garage and guest area on the east side. The central position of the staircase means that the second floor is divided into two main areas linked by a bridge over the living room. In the west wing is the master bedroom with its ancillary rooms, with direct access to an outside terrace, with a Jacuzzi, leading to the garden via an outside spiral staircase. The east wing has two bedrooms and the bathroom, over which a corner window makes an interesting feature on the access façade.

Koechlin House

Herzog & de Meuron

Location: Basle, Switzerland. **Date of construction**: 1994. **Architect**: Herzog & de Meuron. **Scheme**: Home, garden, and garage. **Photography**: Margheritta Spilutini.

The Koechlin House is built from the inside out. The courtyard can be open or enclosed and at certain times of the year can be turned into a conservatory. The upper floor can be closed off with a long wall of glass. This dual purpose has direct consequences for the design of the other parts of the house. The courtyard has no clear boundary and can become part of the first floor living room, with a window in the façade, or take over a section of the second floor framework to create a terrace. According to the architects themselves, this means that the rooms overlap, flow together, and enfold each other.

Another of the major ideas of the design is the intention that the outside forms a constant part of the inside, that the house is part of its surroundings, the garden, and views of the city in the distance. The outside walls are finished in cement gray rendering, which gives the house a sober appearance.

Hakuei House

Akira Sakamoto

Location: Tokyo, Japan. **Date of completion**: 1996. **Client**: Hakuei family. **Associates**: Reinhold Meyer (structural engineer), Kaiser Bautechnik (works supervision), Roger Preston (mechanical and electrical engineer). **Photography**: Nacasa & Partners.

The Hakuei residence is located on a relatively small and narrow suburban plot. For Sakamoto the decision to build a simple building with white walls signifies creating visual silence in the city where passers-by can rest their eyes. In this project, more important even than the composition of the rooms was to define the courtyard as an exterior, but at the same time private, area, around which to organize the day-to-day life of the occupants of the house. Akira Sakamoto built a side wall which runs across the

plot from the entrance to the rear boundary and acts as a screen. The wall is located on the east side and the afternoon sun reflects off it into all areas of the house. Opposite this wall, Sakamoto built three white boxes, two of them exactly alike.

The radical simplicity of this house seems to strip any notion of the superfluous, to slow down sounds which cross the room from one window to the other, and to project the movement of people crossing the rooms onto the white walls.

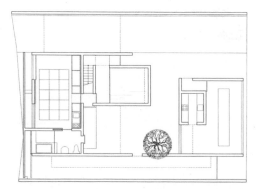

Kidosaki House

Tadao Ando

Location: Osaka, Japan. **Date of construction**: 1990. **Architect**: Tadao Ando. **Scheme**: Single family home.
Photography: Richard Bryant/Arcaid.

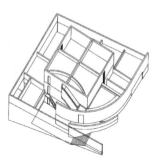

This building stands on an irregularly shaped plot. The main building consists of a perfect cube with 12 m (39 ft) sides, around which is arranged the rest of the house. This cube is located almost in the center of the plot, leaving open space both to the north and south. The area to the north consists of the entrance. This area has the peculiarity of cutting the straight line of the elevations which border the plot. Thus, one of the side walls, that facing west, begins to curve in towards the center, coming out on the north side, producing an open space which becomes the entrance. The interior has clean lines, providing an austere space devoid of embellishments, faithful to Japanese tradition. The rooms are open plan, very large, and empty. You could say this is an amorphous building which is integrated with nature, producing an almost floating space.

House in Yokohama

Kazuo Shinohara

Location: Yokohama, Japan. **Date of construction**: 1987. **Architect**: Kazuo Shinohara. **Scheme**: Construction of a single family home as an annex to an old house. **Photography**: Richard Bryant/Arcaid.

This house was designed as an extension to an old wooden house with the intention of preserving as many trees as possible on the site it was to occupy. The new building takes up only a small part of the original garden.

The house is located in Yokohama, Japan, at the top of a very steep slope on an extensive, quiet plot. The site is covered with a large number of enormous trees, which is why this green belt area was treated with great respect. The new structure, an L-shaped section on two floors, was added to one side of the existing building, a rectangular bungalow, totally regular and uniform. The first floor of the new extension contains the entrance (which is located between the two buildings), the master bedroom, and a bathroom with a *tatami*. The second floor is accessed by a staircase near the entrance and accommodates the

all-important kitchen, together with the dining room, a spacious living room, and a closet.

Blades House

Morphosis

Location: Santa Barbara, California, USA. **Date of construction**: 1996. **Architect**: Morphosis. **Scheme**: Single family house, garden, swimming pool, and garage. **Photography**: Morphosis (also pp 920/921).

In June 1990, a dreadful fire razed to the ground hundreds of single family homes built in the hills of the Santa Barbara coastline near Goleta, California (USA). All that remained, along with the ash, was a gently sloping landscape with scattered rocks and a group of native oaks. Morphosis' strategy was to build an elliptical wall and contain all parts of the house within it. This wall, which has an upper edge or lip suggesting that this exterior room is partly roofed, is made of exposed aggregate concrete. Opposite the ellipsis of the garden, the house roof draws another curve in the vertical plane.

The floor area of the house is about 350 m² (3800 ft²), arranged into three large areas adjacent to five small exterior rooms. Each area is designed as a sequence of superimposed zones in which the boundary between communal and private space has been deliberately blurred.

Check House

KNTA

Location: Singapore, Malaysia. **Date of construction**: 1995. **Architect**: KNTA. **Associates**: Joseph Huang, Ove Arup & Partners, Singapore (structural engineers); Hin Yin Choo, Michael Chorney, Finbarr Fin, Chee Meng Look, Bruce Ngiam, Ben Smart, Mong Lin Yap, Jacks Yeo, CCL Chartered Surveyors; Ee Chiang & Co. Pte Ltd. (main contractor), Ho Kong Aluminium Pte Ltd., Xin Hefen Engineering Pte. Ltd. (specialist contractors). **Photography**: Dennis Gilbert.

The plot on which the Check House stands is elongated, which is reflected in the design of both the house and the gardens. On the first floor, the shapes are curved and fluid, while on the second floor they are straight and angular. The house is designed as a series of stages and areas which follow each other naturally. A small paved road provides car access as far as the house, crossing the back garden. A curved ramp provides access to the entrance from the garage area, dominated by the sculptural image of a metal pergola suspended from a tensioning device on one side.

Concrete walls form the basic structure of the house. The various elements made of other materials are fixed to or hang from them.

All parts of the house converge on the double height living room, from which there are views over the front and rear gardens. The dining room, close to the front garden, is a circular room designed around a central, round table seating 12 people comfortably.

The rear garden houses the swimming pool, which is an open area surrounded by large windows. At the north end of the house, next to the swimming pool, there is a small pavilion made of glass blocks and a roof of two projecting wings supported on a single load-bearing beam.

Psyche House

Rene van Zuuk

Location: Almere, The Netherlands. **Date of construction**: 1991–1992. **Clients**: Rene van Zuuk and Marjo Körner **Architect**: Rene van Zuuk. **Photography**: Herman H. van Doorn.

The project is a composition of interlinking areas, surfaces, and elements. It is designed on the basis of the materials, conscientiously rejecting the use of both passing fads and standard ideas. The house comprises two adjacent, longitudinal strips: one, double height, to the north; the other, with two levels, occupying the southern half. A curtain of translucent glass enters the house from the northwest corner, describing an arc which the sub-frame of the adjacent southern area joins at a tangent. Sheltered by the glass arc are four structures, four steel trees: their trunks split and the branches spread out, supporting the two wings of the roof. One of the trees is in the entrance area and the other three are interlinked by metal cross-tensioners inside the room, which dominate it. The structure is supplemented with another two Y-shaped supports, produced by I-shaped profiles, which support the more projecting wing of the roof running under the south façade.

House in Vaise

Jourda & Perraudin

Location: Vaise, France. **Date of completion**: 1990. **Architect**: Françoise-Hélène Jourda, Gilles Perraudin. **Scheme**: Single family home, garden, and garage. **Photography**: Stéphane Couturier.

This house is a direct representation of the architectural concepts of its designers, which have already been displayed in some of their previous works, such as the Paris City of Music and the Gandhi Cultural Center in New Delhi. The project clearly reflects its architects' concern to bring the inhabitants in contact with the external weather conditions and to integrate the building into its surroundings. The project is a direct testimony to a new philosophical focus on the relationship between living space and nature and connections between culture and countryside. The plot on which the house stands is a six-sided, irregular polygon. To retain as much greenery as possible, the architects decided on a layout of two, reduced height, rectangular floors. This arrangement suited perfectly the client family, with four children continually coming in and going out of the house. The layout consists of a living room/diner, kitchen, bedrooms, bathrooms, playroom, cellar, and terraces representing visual continuity between the inside and the outside. The architects achieved what they were initially seeking: to apply a biotechnological architecture where materials are used according to their specific function within the general structure.

Single family country homes

In modern society, where cities occupy
the center ground and radiate their grid-
like surroundings and their speed, the
country means a move towards another
type of activity. Anyone who decides to
build a house in a meadow or near a
wood takes a basic decision. They are
expressing a desire for isolation, for the
achievement of greater tranquillity, and
for the start of a dual journey: proximity
to more simple, fundamental things and
gradual detachment from urban networks
of relationships and obligations. We have
included here houses which have a
specific and recognizable shape. All the
projects relate to nature in different ways:
they adapt to the countryside, alter it,
embellish it, and reveal the motives of
those who live in them.

Villa M

Stéphane Beel

Location: Zedelgem, Belgium. **Date of construction**: 1994. **Architect**: Stéphane Beel. **Associates**: Dirk Hendriks, Paul van Eygen, Hans Verstuyft, Harm Wassink, Hans Lust, Philippe Viérin (design), SCES (structural engineering), R. Boydens (fittings). **Photography**: Lieve Blancquart.

The site for the Villa M is a clearing in a wood approximately 1 ha (2.5 acres) in area; it is completely flat.

The villa is an elongated structure (60 m, 197 ft in length by 7 m, 23 ft wide), built parallel to one of the existing walls. The different areas are set out along the length of the house in a sequence, separated by patches of architectural silence which may take the form of small patios or areas not dedicated to any particular purpose, which accommodate the services. These silent areas serve the purpose of keeping adjacent rooms at a distance from one another. Although there are no doors to interrupt the spatial continuity, the rooms are nevertheless separated, with the kitchen isolated from the dining room and the living room. From the garden, when the light starts to wane, the interior of the building takes on the appearance of a scenery backdrop: the enormous glass windows allow for movements to be seen, as the people inside pass from room to room.

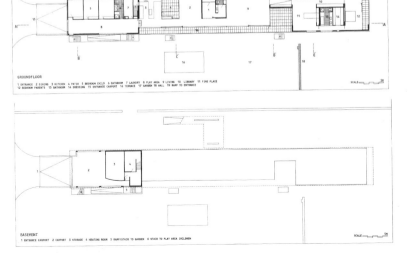

GROUNDFLOOR

1 ENTRANCE 2 DINING 3 KITCHEN 4 PATIO 5 BEDROOM CHILD 6 BATHROOM 7 LAUNDRY 8 PLAY AREA 9 LIVING 10 LIBRARY 11 FIRE PLACE
12 BEDROOM PARENTS 13 BATHROOM 14 DRESSING 15 ENTRANCE CARPORT 16 TERRACE 17 GARDEN 18 WALL 19 RAMP TO ENTRANCE

SCALE

BASEMENT

1 ENTRANCE CARPORT 2 CARPORT 3 STORAGE 4 HEATING ROOM 5 RAMP/STAIR TO GARDEN 6 STAIR TO PLAY AREA CHILDREN

SCALE

Villa M 951

Villa in the woods

Kazuyo Sejima

Location: Chino, Nagano, Japan. **Date of construction**: 1994. **Architects**: Kazuyo Sejima. **Associates**: R. Nighizawa, S. Funaki, Matsuvi Gengo + O.R.S. **Scheme**: Single family home. **Photography**: Nacása and Partners.

The villa in the Tateshina woods occupies a position almost of defense in the face of the wilderness, creating a point with an ordered identity in the midst of natural chaos. Kazuyo Sejima chose a circular site to express the sense of homogeneity which the woodland created within him. This dense encirclement of vegetation does not allow for an axis to be identified; the sun's rays filter through the branches and make orientation difficult. The client, a gallery owner from Tokyo, wanted a house which he could use as a second home, in which he would be able to receive visitors, and was also provided with an exhibition area, the atelier. This scheme is arranged around a central circular space which meets these requirements, and which creates, by its perimeter, a ring in which the architect brings together the areas providing for the basic functions of a home.

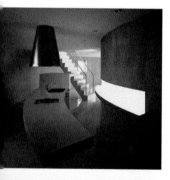

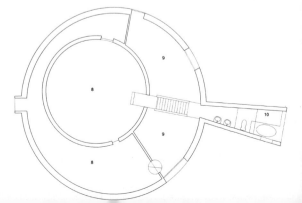

House at Tateshina

Iida Archischip Studio

Location: Tateshina, Nagano, Japan. **Date of construction**: 1994. **Architects**: Yoshihitko Iida. **Associates**: Niitsu (construction). **Scheme**: Single family home, landscaping, and external, double height covered walk. **Photography**: Koumei Tanaka.

The house is located in a holiday area, at the foot of Mount Tateshina, in Nagano. The site is on a gentle slope to the southwest, with the building surrounded by woodlands. Iida's project involved the construction of two parallel elements on a rectangular plot, somewhat displaced in relation to one another. Both are sited so as to follow the slope of the ground; access is through the more elevated end, and from the vestibule a ramp descends, following the natural inclination of the mountain side, and leads the visitor to the living room and the large wooden terrace. The ramp continues until finally losing itself again in the woods. A second ramp rises from the vestibule to a small bridge which connects to the adjacent building. The bathroom is on the second floor. This is an unusually open structure, with panoramic views over the woods, inviting one to spend hours relaxing in the bath and enjoying the scenery.

Barnes House

Patkau Architects

Location: Nanaimo, British Columbia, Canada. **Date of construction**: 1993. **Architects**: Tim Newton, John Patkau, Patricia Patkau, David Shone, Tom Robertson. **Associates**: Fast & Epp Partners (structural engineering), Robert Wall Ltd. (contractor). **Scheme**: Single family home and landscaping. **Photography**: Undine Pröhl.

According to the owners, John and Patricia Patkau, the Barnes House is part of an investigational process exploring architecture which started some years ago and is still going on. This journey is focused on the quest for the specific, the real, and the heterogeneous elements. In the case of the Barnes House, the specific is basically the location and the lively landscape which surrounds the building, rocky outcrops rich in vegetation, with views of the Strait of Georgia and Vancouver Island. The scheme by John and Patricia Patkau plays with both themes; on the one hand, the landscape, the topography, and the panoramic views; and, on the other, the abrupt, rocky site, resplendent with edges, changes of level, and sharp profiles. In a certain way, the forms of the house itself evoke both aspects of the landscape, and bring them to an intermediate scale.

Typical/Variant House

Vincent James, Paul Yaggie

Location: Wisconsin, USA. **Date of construction**: 1996. **Architects**: Vincent James, Paul Yaggie. **Associates**: N. Blantard, N. Knuston, A. Dull, S. Lazen, K. Scheib, Coen + Stumpt (landscaping), Yerigan Construction (building contractors). **Scheme**: Single family home, landscaping, and garage. **Photography**: Don F. Wong.

The owners embodied in the project a concept which fascinated them and for which they coined the term "typical/variant." The Typical/Variant House is a collection of spaces which accord with the rhythms and outlines of domestic life. Making use solely of elements which resemble wooden boxes, a variety of different contiguous architectural situations were created. Each one of them has its own specific proportions, orientation, and natural lighting. In parallel with this, the turns and angles of the different parts of the building define different semi-enclosed spaces on the outside. Both the rooms and the patio areas of the house are conceived as

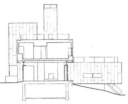

immediate, unadorned spaces, straightforward in form, which acquire life from the daily cycle of use. The structural solutions and the types of finish chosen are inspired by the typical rural architecture of the northern United States. The final result is at once abstract and yet familiar, satisfying the owners' desire for their home to be rustic and warm, allowing them to establish a feeling of intimacy and love. The external materials, mainly copper sheeting and bluish stone, are arranged in distinct sections which create a rich variety of rhythms and textures in the façades. As time passes, so the copper turns from a bright honey tone to a bluish-purple colour, then to a rich brown, and finally to a whitish-green shade.

Huf House

Ernst Beneder

Location: Blindenmarkt, Lower Austria. **Date of construction**: 1990–1993. **Client**: Dr. Josef Huf and Maria Huf. **Architect**: Ernst Beneder. **Associates**: Anja Fischer. **Photography**: Ernst Beneder, Marguerita Spiluttini.

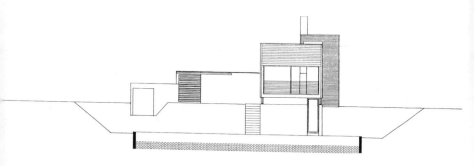

The Huf House was created as a second home, covering an area of 75 m² (807 ft²) and simple in scope. The site, surrounded by the wetland woods of the River Ybbs, is located adjacent to a large artificial pool. Bordered by the roadway on the north side, the house is shaped as a longitudinal prism, faced in timber, supported on the flat surface of the site and rising above the slope down to the edge of the water.

The interior is designed as a single space in which objects are then arranged; the staircase, which rises from the patio to the roof, stands next to the chimney and above the fittings of the kitchen in an entirely natural manner. The prism structure is supported on a concrete base, partially underground, and in turn supports a robust aluminum tower containing the bathroom on the lower floor and a gallery-cum-bedroom on the intermediate floor. The bathroom, which projects outside the perimeter of the prism structure, is separated by a semi-transparent door. One of the bedroom windows faces onto the patio, while the other opens onto the terrace and the dining room, across the stairway. Just at the point at which the site starts to fall away, the interior floor rises by five steps, merging into the parquet floor in the living room area.

Outside on the patio the batten framework adds warmth to the open space.

Häusler House

Karl Baumschlager and Dietmar Eberle

Location: Hard, Austria. **Date of construction**: 1993. **Architects**: Karl Baumschlager and Dietmar Eberle. **Area**: 230 m² (2500 ft²). **Scheme**: Single family house and landscaping. **Photography**: Eduard Hueder/Ardi-Photo Inc.

The Häusler House is a single family home in Hard, Austria, located on a flat and open site, and consisting essentially of a rectangular structure, characterized by a gray concrete texture, within which the project develops. The access façade and the side elements are practically closed off to the outside, and only the southern face is open. This façade consists of a regular concrete structure forming a uniform latticework, with timber facings, and recessed to a greater or lesser extent, from which a number of different floors branch off. The northern façade, the area of access, is a rectangle of gray concrete, which accommodates, as its only compositional elements, the aperture for the entrance and a horizontal window, extended and elongated, on the right, which runs as far as the corner. The house is reminiscent of the concrete creations by the North American artist Donald Judd: pure geometrical forms, of large dimensions, set in open landscapes, and creating a strange and disconcerting form of order.

Dub House

Bolles + Wilson

Location: Münster, Germany. **Date of construction**: 1994. **Architects**: Bolles + Wilson. **Scheme**: Single family home, interior courtyard, and landscaping. **Photography**: Christian Richters.

The scheme for the Dub House involved the reshaping (small-scale modification) of a house dating from the 1960s, in the modern style.

The first "extra," the word which the people involved use themselves, was an earthenware ceramic wall of vivid blue on the interior courtyard, a bold and optimistic explosion of color. The second element was a studio located next to the blue wall, somewhat lower, faced in zinc on the outside and wood on the inside. This second wall incorporates a set of windows of different sizes, as references to a neoplastic style. The third extra, by contrast with the first two, is a flat horizontal surface with a pergola of zinc bars which occupies the space created by the slight displacement of the two walls already described, between which the access to the building has been constructed.

On the inside there are two more new elements, a chimney formed of geometric shapes, with a circular aluminum fume extraction pipe, and a substantial wooden swing door, which almost amounts to a revolving wall in appearance.

Aktion Poliphile

Studio Granda

Location: Wiesbaden, Germany. **Date of construction**: 1989–1992. **Client**: Galerie z.B., Frankfurt. **Architects**: Studio Granda. **Photography**: Norbert Migueletz.

shadowy cold sadness and slowness, of its neighbor Saturn, both houses so forming a single private system. Saturn is solid and impenetrable, its roof formed of lead and the walls of a dark red plaster. Nothing passes across its face, its walls have no characteristic adornments or features, with the exception of a short arcade on the flank of the wall. From the shelter of the garden a deep groove, of double height, reveals the interior, showing through a series of smaller gaps in the side of the wall. Moving to the north wall of the building, we find a latticework of great beauty and originality, which likewise has a strong sense

of symbolism. Saturn and Delia, wood and stone, fragility and strength. Symbolism, beauty, and practicality; three words which when taken together give meaning to the Aktion Poliphile, three words which, in harmony, join within this project, providing a masterly lesson for those who cling to the old adage that beauty always strives against the pragmatic. Symbolism, beauty, and practicality; neither the one nor the two prevail, only the three, and their perfect interdependence is mirrored in the Aktion Poliphile houses.

The scheme involves two houses, located above the fertile fields to the north of Wiesbaden, Germany: the Saturn House and the Delia House. Saturn symbolizes the concept of the paradox of time, which creates only subsequently to destroy its own creation. Its successor, the Delia, is a symbol of the fount of youth, energy, and health. Delia symbolizes modern times. Its hidden side, discreetly concealed, reflects the

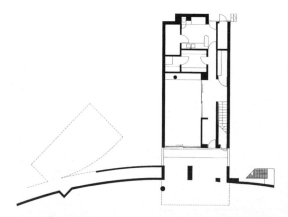

Bom Jesus House

Eduardo Souto de Moura

Location: Braga, Portugal. **Date of construction**: 1994. **Architect**: Eduardo Souto de Moura. **Scheme**: Single family home and landscaping. **Photography**: Luis Ferreira Alves (also pp 948/949).

The conceptual simplicity and the architectural language which characterize the Bom Jesus House are a clear example of how to provide a response to the physical circumstances which already prevail, a response which is appropriate yet understated and subtle. The composition of this single family house incorporates two elements which represent two different schemes and two different construction systems, uniting two houses in the same project. One structure in natural stone, which, springing from the irregular configuration of the ground, spans the building, and a cube of concrete and glass which rests on the platform delimiting the stone wall, symbolize the meeting between that which already exists and that which is

new. The Bom Jesus House stands on a site with a pronounced slope towards the southwest, facing towards the anarchic silhouette of the city of Braga. Access to the property from lower levels, coincides with the upper limit of the site, merging into a paved path which rises gently in a semiritualistic pattern.

Grotta House

Richard Meier

Location: New Jersey, USA. **Date of construction**: 1988. **Architect**: Richard Meier.

This house is sited on a slightly inclined surface, with woodland to the northwest and beautiful views to the south and the east. Two axes drawn from the center of the building form right angles with the main buildings, projecting the interior of the house into the natural landscape surrounding it, and providing a position of privilege in a location which is otherwise difficult to define. The circles and squares are stylistic elements of great importance and value to New York architect Richard Meier. The latest owners of the house, two art collectors, also acquired a love of architecture, inspired by the geometry of this design. The building is constructed around a cylindrical center space, two stories in height; this virtual structure is partially absorbed by the orthogonal body, in which it is integrated in turn within a square base. The house is a clear example of many of the themes which arise in Meier's work, such as the use of white; the building is almost completely white, the architect's preferred color, so sharpening the perception of the colors which exist in natural light and within nature itself. The interplay between light and dark, between mass and volume, can be better appreciated thanks to the contrast with the white surface of the building.

Bernasconi House

Luigi Snorzzi

Location: Carona, Switzerland. **Date of construction**: 1988–1989. **Client**: Raffaele Bernasconi. **Architect**: Luigi Snorzzi. **Associates**: Gustavo Grosman, Hans Peter Jenny. **Photography**: Filippo Simonetti.

The building is located in the Carona valley, in an area characterized by a pronounced upward slope in a southerly direction, and a broad vista to the northern flank. Access to the building is via an area on the highest side of the site, where the parking area is located and the view from the house is to the southwest. The functional arrangement of the interior is of a residential house located on three floors, added to which is a basement where the storage areas are located. The simplicity of the interior is reflected in the façades: visible concrete, simple structures, and strategically located apertures. The view of the building from the access area discloses the presence of two prismatic modules: the first, generally horizontal in arrangement, accommodates the residential areas proper, while the second, with a vertical superimposed perspective, provides the communicating link between the remote surfaces. The peaceful harmony between the visible concrete and the glass is supported by the use of the glass in the transitional area as both the floor paving and for the access stairways. The use of this material brings about a subtle change in the light effects on the changing levels of the stairway and at the ends of the floors.

Neuendorf Villa

Claudio Silvestrin

Location: Majorca, Spain. **Date of construction**: 1988–1991. **Client**: Hans and Carolie Neuendorf. **Architects**: Claudio Silvestrin. **Associates**: Tietz & Partners (engineering), J. Salis Construcciones (construction). **Photography**: Marco de Valdivia.

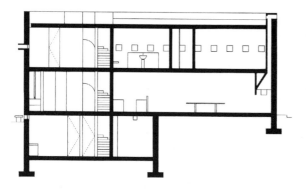

sense of emotion and dynamic energy to the whole complex. The structural forms and limits are a clear manifestation of the minimalist language of the project. Free of any element alien to the spiritual essence of the building, the ideas of space, light, and freedom have full rein.

The house is made of natural local materials. As a response to the arid and reddish surroundings, the walls are practically bare, with vertical clefts echoing the scoring of the ground and the interplay of light and shadow created by the slender trees which surround the building. The house was not designed to be directly accessible by car. The country lane which approaches the site leads to a shady parking area, from which a ramp 110 m (120 yds) in length rises to the villa. The swimming pool is designed to be an extension of the structure, with a length of nearly 40 m (44 yds) but a width of just 3.4 m (3.7 yds.) Despite the simplicity of the building's design, with

its tendency towards cubic shapes, each of the four façades offers a specific and individual aspect to the outside. After passing through the narrow hollow which gives access to the building, an interior patio measuring 12 x 12 m (39 x 39 ft) appears, around which the body of the villa extends in the shape of an L. Simple rectangular apertures, in generous dimensions, provide entry to the basic elements of the building, set out on two stories. The first floor contains the household areas, and the bedrooms and associated facilities are located on the upper floor. The movement of the light over the upper areas and rooms creates dramatic visual effects, and adds a

Single family homes by the sea

The environment has a profound influence
on human development, to the degree that
every site has its own territorial spirit. A
good house needs to be in tune with, and
provide a direct response to, not only the
climate and other environmental
conditions of the area in which it is
located, but also the traditional way of life
of the inhabitants. The coastline is
characterized in minute detail by its highly
significant geographical and social
diversity; this means it is impossible to
generalize about a shoreline, and it is far
better to make a more specific and
detailed study of small stretches. This
section considers schemes which are
located in an environment which is both
beautiful and unique – the seashore. These
are buildings which engage in dialogs with
the landscape that are especially
interesting, a landscape which is
constantly different, and constantly
changing. And, in addition to their
residential function and their vacation and
leisure use, the frontage to the beach
provides the ideal environment to escape
the noise and stress of the big city.

Extension to the Neutra House

Steven Ehrlich Architects

Location: Santa Monica, California, USA. **Date of construction**: 1996–1998. **Architects**: Steven Ehrlich Architects. **Scheme**: Extension/annex to a single family home. **Photography**: Tom Bonner.

The Lewin residence in Santa Monica was designed by Richard Neutra in 1938. It is located at the foot of a rocky outcrop on the beach, and initially occupied an area of 550 m² (5900 ft²). The present owners wished to add a leisure area to this, with a swimming pool, an extension to the garage, and areas for services. To cut out the noise from the adjacent highway, Steven Ehrlich opted to locate the new garage and the service areas in such a way as to form an effective noise barrier. This arrangement creates a first patio common to both sections of the building, while the second patio encountered on the way from the road also has the original Neutra House as a backdrop, and establishes a visual link between the old living room and the new pavilion structure which accommodates the leisure facilities. A glazed bridge element crosses this outside space to connect the two areas. The meticulous care and attention, both in general planning as well as in

House at Sag Pond

Mario Gandelsonas, Diana Agrest

Location: Sagaponack, Southampton, New York, USA. **Date of construction**: 1989-1992. **Client**: Richard Ekstract. **Architects**: Mario Gandelsonas, Diana Agrest. **Associates**: Wal-Siskind (interiors); Claire Weisz (architectural plan); Tom Bader, Peter Frank, Maurice Harwell, Thomas Kalin (consultants); Robert Silman Associates (structural engineering); David Dominsky (contractor). **Photography**: Paul Warchol.

The house, surrounded by fields, consists of six towers connected by bridges, spanning a void some 33 m (108 ft) in length facing north. The void accommodates the communal areas of the building, while the bridges and towers contain the private rooms, in two independent wings. One wing, facing south, houses the main bathroom and the master suite; the other, facing north, contains the bedrooms, which have independent stairways for guests. The formal structure of the building is developed over the width of these two geometric forms, the juncture of which creates the triangular shape of the hall, incurring a reverse perspective distortion of the stairways and imposing torsion on the parabola of the roof. This movement in turn affects the structure of the chimneys and the storeroom which separates the principal spaces and communal areas of the void. The cylindrical greenhouse structure is the only tower of which the structure is composed of vertical steel columns and timber rings.

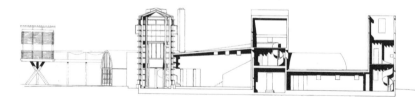

Cashman House

Ed Lippmann

Location: Sydney, Australia. **Date of construction**: 1996. **Architect**: Ed Lippmann. **Associates**: Ove Arup (engineering). **Scheme**: Single family home. **Area**: 200 m² (2150 ft²). **Photography**: Peter Hyatt.

This house was built for a family who wanted to spend their weekends and summer vacations away from the big city. The site is located on a beach which is difficult to access, and is surrounded by thick vegetation that forms part of a nature reserve.
A geotechnical survey indicated that the structure ought to be very light: this is an area prone to torrential rainfall, its soil of very low consolidation and with serious erosion problems. The building was constructed with a light metallic structure and a cladding of undulating metal sheeting.
The house was designed as an open pavilion, with substantial glazing, almost as if it were a large covered terrace. The living area is divided into two parts, one of a single floor which accommodates the communal areas (living room, dining room, and kitchen), and one of two stories, containing the bedrooms and bathrooms.

House at Capistrano

Rob Wellington Quigley

Location: Capistrano Beach, California, USA. **Date of construction**: 1994. **Architect**: Rob Wellington Quigley. **Associates**: T. Cruz, C. Herbst, M. Falcone. **Scheme**: Single family home, kitchen garden, garage. **Photography**: Undine Pröhl.

Capistrano Beach is a locality on the coast of California where a series of single family houses have been constructed on the shoreline, above the sand of the beach itself. They form a gathering of individual fragments, a discontinuous formation spread over the uniformity of the beach. Their architecture is narrative and figurative, and, at the same time, abstract; this paradox and sense of dissonance are their essential aesthetic strategy. This complex of juxtapositions, tensions, and integrated fragmentation creates a difficult final unity, but nevertheless a unity which is capable of forming its spaces into a coherent whole. The faces, to the east and west, form parallel surfaces which contain the mass of the residential section. On the north and south faces, these rigid planes become blurred and at some points open to reveal the interior, such that the sea winds through the openings and domestic life overflows to the beach beneath. This house is a sensitive sequence of spaces with widely differing dimensions, different ways of obtaining light, and contrasting stylistic points of reference.

Schnabel House

Frank O. Gehry

Location: Los Angeles, California, USA. **Date of construction**: 1987–1989. **Architect**: Frank O. Gehry.
Photography: Mark Darley

the west, a slender prism-shaped extension has been built outwards, which accommodates the garage. Above this is another smaller structure, arranged around the axis of the first, which houses the services; to connect this module to the kitchen,

Gehry has provided an arcaded gallery, supported by columns with cladding of natural copper and passing over part of the landscaped area.

The site provided for the building is a large plot of somewhat dull topographic features, a rectangular area which ended in an irregular trapezoidal area, approached by a descent in level to create an area of greater privacy in relation to the building's surroundings.

On the lower level, the main section of the rectangular site contains the kitchen, a split-level living room with central ceiling lighting, and a small studio. On the upper floor there are two bedrooms with en suite bathrooms, arranged around the structural void created at that level by the living room.

The appearance of the outside is characterized by a simple steel-gray stucco effect on the walls.

In the site access area, to

House in Venice

Antoine Predock

Location: Venice, California, USA. **Date of construction**: 1990. **Architect**: Antoine Predock. **Photography**: Timothey Hursley.

bathroom and dressing room, and a large terrace from which a stairway leads to a solarium. The most impressive aspect of this house is the use of materials and techniques, which reflect the actual use of the different areas, where ceramics in dark colours are combined with moquette floorings of natural materials, and the use of the water, in such a way that the image produced is always present but remains inverted.

A retaining wall with black granite facing, over which the water flows, is the only element which separates the building from the public highway. The sash window, with a red metal frame, located at the end of the axis of the building, pivots horizontally and forms an opening 33 cm (13 in) high with views of the ocean. Inside the building, areas illuminated by natural light combine with those of diffused lighting provided by a system of concealed glass panes.

This house, built right on the edge of the beach, is mounted on a rectangular base and extends over three separate floors. A basement, at ground level and partially concealed by concrete walls, serves as a garage and area for services. The first floor accommodates a spacious living room, the dining room, and the kitchen; the other wing contains a studio room and a bathroom. The top floor is the location for the bedrooms, the largest of them with an en suite

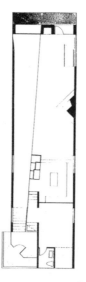

Villangómez House

Salvador Roig, F. J. Pallejà, J.A Martínez Lopeña, Elías Torres

Location: Ibiza, Spain. **Date of construction**: 1988–1990. **Clients**: Mariano and Alejandro Villangómez.
Architects: Salvador Roig, F.J. Pallejà, J.A. Martínez Lopeña, Elias Torres. **Photography**: Hisao Suzuki

The scheme for the building is conventional: a single family house with three bedrooms and an interior patio, the various sections of which are intended to merge as harmoniously as possible with the surrounding landscape, as well as providing interior light. The structure can be divided into two blocks of prismatic design, which are laid out essentially in an L shape. The intersection element between these blocks is oblique, triangular in shape, and intended to define an internal space facing the sea which acts as a patio and, at the same time, establishes and arranges the physical and visual communications of the entire structure. To provide the essential sense of intimacy, the architects have made use of two strategies: firstly, both the house and the patio are elevated some 60 cm (2 ft) above the natural ground level, so as to exploit to the full the views of the outside; and, secondly, the open section of the patio facing the sea is delimited by sketching out a series of open and unconnected facings between which the surrounding landscape can be glimpsed, as well as the permanent view of the sea, providing a vision from the terrace and the inside of the house of vertical fragments which then create one single horizontal reality. The house can be seen by passers-by between the trunks of the trees, as a fragmented vision, an impression which is heightened by the arrangement of different elevations, with specific solutions to suit the opposing landscape.

House on Lake Weyba

Gabriel Poole

Location: Noosa Heads, Australia. **Date of construction**: 1996. **Architect**: Gabriel Poole. **Associates**: Elisabeth Poole (design), Rod Bligh-Bligh Tanner (structural engineering), Barry Hamlet (aluminum). **Photography**: Peter Hyatt.

Poole arranged the space available into three separate and distinct pavilion structures, based on the life inside a residential house. Located at one end, the entrance element contains the kitchen, office, dining room, and living room-cum-studio. The area occupied can be doubled by extending the vinyl and steel panels and so creating a covered walkway area. The limits of the interior space can be constantly changed thanks to the use of movable interlocking elements and the enlargement of the floor surface beyond the line which delineates the structure. The second pavilion element houses the bathroom area, with shower and washroom sections. The colours of the individual facings contrast with the monochrome fiber-cement walls. The third pavilion is occupied by the main bedroom. The roof is the most immediately striking feature of the house; its polycarbonate cladding and its pitch, its edges, and its surrounds demonstrate clearly the way in which the residents face the elements.

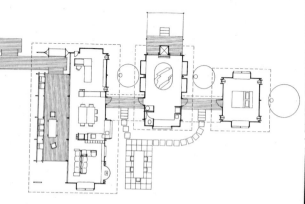

House in Sausalito

Mark Mack

Location: Sausalito, California, USA. **Date of construction**: 1987. **Architect**: Mark Mack.

This is a single family house which extends along the northwest axis of a site located on the crest of the Wolfback ridge in California, and is set in a landscape of exceptional beauty, offering simultaneously views of the Pacific Ocean and of San Francisco Bay.
The house is set on an irregular base, slightly curved, and extending over

two storys. The different parts of the building, separated according to their functions, are divided into the northern face, the public part of the building, closed and solid, and emphasized by the chamfered frames of the windows; and the south facing section, the private area, open and airy, with large windows and terraces giving dramatic views of the Bay and the Pacific.
In addition to this, the interior spaces are developed on both floors around the structure of the chimney, located at the epicentre of the structure, and which serves as both a functional element and a means of division.

Ackerberg House

Richard Meier

Location: Malibu, California, USA. **Date of construction**: 1986. **Architect**: Richard Meier.

Influenced by the traditional style of courtyards typical of Southern California, this house is located among the mountains extending alongside the coastal highway and the beach which borders the Pacific Ocean. The site chosen for the construction of the building consists of three flat areas and the adjacent plots, facing Malibu Beach. The building stands on an L-shaped base, and consists of two floors, the private family area and the living room area. Main access is from the north front, from where, passing through a covered walkway, a vestibule is reached with floors set at different levels, and surfaces set with glass.

This area leads on to the living room, the dining room, the kitchen and the bathrooms, the interior courtyard, and the guest rooms. Going up the stairs to the second floor, which is linked to the first floor by means of the open space of the living room, we come upon a suspended shelving area opening onto the lower level. A number of rooms and a suite with dressing room and washroom complete the basic ground plan. This free spatial sequence is supplemented by a tennis court already in place in the southern section, and a recently constructed swimming pool on the west side.